Psychology of Sex

Attention Authors

'We Convert Fighters into Writers'. That's the motto of Manas Publications since more than four decades. Our message to the world is that India can win the battle not only by the bullet but also by the pen. There is no dearth of intellectuals in our country, but their knowledge is confined to them only. No sincere effort has been made by any other publisher to channelise their knowledge in national interest. That is why the talent of a large number of intellectuals remains latent. An author transforms his knowledge into a manuscript, and it is our job to spread his/her knowledge by converting it into a beautiful book. For over four decades, Manas has been motivating the intellectuals by publishing their manuscripts and would like to publish your manuscript too. So if you or your colleagues have any manuscript ready for publication or are working on it, kindly contact us with detailed synopsis and list of contents. We will transform your work into a valuable publication. If you wish, we can also suggest you the suitable subjects for writing the books related to your area of expertise. Manas is known for its publishing quality and commitments. We take utmost care in production and give wide publicity to the book as well as its author through our national and international distribution network.

Psychology of Sex

The Biology of Sex
The Sexual Impulse in Youth
Sexual Deviation
The Erotic Symbolisms
Homosexuality
Marriage
The Art of Love

by
Havelock Ellis

Manas Publications
(We Convert Fighters into Writers)
New Delhi-110002 (India)

MANAS PUBLICATIONS
(We Convert Fighters into Writers)
(Publishers for IAS, IPS, IFS, IRS, Defence, Press, Judges etc)

4402/5-A, Ansari Road (Opp HDFC Bank)
Darya Ganj, New Delhi-110 002 (India)
Off.: 23260783, 23265523, Fax: 011-23272766
E-mail: manaspublications@gmail.com
manaspublications@yahoo.com

2013

ISBN: 978-81-7049-456-0

Rs. 495/-

Designed at
Manas Publications

Printed in India at
Rajdhani Offsets, Delhi
and published by Mrs Suman Lata for
Manas Publications, 4402/5-A,
Ansari Road (Opp HDFC Bank),
Darya Ganj, New Delhi-110 002 (INDIA)

PREFACE

I HAVE frequently been told by readers of the seven volumes of my *Studies in the Psychology of Sex* that there is need for a small book to serve as a concise introduction to Sex Psychology. Ordinary medical practitioners and students, it is said, are far too over-burdened already to be able to master extensive treatises on an additional subject which is not obligatory. The subject of sex in its psychic and social bearings is so central, and of an importance now so widely recognized, if not indeed exaggerated, among the general public, that the medical man of to-day cannot fail to have it brought before him. He cannot, like his predecessors, conventionally ignore its existence, or feel that its recognition would be resented as impertinent or indecorous. Moreover, a knowledge confined to general anatomy, physiology, and pathology is now altogether inadequate.

My own opinion is in accord with these views. I have indeed felt that medical education displays at this point a vacuum which is altogether lamentable. In my own medical training, which began half a century ago, the psychological aspects of sex had no existence whatever. For my gynæcological teachers the processes of sex in health and disease were purely physical; the only consideration they introduced which could in any way be regarded as psychological in its bearing—and it stands out in memory because so isolated—was an unqualified warning against what would now be called contraception. It might be supposed that great progress has been made since those remote days. Here and there, no doubt, there has. But I have no evidence that the progress in any country is widespread or pronounced. It is less than twenty-five years since Fraenkel stated that "most gynæcologists know practically very little about sexuality," and Van de Velde remarks that that is still true for the great majority though there are now some honourable exceptions. I hear from medical students of to-day that they receive absolutely no instruction in the psycho-physical processes of sex, their liability to disturbance, or their hygiene. Ancient superstitions still prevail in our medical schools, and the medical students of to-day are for the most part still treated with almost the same misplaced reverence as the school children of a century ago, whom it was sometimes considered indecent to instruct in so sexual a subject as botany.

After long hesitation I have decided to prepare the little manual here presented to the reader. There is scarcely need to say that it makes no claim to supplant, or even to summarize, my larger work. It has sometimes been stated that those larger volumes deal chiefly with the pathological side of sex. That is an error. I might even claim that my *Studies* differed from all previous work on the subject by a main concern with the normal phenomena of sex. The same main concern is preserved in the present book. While my experience is partly derived from the abnormal persons who have come to me from widely varied quarters, it is chiefly founded on my knowledge of normal men and women and their problems in ordinary life. At the same time I have always sought to show that no sharp boundary-line exists between normal and abnormal. All normal persons are a little abnormal in one direction or another, and abnormal persons are still guided by fundamental impulses similar to those felt by normal persons.

"The goal of scientific inquiry," it has been truly said, "is the representation of experimentally demonstrable data with the aid of mathematical symbolism." We are far from the goal here. In this field we are only in the first phase—but it is a necessary and helpful phase—of regarding sex psychology as a department of natural history. If we desire more, as Freud has lately said at the end of a long career of fruitful research (in the Preface to the second series of his Introductory Lectures), we meet with uncertainties on every side.

I make no apology, therefore, for the fact that this little book is simple and concise. It may thus indeed the better reach the medical readers and students for whom it is primarily intended, though I need scarcely add that the appeal of this manual is not to medical readers alone, since the subject it deals with is the concern of all. There are certain essentials with which all should be familiar. I furnish the clues to those who desire to go further and to master problems which still lie ahead, and cannot in any case be adequately dealt with in an elementary manual.

Those problems stretch afar. Sexual science—sexology, as some would call it—differs, as an eminent German gynæcologist, Max Hirsch, has lately pointed out, from most other branches of the healing art by having no definitely circumscribed frontiers. From its centre radiate beams not only into all the other departments of medicine but also into many neighbouring regions, some of these with no obvious connection with medicine. It is even concerned with the whole of human culture. It leads us to tradition and custom. It is affected by morals and religion. We may recall the remark of Sir John Rose Bradford that what in the wide sense we to-day call the science of medicine might be summed up as "the natural history of man"

So it is that, to enter this field effectively, a complex experience is necessary, a special training, a personal disposition. It is to-day a field into which many put their foot whose explorations do not always, if often, bear examination. One may well be doubtful as to one's ability to bring back from that field anything likely to be of help to one's fellows. If I have myself waited long before presenting, with much hesitation, a manual which seems to offer itself as a guide, I do not feel that I have waited too long.

There are many, I might add, who before accepting me as a guide will desire to know what my attitude is towards psycho-analysis, the doctrine which until recently, if not indeed still, has aroused so much dispute where questions of sexual psychology arise. I may, therefore, say here at once that—as will be clear in due course—my attitude has from the first been sympathetic though never that of a partisan. A book of mine (*Studies*, Vol. I.) was in 1898 the first in English to set forth the earliest results reached by Freud, and my attitude to subsequent results has remained the same, always friendly but often critical. I would like to commend to all readers of the present book Freud's *Introductory Lectures on Psycho-Analysis* as not only the most authoritative but probably the best book for those who would confine their firsthand knowledge of psycho-analytic literature to a single volume; even those who are opposed to the general doctrine cannot fail to find here the outcome of much wisdom and experience. If a still briefer statement is desired it may be found set forth with the highest competence either in Ernest Jones's little book on Psycho-Analysis or in Professor Flügel's section on the subject in the *Outline of Modern Knowledge*. An elaborate and impartial exposition is *Structure and Meaning of Psycho-Analysis* by Healy, Bronner, and Bowers. For those who require a concise but lucid statement of the varying attitudes of all the chief psycho-therapeutic schools I would recommend Nicole's *Psychopathology*. While Freud must be recognized as the master in the psycho-analytic field there is no occasion to reject altogether those who have separated themselves from him to follow their own paths. They all have hold of some aspect of the many-sided human psyche, and, while avoiding a too indiscriminate eclecticism, we may accept whatever sound element each has to give.

The selected bibliographical data furnished at the end of each section, it will be remarked, are all English, so as to be within reach of the largest number of readers. Many important works are only to be found in other languages, especially German. The reader who is acquainted with those languages will have no difficulty in finding, through the data here furnished, such wider literature as he may require.

I have to add that in the preparation of this manual I have made some use of a chapter on "Sexual Problems, their Nervous and Mental Relations," which I wrote some years ago for the treatise on *The Modern Treatment of Nervous and*

Mental Disease, edited by Dr. William A. White and Dr. Smith Ely Jelliffe, and published by Lea and Febiger. I am obliged to the editors and publishers for permission thus to use this chapter. I have also made use of my contribution on the psychology of the normal sexual impulse to Dr. Albert Moll's *Handbuch der Sexualwissenschaften,* and that on psychopathic sexuality to Dr. A. Marie's *Traité International de Psychologie Pathologique.* It is only necessary to remark in conclusion that Sexual Psychology as here understood means the psychology of the sexual impulse and not the differential psychology of the two sexes, which is dealt with fully in my book, *Man and Woman.*

HAVELOCK ELLIS.

CONTENTS

PSYCHOLOGY OF SEX

CHAPTER I

INTRODUCTION

SEXUAL Psychology, normal and abnormal, as well as Sexual Hygiene, nowadays attracts a general interest and attention which before the present century was undreamed of. The young man of to-day is sometimes remarkably well informed in relation to the literature of sex, and the young woman of to-day often approaches these subjects in an inquiring spirit and with an absence of prudery which would have seemed to her grandmother absolutely impious. Until recent years any scientific occupation with sex was usually held to indicate, if not a vicious taste, at all events an unwholesome tendency. At the present time it is among the upholders of personal and public morality that the workers in sexual psychology and the advocates of sexual hygiene find the warmest support.

It can scarcely be said that until lately the medical profession has taken an active part in the extension of this movement. The pioneers, indeed—at first, nearly a century ago, in Germany and Austria, and later in other countries—have been physicians, but they were often looked at askance by their colleagues. Sexual psychology and sexual hygiene have formed no part of the physician's training. Indeed, scarcely more can be said of sexual physiology and it is little over twenty years ago that the first really scientific and comprehensive manual of sexual physiology (F. H. A. Marshall's) was issued from the press.

Just as the ordinary college manuals have ignored the anatomy and physiology of sex as completely as though this function formed no part whatever of animal life, so medical manuals have completely ignored the psychology of sex. It thus comes about that in the scientific knowledge of these matters, which for the comprehension of some cases is vitally important, the physician is often less well informed than his patient, and not seldom is the victim of false traditions and antiquated prejudices. Religion and morality have been invoked in behalf of silence on such subjects by those who might have remembered that, even from his own standpoint, a great Father of the Church had declared that we should not be ashamed to speak of what God was not ashamed to create.

This ignorance may be even more serious when we are concerned with what was often referred to with horror as "perversion." Again and again, where psychic sexual anomalies are concerned, we find patients complaining that their physician has shown no comprehension of their special difficulties, either brushing aside the condition as of no consequence, or else treating them as vicious, wicked, perhaps disgusting persons. It is doubtless the patient's consciousness of this attitude in his doctor which leads many physicians, even of great experience, to declare that psycho-sexual anomalies are very rare and that they scarcely ever meet with them.

It may no doubt be maintained that in vaguely holding forth an ideal of robust normality, and refusing even to hear of any deviation from that ideal, the physician is stimulating and inspiring his patients to pursue the right course. But it must be pointed out that in this respect psychic health is not different from physical health. An exact and intelligent knowledge of the patient's abnormal condition is necessary in order to restore the normal condition. We cannot bring him to the position where we desire him to be unless we know where he at present is. Moreover, in psychic health, to an even greater extent than in physical health, the range of what may be considered normal variation is very wide. And further, in order to ascertain what precisely is the norm for any given individual in this matter, we must know exactly what is his innate psycho-sexual constitution, for otherwise we may be putting him on a path which, though normal for others, is really abnormal for him.

It is on these grounds that much facile and conventional advice given to psycho-sexual patients is misplaced and even mischievous. This holds good, for instance, of the advice so often given to sexually abnormal persons to marry. Certainly in some cases such advice may be excellent. But it cannot be safely given except with fullness of knowledge and with precise reference to the conditions of the individual case. This warning holds good, indeed, of all advice in the psycho-sexual sphere. Sex penetrates the whole person; a man's sexual constitution is a part of his general constitution. There is considerable truth in the dictum: "A man is what his sex is." No useful advice can be given concerning the guidance and control of the sexual life unless this is borne in mind. A man may, indeed, be mistaken concerning his own sexual nature. He may be merely passing through a youthful and temporary abnormal stage, to reach eventually a more normal and permanent condition. Or he may, by some undue reaction, have mistaken a subordinate impulse of his nature for the predominant impulse, since we are all made up of various impulses, and the sexually normal man is often a man who holds in control some abnormal impulse. Yet in the main a man's sexual constitution is all-pervading, deep-rooted, permanent, in large measure congenital.

At the same time we must be cautious in fixing the barrier between the constitutional and the acquired. We have to recognize, on the one hand, that the acquired may go much farther back than was once believed, and, on the other hand, that the constitutional is often so subtle and so obscure that it remains undetected. For the most part, as is too often forgotten, both sets of factors combine: the germ proves active because the soil happens to be favourable. Here, as elsewhere, the result is not due to seed alone or soil alone, but to their association. Even in children of the same family the results of Mendelian inheritance may bring different seeds into action, and the Director of the London Child Guidance Clinic has lately pointed out how the same stress may make one child steal and another abnormally shy.

This consideration serves to control the advice which the physician may reasonably give in psycho-sexual cases, and even to restrict the influence of any guidance he may offer. There is another reason why the sexual impulse is incomparably less amenable to therapeutical influence than the other impulse with which it may be compared, the nutritive impulse. Certainly the sexual impulse may, within limits, be guided and controlled at will to a much greater extent than some are willing to admit. But the sexual impulse is, to an incomparably greater degree than the nutritive impulse, held in certain paths and shut out of other paths, by traditional influences of religion, morality, and social convention. There are a few physicians who hold that these influences should be ignored. The physician has nothing to do with morals or with conventions, they argue; he must consider what is for his patient's good and advise him accordingly, without any regard to moral and conventional dictates. That, however, is a short-sighted course of action which leads to many awkward positions, to all kinds of inconsistencies, not seldom to a greater evil than the evil it is sought to cure. For it is the special characteristic of the sexual impulse, as distinct from the nutritive impulse, that its normal gratification involves another person. It leads directly into the social sphere, into the sphere of morals. No one is entitled to seek his own good, or can be advised to seek his good, in any line of action which involves evil to other persons. Nor, indeed, can the patient's own good, in any comprehensive and rational sense, be found in a line of action involving injury to those nearest to him, or a violation of his own conscience and convictions. The wise physician cannot afford to neglect these considerations, even though he may be fully resolved that his advice shall not be based on mere conventions. They are real and vital considerations, interwoven with the traditional social edifice in which we all live, and in innumerable cases they render it impossible for the physician to follow purely biological lines in framing his psycho-sexual therapeutics. He must often feel himself helpless because the condition before him is largely the result of factors over which he has no control, just as he must feel himself helpless with patients whose condition is mainly the result of overwork and underfeeding which the conditions of their lives have rendered inevitable.

It may be desirable, at the same time, to point out that, while the patient's moral situation cannot be ignored, it would be a mistake to regard the moral situation as absolutely rigid and unchangeable. Morals are in perpetual transition. Much that is regarded as moral to-day, or at all events as permitted, was fifty years ago regarded as immoral, and was not openly permitted. In harmony with the change in the moral situation, distinguished physicians, with a full sense of responsibility, to-day openly publish advice in matters of sex which not so very long ago they could not have ventured to give even in private. The physician, alive to the large and splendid part he is entitled to play in working for the welfare of the community, and as medical adviser in the education of the whole people, takes part in this transformation of morals. But he has always to consider the special situation of the individual patient.

Thus it would be a serious mistake to conclude that psycho-sexual cases must be viewed pessimistically, or regarded as belonging to a field with which it is not worth while for the physician to concern himself. On the contrary, psycho-sexual cases, precisely because they are in the psychic sphere, can be affected by indirect influences which have little effect on the more physical factors of disease, like overwork and underfeeding, which are likewise often beyond the physician's direct reach. It is at times astonishing to the physician to find in such cases, even when he has seemed to himself most helpless, how genuinely grateful the patient is for the benefit received. This is not always the result of suggestion, but rather of the opposite and equally natural process on which Freud had at the outset based his method of psycho-analysis—the cathartic process of yielding up and bringing to the surface suppressed elements of consciousness and so relieving the tension caused by the suppression. In this very process of self-confession, in which the physician, even by the intelligence and sympathy he brings to the task, is really taking an active part, an abnormal condition is removed, and while this may not suffice to render the sexual impulse normal, it certainly renders it less injurious, and at the same time restores the whole psychic life to some degree of harmonious equilibrium. The religious process, so completely developed in Catholicism of confession and absolution, rests psychologically on this same basis, and (though it has other reasons for existence) it tends, without doubt, to produce the same beneficial results. It is noteworthy that many persons, suspecting that they will find little intelligent sympathy from their doctor, spontaneously take their sexual anomalies to their minister, of whatever denomination, for the sake of the relief of self-confession to one whose function it is to restore and console. There is an important field of such psychic therapeutics, apart from religious operation and even apart from hypnotic and other forms of suggestion, which legitimately belongs to the physician, and will be found peculiarly helpful in the psycho-sexual sphere. It is among Freud's special merits—whatever we may think of the developments of which his doctrine proved susceptible in his own hands or the hands of others—that he early recognized this special province of psycho-therapeutics, and realized—in the simile he adopted from the arts of painting and sculpture—that psycho-therapeutics may operate not only *per via di porre*, by putting in, but also *per via di levare*, by taking out, by removing unnecessary inhibitions and suppressions and thus restoring the normal relationships of the psychic organism.

BIBLIOGRAPHY

F. H. A. Marshall, *The Physiology of Reproduction.*
S. Freud, *Introductory Lectures on Psycho-Analysis.*

CHAPTER II

THE BIOLOGY OF SEX

The Physical Basis of Sex

REPRODUCTION is so primitive and fundamental a function of vital organisms that the mechanism by which it is assured is highly complex and not yet clearly understood. It is not necessarily connected with sex, nor is sex necessarily connected with reproduction. Yet the full development of the sexual apparatus with the related secondary sexual characters, as of the body generally, depends on the integrity of the gametes or reproductive cells—the ova provided by the female and the spermatozoa by the male—during the whole of their course in giving origin to the zygote or fertilized egg, and later on the course of the zygote's development. The best authorities hesitate to define exactly what "sex" is, but at all events it is at the outset conditioned by the chromosome constitution of the at first relatively undifferentiated gonad cell. During the process of cell-division, the contained chromatin of its nucleus resolves itself into a certain number of filaments of definite rod-like shape—these being the chromosomes—which fall into order and are constant in number for the species to which the cell belongs. They are alike in all races of man, whether in the male or the female, though it is the male that is digametic, or, as it is termed, XY, and distinguishable by its smaller size. In mammals generally, indeed (it is the reverse in birds), the male elaborates two kinds of gametes, X-bearing, and non X-bearing, or Y-bearing, while the female elaborates but one. An X-bearing egg can be fertilized either by an X-bearing sperm, to become XX and female, or a Y-bearing sperm to become XY and male. Therewith we have the starting-point of the whole process (made clear by the extended and comprehensive investigations of Evans and

Swezy) which there is no occasion to follow in detail here in its variations along, as is now held, Mendelian lines. The Mendelian processes of heredity are much more varied and complicated in man than in those lower organisms in which they were first studied.

We have to conclude that sex is, normally, determined at conception, and to put aside all the various devices for determining sex during pregnancy. It is certainly necessary to postulate, in Crew's words, that " in every zygote, be it XX or XY in sex chromosome constitution, there are the physical bases of developmental impulses which strive to impose upon the developing individual a male type and a female type of differentiation respectively."

It is necessary to refer to the recent developments of knowledge in this field—recent as belonging to the present century—because they happen to be of peculiarly close relationship to the psychology of sex.

At the outset we assume as accepted that when a complex of glands to which the testis is central predominates in the organism we have an individual of male sex ; when a complex of glands to which the ovary is central predominates we have a female. Thus are secured normally the primary sexual characters. Associated with them is the development of the respective sexual organs. Finally sexual maturity is established with the full acquisition of the manifest secondary characters, with which are associated, as tertiary sexual characters, many differences which are not obvious but are clear when we deal with averages. All these processes are liable to much variation. The sex glands and the secondary sexual characters may shift towards an inter-sexual type, which in one way or another—physically, psychically, or both—may approximate to the opposite sex.

The syndromes thus observed are, as we now believe, in the majority of cases traceable either to the stimulating influence, or to the defect of such influence, of the internal secretions—the hormones or chemical messengers—entering the blood from the various ductless glands of the body. By over-secretion, under-secretion, or disordered secretion, the physical conformation of the body, and the psychical disposition and aptitudes, may be modified, and even the sex virtually changed. Any dysfunction of one is apt to unsettle the balance of the others. We are concerned with the harmonious adjustment of many ductless glands. To the interpretation of the intricate relations thus resulting much study is now being directed in many countries. New facts and new viewpoints are constantly appearing, and great importance now attaches to the activating influence of the anterior lobe of the pituitary gland, and also to the adrenals, for it is possible, as Blair Bell has long held, to regard ovaries, or testes, as but " one link in the chain of organs such as the pituitary and thyroid which form a gametal system." The testicular hormone, called proviron, is mainly responsible for the development of the secondary sexual characters and has now been standardized. There are at least two ovarian hormones, œstrin and progestin. The results are at many points still uncertain. But it is essential to the study of the psychology of sex to have some acquaintance with the physiological and biochemical researches carried on along these lines, although it would be out of place to deal with them here. They are developing day by day and the progress of knowledge is recorded in the current medical journals and in biochemical literature.

It suffices here to take a surveying glimpse from above and to see that the general change effected has been that, while previously we regarded the nervous system as the active agent in these processes, we now regard the chemical endocrine system as even more active, sometimes under the influence of the nervous system, and frequently apart from nervous action, the nerves and nerve-centres being themselves sometimes subject to chemical regulation.

If we follow Langdon Brown, we may say that the endocrines are an elaboration of those chemical mechanisms to which animals responded before the nervous system was developed. It is an interesting proof of the primitive nature of endocrine regulation of the organism that all the hormonic messengers proceed from very ancient and even vestigial structures in the body, like the pituitary and the pineal. At the same time we may also bear in mind, as Bolk emphasized some years ago, that the stimulation or retardation due to hormonic influences is peculiarly influential in developing the specific human qualities, and even, as Keith has more recently pointed out, the various racial human characteristics. When the nervous system began to take shape, and even to acquire dominance, it entered into alliance with the pre-existing chemical mechanisms, especially through its lowest level, the visceral nervous system, subdivisible into the sympathetic system and the para-sympathetic (or extended vagus) system. The sympathetic, which may be regarded as tending to be katabolic and active, is associated with the pituitary, thyroid, and adrenals. The para-sympathetic, which may be regarded as largely anabolic and passive, is associated with the pancreas and, indirectly, the parathyroids. These katabolic and anabolic systems are antagonistic, the rhythm of life, it has been said, depending upon their balance. The gonads interact especially with the sympathetic-endocrine group. The pineal and thymus, though not true endocrine glands (since they have no known secretions), affect the endocrine system chiefly by a retarding influence on sexual maturity, and a favouring influence on somatic growth.

The pituitary is now seen to be what has been termed "the leader of the endocrine orchestra." Ancient anatomists, viewing this small body joined by a stalk to the brain above, regarded it as a miniature brain and to-day the notion is seen to be not altogether absurd. "Here, in this well-concealed spot," says Harvey Cushing, "lies the very mainspring of primitive existence—vegetative, emotional, and reproductive—on which, with more or less success, Man, chiefly, has come to superimpose a cortex of inhibitions." Evans and Simpson have worked out the relation of certain of its cells to growth and to sexual development.

The thyroid, again, which has been termed "the gland of creation," is also essential to reproduction, if, indeed, it is not, as has been claimed, essential to all kinds of creative activity, artistic and intellectual. Its extract, thyroxine (which can be synthetically prepared) also has a slow and gradual influence on general nutrition.

Adrenaline (which may also be prepared synthetically) from the suprarenals has a more rapid influence on the heart, vessels, liver, salivary glands, intestines, pupils, and spleen. While adrenaline has this wide influence, its secretion itself, as Tournade has shown, is intimately dependent upon the nervous system.

The endocrine organs may influence each other. Removing the thyroid may lead to pituitary enlargement, though to remove the pituitary at a youthful stage in an animal may arrest the thyroid. The thyroid stimulates the suprarenals, which stimulate the hepatic cells to discharge glycogen into the blood, and this stimulates the pancreas to increased secretion of insulin. The anterior part of the pituitary, again, appears to yield three hormones, one which promotes growth, one which stimulates the ovaries, causing maturation of the Graafian follicles, which produce œstrin, which initiates changes in the uterus to receive the fertilized ovum ; while a third hormone leads to further uterine changes for the fixation of the ovum. Œstrin (also called by other names) is an ovarian hormone of special practical importance as its presence in the urine is the basis of the Zondek-Aschheim test of pregnancy.

There is a close resemblance between the action of internal secretions and drugs. Sharpey-Schafer would restrict the use of the term " hormone " to those having an exciting influence, and would term those with an opposing inhibitory influence " chalones." He would call both together " autacoids," to signify that they are drug-like principles produced by the body itself.

It will be seen that we now have to define physiological phenomena in terms of chemical as well as of nervous regulation. We see also that both sets of terms, and the chemical perhaps even more than the nervous, lie on the other side of psychic phenomena. We have to realize the existence of a large number of substances in the body, very minute but very potent—hormones and vitamins as well as the derivative serums and vaccines—which may properly be termed biochemical drugs. Their significance seems greater the more our rapidly growing knowledge of them extends. But we are not therefore justified in importing biochemical phraseology into psychology. It has long been clearly understood that it was a mistake to attempt to introduce histological terminology into psychology. It would be equally a mistake to introduce biochemical terminology. An emotion remains an emotion, alike whether a hormone or a chalone has on the physical side taken part in its production.

BIBLIOGRAPHY

F. A. E. Crew, *The Genetics of Sexuality in Animals*, also article "Sex" in Rose's *Outline of Modern Knowledge*.

A. Lipshütz, *The Internal Secretions of the Sex Glands*.

Joseph Needham, *Chemical Embriology*, 3 Vols.

F. H. A. Marshall, *The Physiology of Reproduction*, also on the Sex Hormones, *British Medical Journal*, August 6th, 1932.

C. C. Hurst, *The Mechanism of Creative Evolution*.

H. M. Evans and Olive Swezy, "The Chromosomes in Man," *Memoirs of the University of California*, Vol. IX, 1929.

W. Blair Bell, "Conservative Gynæcological Surgery," *British Medical Journal*, April 18th, 1931.

Langdon Brown, "Endocrines and Associated Psychoneuroses," *British Medical Journal*, February 6th, 1932.

J. H. Burn, *Recent Advances in Materia Medica* (the biochemical drugs), 1931.

Sir E. Sharpey-Schafer, "Endocrine Physiology," *British Medical Journal*, August 22nd, 1931.

The Nature of the Sexual Impulse

Turning from the strictly physiological aspects of the organic activities that work together to effect sexual development, it is necessary to obtain a comprehensive view of the biological process of sex as expressed in the psychic phenomena with which we are here immediately concerned.

There is, indeed, no universally accepted theory of the process on its psychic side. In the old popular belief the sexual impulse is simply the expression of a need of evacuation, comparable to that experienced periodically in the bowels and bladder. That was an inaccurate and misleading view; the male semen is not a waste product for excretion and the female scarcely presents even the semblance of a sexual desire for excretion. A more respectable theory sometimes put forward defined the sexual impulse as an "instinct of reproduction." There is, however, strictly speaking, no such instinct, nor is it needed in bisexual organisms. All that is needed is the motor impulse to bring male and female together in such a way as to insure fertilization; that once achieved, the future of the offspring is ensured by the stimulus furnished to the parental impulses; no instinct of reproduction is called for.

In what has perhaps been the most popular manual of its subject, Professor W. McDougall's *Introduction to Social Psychology*, no treatment of sex was to be found at all (beyond a reference to the "instinct of reproduction") until the eighth edition appeared in 1914 with a supplementary chapter on "the sex instinct." It is here defined as a complex, innately organized, psycho-physical disposition, consisting of three parts, each subserving one of the three phases that we distinguish in every complete mental or psycho-physical process, namely the cognitive, the affective, and the conative; three parts which, from the point of view of nervous function and structure, we may call the afferent or sensory, the central, and the efferent or motor. He points out that on the cognitive side there is involved an innate disposition to perceive or perceptually discriminate those things towards which such reactions are demanded by the welfare of the species; that is to say, an ability to discriminate the opposite sex, with, in the higher species, a chain of reactions to ensure complete adaptation in the sexual act.

McDougall's definition is, as he himself remarks, that which he would give for all instincts, and he defines instincts as "certain innate specific tendencies of the mind that are common to all members of any one species." It is, in fact, a generalized statement which scarcely helps us to grasp what takes place in the process of bisexual approximation and union.

There is, indeed, a tendency, which I have long followed, to discard in this connection, so far as possible, the use of the word "instinct," though Piéron and many others would still preserve it. It may even be undesirable to use the word "instinct" at all. The word has, as Bohn remarks, a compromising history, nor is there any complete agreement as to the sense in which it should be used, though, for ordinary purposes, "instinct" may be regarded as, according to the definition of Herbert Spencer, "compound reflex action," the question as to whether it is accompanied by consciousness being regarded as non-essential.

It may even be said that biological psychologists generally, and not only those who had been subjected to the influence of Loeb, are inclined to return to the position of Condillac and to drop the use of the word "instinct." It is our business, these investigators hold, to analyse the automatic psychic processes we meet with, and we are not called upon to increase the difficulties of doing so by applying to them a word with so many varied and unfortunate associations. I have always preferred the less questionable term "impulses"; as Freud has remarked, "impulsion is in fact the very essence of an 'instinct'." We may, therefore, put aside the discussion of sex as an "instinct," and certainly as "an instinct of reproduction," which is but a crude euphemism, for an impulse is not analysed by merely stating the end which it may indirectly effect. We are solely concerned with the sexual impulse and its analysis.

The question of the analysis of the sexual impulse was placed upon higher ground when, in 1897, Moll set forth his theory of the constitution of this impulse. As Moll understood it, there are two components in the sexual impulse: one which urges to a local genital function, which in man is the expulsion of semen, and is thus a process of evacuation comparable to the emptying of the bladder, and the other which urges each partner to physical and psychic contact with the other partner. The first component Moll termed *the impulse of detumescence*, the second the *impulse of contrectation*. Both these components may be traced back to the sexual glands, the first being primary and the second secondary, but they are distinct and each may exist separately. Their union constitutes the complete normal sexual impulse.

Moll's analysis had much to commend it, as a scientific and comprehensive statement, and it has in consequence been widely accepted. It presents, however, certain difficulties : it is, for instance, less satisfactory when applied to women than to men, and it has the disadvantage, pointed out by Robert Müller, Saint-Paul, and others, that it divides the sexual process. In order to avoid this and other difficulties, the theory of Moll was by me somewhat modified with the aid of the least contested part of the Darwinian doctrine of sexual selection. If we look into the sexual process as it exists among animals generally, and among men in the savage state, we soon realize that we cannot start with detumescence. Before *detumescence* can take place, *tumescence* must be achieved. In domesticated animals and in civilized man that is often an easy process. It is not usually so in the natural state. There it is achieved through much activity and display on the part of the male, and long contemplation and consideration on the part of the female, the part taken by each in this process serving to increase tumescence alike in both. "Contrectation," whether physical or psychic, simply has as its end the heightening of tumescence and may be regarded as part of the process.

It is during the slow process of tumescence that sexual selection is decided, the crystallizations of love (as Stendhal called them) elaborated, and the individual erotic symbols, normal or abnormal, determined. Yet detumescence is the end and climax of the whole drama ; it is an anatomic-physiological process, certainly, but one that inevitably touches psychology at every point. It is, indeed, the very key to the process of tumescence, and unless we understand and realize very precisely what it is that happens, our psychological analysis of the sexual impulse must remain vague and inadequate.

Detumescence is normally linked closely to tumescence. Tumescence is the piling on of the fuel ; detumescence is the leaping out of the devouring flame whence is lighted the torch of life to be handed on from generation to generation. The whole process is double and yet single ; it is analogous to that by which a pile is driven into the earth by the raising and then the letting go of a heavy weight which falls on to the head of the pile. In tumescence the organism is slowly wound up and force accumulated ; in the act of detumescence the accumulated force is let go, and by its liberation the sperm-bearing instrument is driven home. Courtship, as we commonly term the process of tumescence which takes place when a woman is sexually approached by a man, is usually a highly prolonged process. But it is always necessary to remember that every repetition of the act of coitus, to be normally and effectively carried out on both sides, naturally demands a similar double process ; detumescence should be preceded by an abbreviated courtship.

This abbreviated courtship, by which tumescence is secured or heightened even in the repetition of acts of coitus which have become familiar, is mainly tactile. As tumescence, under the influence of sensory stimulation, proceeds toward the climax when it gives place to detumescence, the physical phenomena become more and more acutely localized in the sexual organs. The process which was at first predominantly nervous and psychic now becomes more prominently vascular. The ancient sexual relationship of the skin asserts itself; there is a marked surface congestion showing itself in various ways. The face tends to become red, and exactly the same phenomenon is taking place in the genital organs; "an erection," it has been said, "is a blushing of the penis." The difference is that in the genital organs this heightened vascularity has a definite and specific function to accomplish—the erection of the male organ which fits it to enter the female parts—and that consequently there has been developed in the penis that special kind of vascular mechanism, consisting of veins in connective tissue with unstriped muscular fibres, termed erectile tissue. This process may be set in action either centrally or peripherally.

It is not only the male who is supplied with erectile tissue which in the process of tumescence becomes congested and swollen. The female also in the corresponding external genital region is likewise supplied with erectile tissue now also charged with blood, and exhibits the same changes as have taken place in her partner, though they are not conspicuously visible. In the anthropoid apes, as the gorilla, the large clitoris and nymphæ become prominent in sexual excitement, but the less development of the clitoris in women, together with the specifically human evolution of the *mons veneris* and larger lips, renders this sexual turgescence practically invisible, though it is perceptible to touch in an increased degree of spongy and elastic tension. The whole feminine genital canal, including the uterus, indeed, is richly supplied with blood-vessels, and is capable during sexual excitement of a high degree of turgescence, a kind of erection.

The process of erection in woman is accompanied by the pouring out of fluid which copiously bathes all parts of the vulva around the entrance to the vagina. This is a bland, more or less odourless mucus which, under ordinary circumstances, slowly and imperceptibly suffuses the parts. There is, however, a real ejaculation of fluid which, as usually described, comes largely from glands, situated near the mouth of the vagina, which are already able to secrete at birth. The fluid poured out in this manner whenever a high degree of tumescence is attained, and before the onset of detumescence, performs an important function in lubricating the entrance to the genital canal and so facilitating the entrance of the male organ. A similar process takes place during parturition when the same parts are being stretched for the protrusion of the fœtal head. The occurrence of the mucous flow in tumescence always indicates that that process is actively affecting the cerebral centres, and that voluptuous emotions are present. Hence it is of high significance in the art of love.

When erection is complete in both the man and the woman the conditions for conjugation have at last been fulfilled.

At this point, when the woman is a virgin, the problem of the hymen is encountered. In ancient days, this little flap of tissue—the maidenhead as it was suggestively termed—was frequently regarded as of immense significance in determining the status of a woman. Its presence was held to decide the moral character of an unmarried woman. There are reasons now why it cannot retain that position, even apart from the fact that the virtue of a woman is less commonly supposed to rest on a merely anatomical foundation. There are many natural variations in the shape and size of the hymen; various accidents (as well as virginal masturbation) may cause its disappearance; while it may occasionally persist after intercourse, even in prostitutes.

Its rupture on the first act of intercourse is apt to cause pain and discomfort. Occasionally its toughness leads to difficulty in penetration. A slight incision may then be necessary. Graduated pressure, as with the finger, which may be practised by the woman herself, has also been recommended. Among some peoples the insertion of the finger is practised by mothers on their girl children from an early age, sometimes for hygienic reasons and sometimes to facilitate intercourse in future years. There may be something to be said for this practice.

In all animals, even those most nearly allied to Man, coitus is effected by the male approaching the female posteriorly. In Man, the normal method of male approach is anteriorly—face to face—the position of so-called *Venus observa*. While, however, the *Venus observa* may be regarded as the specifically human method of coitus, there are modifications of it, and other more animal-like methods which have been adopted by various peoples as national customs, and which, therefore, come within the normal range of variation. It is a mistake to regard them as vicious perversions.

Now a new element comes in: muscular action. With the onset of muscular action, which is largely involuntary, even when it affects the voluntary muscles, detumescence proper begins to take place. Hence full purposeful action is, except by an effort, virtually abolished. We approach the decisive moment when, under the influence of the stimulus applied to the penis by friction with the vagina, the tension of the seminal fluid poured into the urethra arouses the ejaculatory centres located in the lower part of the spinal cord and also, it appears, in the pelvic plexuses.

and the bulbo-cavernosus muscle surrounding the urethra responsively contracts in rhythmic spasms. Then it is that ejaculation occurs.

The phenomena of coitus may all be directly or indirectly reduced to two groups: the first circulatory and respiratory, the second motor, though it must be borne in mind that these are not really separable. The respiration becomes shallow, rapid, and to some extent arrested. This arrest of respiration tends to render the blood venous, and thus aids in stimulating the vasomotor centres, raising the blood-pressure in the body generally, and especially in the erectile tissues. High blood-pressure is one of the most marked features of the state of detumescence; according to Poussep there are in animals during coitus rapid alternations of vaso-constriction and vaso-dilatation, both in the brain and the vascular system generally. The heart-beats are stronger and quicker, the surface arteries are more visible, the conjunctivæ become red. At the same time we find a general tendency to glandular activity. Various secretions are formed abundantly. Perspiration is copious, with a general activity of the skin and its odoriferous secretions; salivation also occurs. In men, corresponding to the more copious secretion in women, there is, during the latter stages of tumescence, a secretion of mucus which appears in drops at the urethral orifice and comes from the small glands of Littré and Cowper which open into the urethra. This phenomenon was called *distillatio* by the old theologians, who realized its significance, as distinct from semen but an indication that the mind was dwelling on voluptuous images; it was also known in classic times; more recently it has often been confused with semen and has thus sometimes caused needless anxiety to nervous persons. There is also an increased secretion by the kidneys and probably by the glands throughout the body generally.

Motor activity is of the essence of detumescence because without it the sperm-cells could not be effectively brought into the neighbourhood of the germ-cell and be propelled into the womb. This activity is general as well as specifically sexual. There is a tendency to more or less involuntary movement, without any increase of voluntary muscular power, which is, indeed, decreased. The tendency to diffused activity of involuntary muscle is illustrated by the contraction of the bladder associated with detumescence. While this occurs in both sexes, in men erection usually produces a mechanical impediment to any evacuation of the bladder. In women there may be not only a desire to urinate, but, occasionally, actual urination. The tendency to trembling, constriction of the throat, sneezing, emission of internal gas, and the other similar phenomena occasionally associated with detumescence, likewise witness to diffusion of the motor disturbance.

More important, and more purposive though involuntary, are the specifically sexual muscular movements. From the very beginning of detumescence, this muscular activity makes itself felt. In the male these movements are fairly obvious and fairly simple. It is required that the semen should be expressed from the vesiculæ seminales, propelled along the urethra, in combination with the prostatic fluid which is equally essential, and finally ejected with a certain amount of force from the urethral orifice. Normally, under the influence of the stimulation furnished by the contact and friction of the vagina, this process is effectively carried out, mainly by the rhythmic contractions of the bulbo-cavernosus muscle, and the semen is emitted in a jet.

The specifically sexual muscular process is less visible in the woman, more obscure, more complex and uncertain. Before detumescence actually begins there are at intervals involuntary rhythmic contractions of the walls of the vagina, seeming to have the object of at once stimulating and harmonizing with those that are about to begin in the male organ. It would appear that these rhythmic contractions are the exaggeration of a phenomenon which is fairly constant, just as slight contractions are normal and constant in the bladder. This vaginal contraction, which may become well marked just before detumescence, and is due mainly to the action of the sphincter cunni (analogous to the bulbo-cavernosus in the male), is only a part of the localized muscular process.

The active participation of the sexual organs in woman, to the end of directing the semen into the womb at the moment of detumescence, is an ancient belief, and harmonizes with the Greek view of the womb as an animal in the body endowed with activity, but precise observation in modern times has offered but little confirmation of the reality of this participation. Such observations as have been made have usually been the accidental result of sexual excitement and orgasm occurring during a gynæcological examination. So far as the evidence goes, it would seem that in women, as in mares, bitches, and other animals, the uterus becomes shorter, broader, and softer during the orgasm, at the same time descending lower into the pelvis, with its mouth open intermittently.

It would seem probable that in this erection, contraction, and descent of the uterus, and its simultaneous expulsion of mucus, we have the decisive moment in the completion of detumescence in woman, and that the thick mucus, unlike the earlier more limpid secretion, which women are sometimes aware of after orgasm, is emitted from the womb at this time. Some authorities regard detumescence in women as accomplished in the pouring out of secretions, others in the rhythmic genital contractions, especially at the cervix of the womb. The sexual parts may, however, be copiously bathed in mucus for an indefinitely long period before the final stage of detumescence is achieved, and the rhythmic contractions are also taking place at a somewhat early period ; in neither respect is there necessarily any obvious increase at the final moment of orgasm. In women this would seem to be more conspicuously a nervous manifestation than in men. On the subjective side it is pronounced, with its feeling of relieved tension and agreeable repose, but on the objective side the culminating moment is often less easy to define, and is not invariably, as it tends to be in men, a general motor convulsion.

The active part played by the womb in detumescence can no longer be questioned, but it must not be too hastily assumed that the belief in the active movements of the spermatozoa must therefore be denied. If it is correct, as some authorities believe, that the spermatozoa may retain their full activity in the female organs even for a week or more (though it is questioned whether this is a general rule) they have ample time to exert their energies. It must be added, however, that even if the semen is effused merely at the mouth of the vagina, without actual penetration, the spermatozoa are still not entirely without any resource save their own motility in the task of reaching the ovum. Since it is not only the uterus which takes an active part in detumescence but the vagina also is in active movement, it seems probable that, at all events in some women and under some circumstances, such movement, favouring aspiration toward the womb, may be communicated to the external mouth of the vagina. It is also believed by some that, especially in women of races of more primitive type, the vagina may be capable of obeying the same impulse to expel the semen as to expel the child during parturition, and that this may be utilized for contraceptive ends. Owing to the combined activities of the semen and vagina during sexual excitement, it is possible for the semen to reach the uterus even when it has only been effused at the entrance of the vagina, and even when the hymen is intact. Thus extra-vaginal effusion of semen is not an adequate contraceptive method, and consequently, even when a husband is convinced that he has had no actual coitus with his wife, this is no proof, should pregnancy follow, that there has been adultery.

Even though the specifically sexual muscular process of detumescence in women—as distinguished from the general muscular phenomena of sexual excitement which may be fairly obvious—is thus seen to be complex and obscure, detumescence is, in both sexes, a convulsion which discharges a slowly accumulated store of nervous force. In women, as in men, the motor discharge is directed to a specific end—the intromission of the semen in the one sex, its reception in the other. In both sexes the sexual orgasm and the pleasure and satisfaction associated with it involve, as their most essential element, the motor activity of the sexual sphere.

Although the facial expression, when tumescence is completed, may be marked by a high degree of energy in men and of loveliness in women, at the beginning of detumescence the features are frequently more discomposed. The dilatation of the pupils, the expansion of the nostrils, the tendency to salivation and to movements of the tongue, all go to make up a picture which indicates an approaching gratification of sensory desires; it is significant that in some animals there is at this moment erection of the ears. There is sometimes a tendency to utter broken or meaningless words. The dilatation of the pupils produces photophobia, and in the course of detumescence the eyes are frequently closed from this cause. At the beginning of sexual excitement, tonicity of the eye-muscles seems to increase; the elevators of the upper lids contract, so that the eyes look larger and their mobility and brightness are heightened; with the increase of muscular tonicity strabismus may occur.

So profound is the organic convulsion involved by the process of detumescence that serious effects have sometimes followed coitus. Even in animals this has been noted. In the human species, especially in men—probably because women are protected by the greater slowness with which detumescence occurs in them—not only death itself, but numerous disorders and accidents have been known to follow immediately after coitus, these results being mainly due to the vascular and muscular excitement involved by the process of detumescence. Fainting, vomiting, involuntary urination and defæcation, have been noted as occurring in young men after a first coitus. Epilepsy has been not infrequently recorded. Lesions of various organs, even rupture of the spleen, have sometimes taken place. In men of mature age the arteries have at times been unable to resist the high blood pressure, and cerebral hæmorrhage with paralysis has occurred. In elderly men the excitement of intercourse with young wives or with prostitutes has sometimes caused death.

Such results are, however, exceptional. They tend to occur in persons who are abnormally sensitive, or who have imprudently transgressed the obvious rules of sexual hygiene,

Detumescence is so profoundly natural a process, it is so deeply and intimately a function of the organism, that it is frequently harmless even when the bodily condition is unsound. Its usual results, under favourable circumstances, are entirely beneficial. In men there normally supervenes, together with the relief from the prolonged tension of tumescence, with the muscular repose and falling blood pressure, a sense of profound satisfaction, a glow of diffused well-being, an agreeable lassitude, often a sense of mental liberation from an over-mastering obsession. Under reasonably happy circumstances there is no pain, or exhaustion, or sadness, or emotional revulsion. In women the results of detumescence are the same, except that the tendency to lassitude is not marked unless the act has been several times repeated; there is a sensation of repose and self-assurance, often an accession of free and joyous energy. After satisfactory detumescence women may experience a feeling as of intoxication, lasting for several hours, that is followed by no evil reaction.

Thus we see that tumescence and detumescence are not two distinct processes but one process with two phases. That process represents Nature's method of highly charging the organism in order to discharge it in the act of orgasm which, by liberating the generative cells and effecting their union, achieves the supreme end of reproduction, and, when that end is inhibited, still effects changes throughout the organism which are physically and psychically beneficial.

BIBLIOGRAPHY

A. Moll, *Sexual Life of the Child.*

Havelock Ellis, "Analysis of the Sexual Impulse," Vol. III, and "The Mechanism of Detumescence," Vol. V, of *Studies in the Psychology of Sex.*

Th. Van de Velde, *Ideal Marriage; Fertility and Sterility in Marriage.*

Erogenic Zones

This is the name now given to regions of the body which in the process of tumescence are found to be sexually hyperæsthetic. Some regions are normally so in all healthy persons; other regions of the body, indeed almost or quite any region of the body surface, may be sexually sensitive in special cases, the degree of such sensitiveness being liable to vary at different times and being naturally greater when there is a state of emotional predisposition. The genital region, the mouth, and in woman the nipples may be said to be normal erogenic zones. The ears, the nape of the neck, the nipples in men, the armpits, the fingers, the anus, the thighs are all not uncommon erogenic zones.

The conception of erogenic zones may be said to be developed out of the ancient view of "sympathy." It was first definitely formulated in medicine in the sphere of pathology, as the hysterogenic zones of Charcot, certain regions being found—at first ovarian and later more widely dispersed—which were connected, on pressure, with the causation or the arrest of spasmodic attacks; but Charcot did not associate them with sexual emotion. In 1881, however, Chambard of Paris showed that, in the normal condition and especially in women, there are on the surface of the skin a certain number of regions comparable to the epileptogenic centres, to which the name of erogenic centres may be applied, light and rapid excitations here practised under certain conditions not only causing voluptuous emotions but preparing, determining, or accompanying the orgasm. Féré later came on this observation, and noting the analogy of the centres to Charcot's hysterogenic zones, which Chambard had apparently overlooked, he termed them "erogenic zones," the name they have ever since borne. It is now widely held that erogenic zones in a normal subject are what in a pathological subject become hysterogenic zones, so that there is more than analogy between them. They have been penetratingly studied by Freud who has described the first or auto-erotic stage of libido as that in which the sex impulses have no object, so that their aim is arrested in the erogenic zones themselves, while after puberty more truly sexual ends emerge, so that the fore-pleasure, alone gained in early life, now becomes a step to a further pleasure.

Thus viewed, it will be seen, the erogenic zones constitute

a legitimate and important part of the normal sexual life. They cannot but play their part in any education for the full gratification of love. Every woman has her own system of manifest or latent erogenic zones, and it is the lover's part in courtship to discover these zones and to develop them in order to achieve that tumescence which is naturally and properly the first stage in the process of sexual union.

The organic constitution varies, even though the general pattern may be the same for all. It is because of these variations that the factors of sexual selection differ for each. On the tactile foundation the varying erogenic zones may most easily be demonstrated.

BIBLIOGRAPHY

HAVELOCK ELLIS, " Erogenic Zones " in *Studies in the Psychology of Sex*, Vol. VII.

FREUD, *Three Contributions to Sexual Theory*.

The Biology of Courtship

Courtship, properly understood, is a biological process which may be found throughout the bisexual animal world. It represents the psychic aspect of the slow attainment of tumescence, the method of securing contrectation.

Even among the hermaphroditic slugs an elaborate courtship is found ; each partner slowly follows the other's movements ; they crawl round each other ; one rests its mouth on the caudal end of the other ; they emit large quantities of mucus ; finally the organs of generation are protruded, to twist and curve around each other, assuming beautiful shapes and taking on iridescent colours until tumescence is completed. That is the manifestation of a process which we may trace throughout Nature, even, in its psychic aspects, in the highest stages of civilization.

The phenomena of courtship are most conspicuous, and have been most carefully studied, among various species of birds in widely different parts of the world. The beautiful plumage of birds, their song, their self-display, their parades, their dances, are all (as most authorities now agree) primarily a part of courtship, a method of attaining in the male himself, and exciting in the female he desires for his partner, an adequate stimulation of the pairing impulse. The same influence survives even in human civilization. A Dutchman at the Hague told Hirschfeld that during the Great War, when English troops were frequently there, several hundred Dutch girls had become mothers through the fascinating walk of the English soldiers; referring to their special swift and light step.

In civilization, indeed, owing to the idleness, luxury, and over-nutrition which make sexual erethism comparatively easy, and tumescence sometimes almost constant, the phenomena of courtship become less important. Yet they still prevail, though in more varied, delicate, and often mainly psychic forms.

The phenomena of courtship are biologically connected with the fact that in animals, in savage man, to some extent perhaps in civilized man, and especially in women, sexuality is periodic, and not constant, in its manifestations. If the sexual apparatus were at every moment, in both sexes, quick to respond to stimulation at once, courtship would be reduced to a minimum and the attainment of tumescence would present no difficulties. But for long periods the sexual impulse is quiescent, and courtship may be regarded as the psychic aspect of the effort by which it re-awakens.

Most of the higher animals have a breeding season once or sometimes twice a year, in spring or in autumn or both. Savage man also sometimes has similar breeding seasons, and in widely separated parts of the world erotic festivals are held in spring or at harvest, or both, sexual union taking place on these occasions and marriages formed. The periodicity of the conception-rate in all civilized countries, with a tendency to a heightening of the curve in spring and sometimes in autumn, seems to be a vestige of this primitive breeding season, due to the same cause, whatever that cause may be. As to the exact nature of the cause, there is no agreement. Some (with Durkheim) argue that this and all similar periodicities (as of criminality and suicide) are mainly due to social causes; others (like Gaedeken) assert that the chemical rays of the sun, most powerful in spring, are the true cause ; others (as Haycraft) put the phenomenon down to the heat ; others, perhaps more plausibly, regard them as largely due to the stimulation of the early heat of spring and to the corresponding stimulation of the early cold in winter.

Of recent years traces of sexual periodicity have been found among civilized men, quite apart from their relationships to women. Seminal emissions during sleep in persons leading a continent life have furnished the data on which interesting conclusions have been formed. Julius Nelson in 1888 first brought forward evidence in favour of a monthly sexual cycle in men of a twenty-eight day length. Perry-Coste, on the strength of a more prolonged and elaborate investigation, also found some reason to accept a menstrual rhythm of a strictly lunar character (twenty-nine and a half days), though the conclusions he drew from his data have been disputed. Von Römer found ground for bringing the evidence from involuntary emissions into line with that from voluntary emissions in coitus, by showing that the acts of coitus of an unmarried man fall into a monthly cycle, with two maxima somewhat approximating to Perry-Coste's ; he noted, moreover, that the chief maximum occurs at the time of the full moon, and the secondary maximum at the time of the new moon. This would indicate that heightened sexual activity tends to coincide (whatever explanation of the coincidence may be offered) with the times when, among primitive peoples in many parts of the world, erotic festivals are held. It must, however, be added, that these conclusions are only tentative, and the data have been questioned by Munro Fox and others.

A weekly cycle of involuntary sexual activity, with a maximum at or near Sunday, is often marked. This is probably due to social causes. The same cannot be said, however, of the annual cycle of involuntary sexual activity which I first showed in 1898 and which I have since been able to confirm by additional evidence. This evidence shows clearly that there are two periods in the year of increased spontaneous sexual activity, one in early spring and the other in autumn ; it is often found that the autumn maximum is the highest.

There is no detailed and extensive evidence at present concerning the existence of any yearly cycle of involuntary sexual activity in women. It is, however, in women, as the existence of menstruation shows, that sexual periodicity is most normal and pronounced. In this respect women are more profoundly primitive than men. The origin of menstruation has been much discussed. It used to be thought that lowly organisms living within the influence of the tides would show a lunar periodicity. This, however, is seldom found. Shell fish are not usually affected by the moon. But, in the gulf of Suez, sea urchins do obey the moon. They increase as she increases and decline as she declines. Their size is due to the roe and they spawn at full moon. So zoologically remote an influence could not extend to quadrupeds, and among mammals a menstrual rhythm does not even begin to appear until we reach some of the anthropoids allied to Man. The suggestion of Arrhenius (accepted by Munro Fox who has specially studied this subject) is that the source of menstrual periodicity is electrical. He has shown that atmospheric electricity varies in a rhythmical manner, with a maximum every twenty-seven and a third days which is the time taken by the moon to revolve round the earth. He also found a slight menstrual rhythm in the curve of births.

In the apes among whom menstruation begins to appear, it co-exists with the more primitive seasonal influence, so that the apes which menstruate at approximately monthly intervals still only procreate at certain periods of the year. A vestige of this tendency remains in the human species. It is during the *œstrus*, or " heat," only that female animals generally allow intercourse. In women, the period of maximum sexual desire tends to occur around menstruation, but, especially in civilization, sexual desire is more diffused. The majority of the earlier authorities admitted a heightening of sexual emotion before or after the menstrual crisis, *e.g.*, Krafft-Ebing, who placed it at the post-menstrual period. Otto Adler stated that sexual feeling is increased before, during, and after menstruation. Kossmann advised intercourse just after menstruation, or even during the latter days of the flow, as the period when it is most needed. Guyot said that the eight days after menstruation are the period of sexual desire in women. Harry Campbell, who investigated the periodicity of sexual desire in healthy women of the working classes by inquiries made of their husbands who were patients at a London hospital, found that in two-thirds of the wives, desire was increased before, during, or after the flow, or at all three times.

We now possess the results of inquiries on a more definitely statistical basis. Thus Dr. Katharine Davis, in her study of the sex life of over 2,000 women, found that maximum sexual desire nearly always fell within the period from two days before to a week after menstruation, although, unlike most investigators, she found that it was more often before than after the menstrual flow (69 to 38 cases). Dr. G. V. Hamilton in his examination of 100 married women of educated class—a small number, but carefully studied—found that 25 had sex desire just after menstruation only, 14 just before only, 21 just before and just after, 11 during menstruation and just before and just after, 19 had no periodicity at all, while the remaining 10 gave no information.

The modesty of women, which, in its most primitive form among animals, is based on sexual periodicity, is, with that periodicity, an essential condition of courtship. At the outset modesty may be said to be the gesture of sexual refusal by a female animal who is not yet at the period of *œstrus*. Modesty, however, tends to overlap that period, as we should expect with an impulse which is active during the greater part of the year, and combines with the sexual impulse, constituting coquetry ; then the female alternately approaches and runs away from the male, or runs away from him in a circle. While modesty is primarily the gesture of sexual refusal it speedily combines with other impulses and may finally in man be said to combine the following constituents : (1) the primitive animal gesture of sexual refusal on the part of the female, when she is not at that moment of her generative life at which she desires the male's advances; (2) the fear of arousing disgust, a fear primarily due to the close proximity of the sexual centre to the points of exit of those excretions which are useless and unpleasant, even in many cases to animals; (3) the fear of the magic influence of sexual phenomena, and the ceremonial and ritual practices primarily based on this fear, and ultimately passing into simple rules of decorum which are signs and guardians of modesty; (4) the development of ornament and clothing, concomitantly fostering alike the modesty which represses male sexual desire and the coquetry which seeks to allure it; (5) the conception of women as property has sometimes been added, imparting a new sanction to an emotion already based on more natural facts.

Thus constituted, modesty is a very powerful motive even amongst the lowest savages—although the forms it assumes vary widely—and it remains powerful also in barbarism. At no stage of culture does modesty necessarily involve the use of garments. Some savages who are habitually almost or completely naked still exhibit modesty, while in modern life new customs of complete nakedness—"nudism," sun-bathing, the popular German Nackt-Kultur, etc.—leave modesty intact. In civilization, however, its potency is attenuated. It persists, in part as a ritual and in part as a grace, but it no longer has the irresistible force which it usually possesses among the lower races. Still, in any case, modesty remains from first to last an essential condition of courtship. Without the reticences and delays of modesty, tumescence could not be adequately aroused in either sex, nor would the female have time and opportunity to test the qualities of the candidates for her favours, and to select the most fitting mate.

BIBLIOGRAPHY

Havelock Ellis, "Analysis of the Sexual Impulse," in Vol. III; "The Evolution of Modesty" and "The Phenomena of Sexual Periodicity," in Vol. I, *Studies in the Psychology of Sex*, and "The Menstrual Curve of Sexual Impulse," in Vol. VII.

Wallaschek, *Primitive Music*.

COLIN SCOTT, "Sex and Art," *American Journal of Psychology*, Vol. VII, No. 2.
HEAPE, "The Sexual Season of Mammals," *Quarterly Journal of Microscopical Science*, 1900, and "The Proportion of the Sexes," *Philosophical Transactions of the Royal Society*, Series B, Vol. 200, 1909.
WESTERMARCK, *The History of Human Marriage*, Vol. I.
J. R. BAKER, *Sex in Man and Animals.*
ZUCKERMAN, *The Social Life of Monkeys and Apes.*
MUNRO FOX, *Selene.*
MAURICE PARMELEE, *Nudism in Modern Life.*

Preferential Mating : The Factors of Sexual Selection

The process of tumescence is achieved, directly or indirectly, by the stimulating influence of impressions received through the various senses. Contrectation, as Moll terms it, is indeed simply the sum of the physical and psychic impressions so received, normally from a person of the opposite sex. Sexual selection is the choice of the person who most adequately imparts these impressions.

In using the term "sexual selection" we may seem to assume a theory in the Darwinian doctrine of evolution which, in its original form, is not always accepted. We must especially remember that such selection is not to be reckoned as primarily æsthetic. It is not beauty but greater vigour, or greater conspicuousness, that counts. The precise degree of validity which Darwinian sexual selection (even apart from its misinterpretation by Wallace) possesses among animals generally is still doubtful even to many careful students of animal life. It is doubtful, in other words, how far such instinctive choice in mating as is so far demonstrable can lead to a biological selection of some characters and the rejection of other characters, so affecting inheritance. The increasing knowledge in recent years of the Mendelian factors of inheritance still further obscures the question of sexual selection. What we are certainly concerned with is *Preferential Mating*, which leaves open the question of sexual selection in relation to racial inheritance. It is not clear that the less preferred are usually shut out from mating, and those who are excluded altogether, whether among the higher animals or the lower human races, seem generally an almost negligible number. Courtship among birds is often a serious, prolonged, and highly arduous affair. Yet it is still not always clear that any Darwinian " selection " has been achieved. Eliot Howard, a very thorough student of bird life, while not absolutely rejecting such " selection," in his great work on *British Warblers*, yet speaks with much hesitation concerning its extent and significance. Various other authorities on bird life are equally cautious.

For Man in the far past preferential mating may really have rendered it difficult for the less preferred to mate and so pass on their less preferred characters. Among the Babylonian women whose duty it was once in life to prostitute themselves at the shrine of Mylitta (though we are not here concerned with a very primitive phase of culture) Herodotus mentions that those who were less charming might have to wait three or four years before they were chosen by a man. The same influence has no doubt largely operated for marriage also in the past. But nearly all women in lower stages of culture seem sooner or later to become pregnant (some observers have noted this of even the least attractive women among savages), so that, while the delay in selection may diminish the opportunities of passing on the less preferred characters, any racial selection must be limited.

The possibilities of sexual " selection " in the Darwinian sense seem indeed to be capable of greater and more rapid development in the future. Even in our present phase of civilization a large number of women and men remain unmated, many of them because they have failed to evoke the pairing impulse in the opposite sex. If civilization in the future tends to free mating from the influence of those extraneous considerations which to-day enable the unattractive and the unfit to pair, and ideals of desirability become a more stringent motive in pairing, the process of selection which leaves a large number altogether unpaired would obviously be a strongly directive force in human evolution. " If men wished women to be taller or less emotional than they are," remarks Heymans, "there are many tall women and unemotional women whom they could select to marry. But it will be long," he adds, "before such tendencies have free play."

It is not possible therefore, at present, to regard Darwinian sexual "selection" as the chisel in the hands of Nature to mould the living being of the future into perpetually new forms while the refuse is being constantly flung away. Within certain limits, as Heymans truly says, the feminine type must have a tendency to adapt itself to the ideals of men, and the masculine type to the ideals of women. But the limits seem uncertain and narrow; we cannot at present regard either sex as the absolute creation, through "selection," of the opposite sex.

It is necessary to make clear this elementary preliminary consideration when approaching the fundamental facts of sexual psychology. Even when the term "sexual selection" is used, what we are really concerned with is preferential mating as mediated by the varying attractions of the sensory stimuli which evoke courtship.

Courtship, we cannot make too clear, by no means necessarily involves, as some still believe, a struggle or a choice between rival candidates for a sexual partner. It is just as pronounced and just as necessary, even though only in an abbreviated form, when rivalry is excluded, and throughout the sexual life. The act of union is not accomplished in an effective and happy manner except as the climax of an ever fresh courtship. Even investigators like Eliot Howard who are most in doubt as to the significance of sexual "selection" among animals are emphatic in their insistence on those elaborate and prolonged phases of excitement in which courtship consists. For courtship is involved in that whole process of tumescence and detumescence which is the foundation of the sexual life.

The senses concerned are touch, smell, hearing, and vision. There seems no good reason to include taste even in abnormal individuals, when we have eliminated from what are usually considered taste-sensations the large part really furnished by olfaction through the posterior nares.

There is probably indeed good reason why taste proper should not have any share in this matter, for taste is the slave of the other great primary organic need, the need of nutrition, and if taste had also become associated with the primary need of reproduction, instinct might be confused and the lover might seek to devour his partner rather than to have sexual union with her. There are only a few animals that occasionally eat their partners and then it is usually the female who does so, and not until after impregnation has taken place.

(I) TOUCH

Touch is the primary and most primitive form of contrectation. The sexual act itself is essentially an act of contrectation, in which touch is supreme. Among children, hugging, kissing, and embracing are the main signs of affection in general and of sexual affection in particular. They equally express the elementary desire of the adult lover.

In this primary impulse, indeed, there is nothing specialized or specific. The skin is the foundation on which all forms of sensory perception have grown up, and as sexual sensibility is among the most ancient of all forms of sensibility, it is necessarily, in the main, a modified form of general touch sensibility. This primitive character of the great region of tactile sensation, its vagueness and diffusion, serve to heighten the emotional intensity of skin sensations. So that, of all the great sensory fields, the field of touch is at once the least intellectual and the most massively emotional. These qualities, as well as its intimate and primitive association with the apparatus of tumescence and detumescence, make touch the readiest and most powerful channel by which the sexual sphere may be reached.

As we might expect, touch is frequently predominant in the courtship of the lower animals. Touch determines mating among crabs and crayfish and is usually the chief sexual sense for spiders. In cattle, deer, horses, dogs, etc., licking is an important part of courtship. Neumann, who watched elephants love-making, observed that the male fondled the female with his trunk, and then, standing side by side, they crossed trunks, putting the tips in each other's mouths. Human beings are impelled to analogous acts. For many people, especially women who have not become habituated to complete intercourse, close tactile contacts furnish in themselves adequate sexual pleasure and satisfaction.

The tactile element is indeed specially prominent in the emotional life, and notably the sexual life, of women. Lillian Martin, investigating the æsthetic sentiment in woman students, observed the prominence of emotions of tactile foundation. Pearce Clark described the case of an epileptic girl of nine who only cared for people whose touch she liked, and classified her acquaintances by her reaction to their handshake or kiss. The sexual awakening of girls at puberty shows itself in a desire for kisses and caresses rather than for intercourse. Sadger remarks that "the halo of chastity surrounding so many young girls rests on the absence of the genital impulse combined with strong eroticism in the skin, the mucous membranes, and the muscular system." This trait is frequently pronounced in women not only at the beginning of the sexual life but throughout, and even to the climax of detumescence. "With all her straining, her wrestling, and striving to break from the clasp of his arms," we read in an erotic novel of the eighteenth century, "it was visible she aimed at nothing more than multiplying points of touch with him." It was a woman poet, Renée Vivien, who wrote that "the strange and complex art of touch equals the dream of perfumes and the miracle of sound." The instinctive recognition by women of the importance of touch in love is additional evidence of the fact that touch is really the primary and primitive erotic sense.

The morbid hyper-æsthetic anomalies on a tactile foundation occur in both men and women, such as the stuff-fetishisms (contacts with fur, velvet, silk, etc.), and may have consequences of social importance, such as kleptolagnia; this is found chiefly in women. The special perversion of frottage, as it is termed, on the other hand, is only found in a pronounced degree in men and consists in a desire to bring the clothed body, and usually though not exclusively the genital region, into close contact with the clothed body of a woman, and in seeking to gratify this passion in places of public resort with women who are complete strangers. Many women have at some time, when standing in a crowd (as at the back of a theatre gallery, or sometimes even in church), become unpleasantly aware of a deliberate contact of this kind. This morbid deviation is of medico-legal interest, and its victims may be otherwise fairly normal men of good social position and superior intelligence.

Ticklishness may here be noted as a kind of by-product of tactile sensation, founded on reflexes developing even before birth, which is closely related to sexual phenomena. It is, as it were, a play of tumescence, on which laughter comes as a play of detumescence, to disperse undesired sexual emotions (as often among bashful sex-conscious girls). Ticklishness leads on to the more serious phenomena of tumescence, and it tends to die out after adolescence, at the period during which sexual relationships normally begin.

Such a view of ticklishness, as a kind of modesty of the skin, existing only to be destroyed, is indeed but one of its aspects. Ticklishness certainly arose from a non-sexual starting-point, and may well have protective uses, for, as Louis Robinson pointed out, in young animals the most ticklish regions are the most vulnerable and those most needing protection. Tickling, however, within the sexual sphere, and in those more remote erogenous zones which are sometimes apt for sexual sensation, acts differently, and this by virtue of what Herrick calls its power of summating successive stimuli, an avalanche-like process by which through the excitation of peripheral cells a vast number of cortical cells may be slowly charged with energy. It is a process of tumescence culminating in an act of detumescence; which, while outside the sexual sphere it may take the form of a muscular reaction or an outburst of laughter, within that sphere its reactions are sexual. All forms of amorous contrectation, and especially the sexual embrace, have an intimate connection with the phenomena of ticklishness. That, indeed, is the basis of Spinoza's famous definition of love: *Amor est titillatio quaedam concomitante idea causæ externæ*, for, as Gowers said, the sexual act is primarily a skin reflex.

It may be worth while to remark that, although tickling (even if practised by young girls as a source of probable sexual pleasure) has become unimportant in the erotic life of civilization it has more significance among some savage peoples, as formerly indeed even in Europe. To tickle among some peoples has been to make love, and sometimes, as among the Fuegians, the same word is applied to the sexual embrace as to tickling. The German word for the clitoris, "Kitzler" or tickler, indicates a similar connection of ideas. The word *pruritus* was used by the Romans as a synonym of lasciviousness, and it is significant that localized pruritus occurs in zones that are in early life auto-erotic and tends to appear at the menopause. In Russia, in the eighteenth century, the Czarina, B. Stein states, retained at Court official foot-ticklers, whose duty it was to give the Empress pleasure by tickling her feet and at the same time telling wanton stories and singing obscene songs; they also possessed the special privilege of refreshing the Czarina, when exhausted from excesses, by smacking the Imperial buttocks. This office was of course reserved for ladies of aristocratic birth. The physiological ground of the proceeding lies in the fact that, as Féré demonstrated, tickling is in moderation a stimulant increasing energy, though in excess it is a depressant.

The relationship between ticklishness and sexual feeling is indicated by the experience of a lady who states that if she is touched in the sexual region when not inclined for sexual relationships, ticklishness is aroused, but that when sexual desire arises ticklishness disappears. It is, we see, a vicarious sexual feeling, or we may say that sexual feeling is a transmuted form of ticklishness. In its original aspect a sentinel to repel contact, it becomes under another aspect a minister to attraction.

The intimate connection between the skin and the sexual

sphere is indicated, not only by the phenomena of tickling, but by the behaviour of the sebaceous glands, which are the vestiges of former hair-glands, and survive from a period when hair covered the body. The attempts of these glands at puberty, or when the sexual system is disturbed, to produce hairs frequently lead to pimples, and actual hairs often appear in women after the menopause.

Thus the hair itself and its disturbances are associated with the sexual system. Partial baldness or *alopecia areata*, as Sabouraud pointed out, tends to occur with special frequency in women towards puberty and again about the age of fifty, though in men there is no corresponding frequency curve. It may also occur after suppression of the menses, as after ovariotomy, and sometimes even in pregnancy.

While the sexual embrace itself is, in large measure, a specialized kind of skin reflex, between the generalized skin sensations and the great primary sexual centre of sensation there are certain secondary sexual centres which have already been brought forward in their general aspect as to be included among erogenic zones.

These secondary centres have in common the fact that they involve the entrances and the exits of the body regions, that is, where skin merges into mucous membrane, and where, in the course of evolution, tactile sensibility has become highly refined. It may, indeed, be said generally of these frontier regions of the body that their contact with the same or a similar frontier region in another person of opposite sex, under conditions otherwise favourable to tumescence, will tend to produce a minimum and even sometimes a maximum degree of sexual excitation. Contact of these regions with each other or with the sexual region itself so closely simulates the central sexual reflex that channels are set up for the same nervous energy and secondary sexual centres are constituted.

It is important to remember that these phenomena are essentially normal. Many of them are commonly spoken of as " perversions." In so far, however, as they are aids to tumescence, they must be regarded as coming within the range of normal variation. They may be considered unæsthetic, but that is another matter. It has, moreover, to be remembered that æsthetic values are changed under the influence of sexual emotion ; from the lover's point of view, many things are beautiful which are unbeautiful from the point of view of him who is not a lover, and the greater the degree to which the lover is swayed by his passion, the greater the extent to which his normal æsthetic standard is liable to be modified. From the non-sexual standpoint, indeed, the whole process of sex may be considered unæsthetic, except the earlier stages of tumescence.

That the utilization of the sexual excitation obtainable through the channels of the erogenic zones must be considered within the normal range of variation we may observe, indeed, among many animals. It is only when they are used to procure not merely tumescence, but detumescence, that such excitations can be termed in any sense, "perversions," and then they are so only in the same ambiguous sense as are the methods of intercourse which involve the use of checks to prevent fecundation.

The kiss is the typical example of this group of phenomena. We have in the lips a highly sensitive frontier region between skin and mucous membrane, in many respects analogous to the vulvo-vaginal orifice, and reinforceable, moreover, by the active movements of the still more highly sensitive tongue. Close and prolonged contact of these regions, therefore, under conditions favourable to tumescence sets up a powerful current of nervous stimulation. After those contacts in which the sexual regions themselves take a direct part, there is no such channel for directing nervous force into the sexual sphere as the kiss. This is specially marked for the so-called columbine kiss, widely practised by lovers in classic as well as in modern times. A form of it called *maraichinage* is generally practised in a part of France, though some theologians would regard it as a mortal sin. Manifestations resembling the kiss are found among various animals lower than man, as in the palpations of the antennæ by snails and insects, the caresses of birds by their bills, the licking and gentle biting of dogs and various other animals in coitus. In man, the kiss has two elements, one tactile and the other olfactory, but the tactile element is at once the most ancient and in Europe the most predominant part of the kiss ; the olfactory kiss, however, or smell-kiss, has a much wider distribution over the world than the European (or Mediterranean) tactile kiss ; it reaches its most complete development among peoples of Mongolian race.

While the kiss may be regarded as the typical and normal erogenic method of contrectation for the end of attaining tumescence, there are others only less important. Any orificial contact between persons of opposite sex is sometimes almost equally as effective as the kiss in stimulating tumescence ; all such contacts, indeed, belong to the group of which the kiss is the type. *Cunnilinctus* (often incorrectly termed *cunnilingus*) and *fellatio* cannot be regarded as unnatural for they have their prototypic forms among animals, and they are found among various savage races. As forms of contrectation and aids to tumescence they are thus natural and are sometimes regarded by both sexes as quintessential forms of sexual pleasure, though they may not be considered æsthetic. They become deviations, however, and thus liable to be termed " perversions," when they replace the desire for coitus.

The nipples constitute yet another orificial frontier region which is a highly important tactile sexual focus. The breasts have a special significance among the sexual centres since they primarily exist, not for the lover, but for the child. This is doubtless, indeed, a fundamental fact on which other erogenic contacts have grown up. The sexual sensitivity of lovers to the lips has been developed from the sensitivity of the infant's lips to contact with his mother's nipple.

As the secreting organs of milk, it is essential that the connection between the sexual organs and the breasts should be intimate, so that the breasts may be in a condition to respond adequately to the demand of the child's sucking lips at the earliest moment after birth. Suction of the nipple causes objectively a reflex contraction of the womb. On the subjective side no one seems to have recorded that the act of suckling tends to produce in women voluptuous sexual emotions until Cabanis, in the early nineteenth century, noted that several suckling women had told him that the child in suckling produced such feelings.[1] It is easy to see why this normal association of sexual emotion with suckling should have come about. It is essential for the preservation of the lives of young mammals that the mothers should have an adequate motive in pleasurable sensation for enduring the trouble of suckling. The most obvious method for obtaining the necessary degree of pleasurable sensation, beyond the relief of the tension caused by the secretion, lay in utilizing the reservoir of sexual emotion, with which channels of communication might already be said to be open, through the action of the sexual organs on the breasts during pregnancy.

It must be added that while the connection between the nipple and the sexual apparatus thus appears to be so intimate it is probably not specific. Kurdinovski found by experiments on rabbits that the stimulation of other orifices, as the ear, will also produce strong contractions of the womb. Perhaps any stimulus anywhere applied to the periphery may by reflex paths evoke a uterine contraction. This supposition is in relation with the general sexual sensitiveness of the skin and the existence of erogenic zones.

The importance of the erotic interest in the breasts is indicated by the amount of attention which has been given to the subject by Catholic theologians. A great controversy arose over mammillary contacts in the eighteenth century. Eminent Jesuit theologians, but in opposition to the Inquisition and the Church generally, maintained that to handle the breasts even of nuns was venial, provided there was no depraved intention. In one Jesuit Penitentiary it was even asserted that to deny the intrinsic innocence of such acts

[1] I should like to point out, however, that, before Cabanis, C. Bonnet in 1764 (in his *Contemplation de la Nature*), had remarked on "the sweet commotion accompanied by a feeling of pleasure," as supporting the natural affection of the mother for the child, "if it is not one of the principal causes," while for creatures below the mammals, he added, "we have also to consider the agreeable reciprocal warmth of mother and offspring."

was dangerously near to an error in faith, and only committed by Jansenists.

(2) Smell

Olfactory sensibility was not at first clearly differentiated from general tactile sensibility. The sense of smell was gradually specialized, and, when taste also began to develop, a kind of chemical sense was constituted. Among vertebrates smell became the most highly developed of the senses; it gives the first information of remote objects that concern them, it gives the most precise information concerning the near objects that concern them; it is the sense in terms of which most of their mental operations must be conducted and their emotional impulses reach consciousness. For reptiles and later for mammals not only are all sexual associations mainly olfactory, but the impressions received by this sense suffice to dominate all others. An animal not only receives adequate sexual excitement from olfactory stimuli, but those stimuli often suffice to counterbalance all the evidence of the other senses. This is not surprising when we remember how extensive is the place of the olfactory region in the brain. The cerebral cortex itself, indeed, as Edinger and Elliot Smith show, was originally little more than the receptive centre for impressions of smell and the instrument for enabling that sense to influence the animal's behaviour; and these olfactory impulses reached the cortex directly and not by passing through the thalamus. So that, psychologically, smell occupies a unique position. It represents "the germ of all the higher psychical powers," or at all events the cement that binds them together. In the primitive vertebrates living in the water, smell (which is then more akin to taste than in Man and also more affective than any other sense) dominates the whole behaviour and is of immense biological significance.

When we reach the higher apes and Man, all this has been changed. The sense of smell, indeed, still persists universally, and it is also exceedingly delicate, though often neglected. It is, moreover, a useful auxiliary. Savages are often accused, more or less justly, of an indifference to bad odours. They are often, however, keenly alive to the significance of smells and their varieties, though it does not appear that the sense of smell is notably more developed in savage than in civilized peoples. Odours also continue to play a part in the emotional life of civilized man, more especially in hot countries.

Nevertheless, both in practical life and in emotional life, in science and in art, smell is, at the best, under normal conditions, merely an auxiliary, and its study fell into some discredit until Zwaardemaker of Utrecht restored it to its proper position by the invention of his olfactometer in 1888 and by the subsequent publication of his work on the physiology of smell. A few years later Heyninx of Brussels still further developed the subject of olfaction, and seeking to put it on a rigid physical basis, he set up a spectrum, as it were, for smell, with a classification dependent on variations of wave-length. It would thus be by a moleculo-vibratory, rather than by a chemical, energy that smells activate the affective paths. Other authorities, however, like G. H. Parker, are content to regard smell as the chief of the "chemical" senses, after we have separated the "mechanical" senses (stimulated by pressure, or sound, or light); the chemical senses date from primitive aquatic life and, while dominated by smell, would also include taste, the function of the organ of Jacobson (opening into the nose), and a common chemical sense. Even yet, however, it can scarcely be said that any large body of assured conclusions has been reached.

The sense of smell still remains close to touch in the vagueness of its messages, though its associations are often highly emotional. It is the existence of these characteristics—at once so vague and so specific, so useless and so intimate—which has led various writers to describe the sense of smell as, above all others, the sense of imagination. No sense has so strong a power of suggestion, the power of calling up ancient memories with a wide and deep emotional reverberation, while at the same time no sense furnishes impressions which so easily change emotional colour and tone, in harmony with the recipient's general attitude. Odours are thus specially apt both to control the emotional life and to become its slaves. Under the conditions of civilization the primitive emotional associations of odour tend to be dispersed, but, on the other hand, the imaginative side of the olfactory sense becomes accentuated, and personal idiosyncrasies tend to manifest themselves in this sphere.

Odours are powerful stimulants to the whole nervous system, causing, like other stimulants, an increase of energy which, if excessive or prolonged, leads to nervous exhaustion. Thus, it is well recognized that the aromatics containing volatile oils are antispasmodics and anæsthetics, and that they stimulate digestion, circulation, and the nervous system, in large doses producing depression. Féré's experiments with the dynamometer and the ergograph greatly contributed to define the stimulating effects of odours.

We approach the specifically sexual aspect of odour in the human species when we note that all men and women are odorous. This is variously marked among all races. It is a significant fact, both as regards the ancestral sexual connections of the body odours and their actual sexual associations to-day, that, as Hippocrates long ago noted, it is not until puberty that they assume their adult characteristics. The infant, the adult, the aged person, each has his own kind of smell, and, as Monin remarks, it might be possible, within certain limits, to discover the age of a person by his odour. In both sexes, puberty, adolescence, early manhood and womanhood are marked by a gradual development of the adult odour of skin and excreta, in general harmony with the secondary sexual developments of hair and pigment. Venturi, indeed, described the odour of the body as a secondary sexual character.

As the sole factor in human sexual selection olfaction must be rare, not so much because the impressions of this sense are inoperative, but because agreeable personal odours are not sufficiently powerful, and the olfactory organ is too obtuse, to enable smell to take precedence of sight.

Nevertheless, in many people, certain odours, especially those that are correlated with a healthy and sexually desirable person, tend to be agreeable; they are fortified by their association with the loved person, sometimes to an irresistible degree ; and their potency is doubtless increased by the fact that many odours, including some bodily odours, are nervous stimulants.

There seems to be little doubt that an intimate relation exists, both in men and women, between the olfactory mucous membrane of the nose and the whole genital apparatus, that they frequently show a sympathetic action, and that influences acting on the genital sphere will affect the nose occasionally, influences acting on the nose reflexly affect the genital sphere.

In a few exceptional, but still quite normal, people smell would appear to possess an emotional predominance which it cannot be said to possess in the average person. These exceptional people are what Binet in his study of sexual fetishism called olfactive type ; such persons form a group which, though of smaller size and less importance, is fairly comparable to the well-known groups of visual type, of auditory type, and of psycho-motor type. Such people would be more attentive to odours, more moved by olfactory sympathies and antipathies, than are other people. The term "ozolagny" was devised by Kiernan for sexual gratification derived from the sense of smell. Many women who may be considered normal are sexually excitable (occasionally even to the point of orgasm) by special odours, as of the general body odour of a beloved man (sometimes when blended with that of tobacco) or of leather (which is ultimately a skin odour), and are sometimes overcome by a sudden almost hallucinatory recollection of the body odour of a lover.

Even in ordinary normal persons, personal odour tends to play a not inconsiderable part in sexual attractions and sexual repulsions. This is sometimes termed "olfactionism." The comparative bluntness of the sense of smell in Man, however, makes it difficult for olfactory influences to be felt, as a rule, until the preliminaries of courtship are already over ; so that smell cannot normally possess the same significance in sexual attraction in Man that it possesses in the lower animals. With that reservation there can be no doubt that odour has a certain favourable or unfavourable influence in sexual relationships in all human races from the lowest to the highest. The fact that it may be so, and that for most people such odours cannot be a matter of indifference in the most intimate of all relationships, is usually only to be learned casually and incidentally.

There can be no doubt, however, that, as Kiernan points out, the extent to which olfaction influences the sexual sphere in civilized man has been much under-estimated, though we need not run to the opposite extreme, with Gustav Jäger, and regard the sexual instinct even in Man as mainly or altogether an olfactory matter.

In Man, not only is the sexual significance of odour altogether much less than in lower animals, but the focus of olfactory attraction has been displaced from the sexual regions themselves to the upper part of the body. In this respect the sexual olfactory allurement in man resembles what we find in the sphere of vision, for neither the sexual organs of man nor of woman are usually beautiful in the eyes of the opposite sex, and their exhibition is seldom regarded as a preliminary stage in courtship. The careful concealment of the sexual region has doubtless favoured this transfer. It has thus happened that when personal odour acts as a sexual allurement it is the armpit, in any case normally the chief focus of odour in the body, which chiefly comes into play, together with the skin and the hair. We have further to recognize the significant fact that even those personal odours which are chiefly liable under normal circumstances to come occasionally within the conscious sexual sphere, and indeed purely personal odours of all kinds, may fail to exert any attraction, but rather tend to cause antipathy, unless some degree of tumescence has already been attained, and even then may prove repulsive, and so be liable to constitute what may be an even serious trouble in sexual relations. That is to say, our olfactory experiences of the human body approximate rather to our tactile experiences of it than to our visual experiences. Smell with us has ceased to be a leading channel of intellectual curiosity. Personal odours make an appeal that is mainly of an intimate, emotional, imaginative character. They are thus liable to arouse what James called the anti-sexual instinct.

Among animals, it seems probable, both sexes are alike influenced by odours, for, while it is usually the male whose sexual regions are furnished with special scent glands, when such occur, the peculiar odour of the female during the sexual season is certainly not less efficacious as an allurement to the male. If we compare the general susceptibility of men and women to agreeable odours, apart from the question of sexual allurement, there can be little doubt that it is most marked among women. Groos pointed out that even among children little girls are more interested in scents than boys, and the investigations of various workers, especially Garbini, have shown that there is actually a greater power of discriminating odours among girls than among boys. In America Alice Thayer showed that girls are considerably more influenced by odour in their likes and dislikes than are boys. Marro went further, and in an extended series of observations on girls before and after the establishment of puberty, he found reason to believe that girls acquire an increased susceptibility to odours when sexual life begins, although they show no such increased powers as regards the other senses. It may be added that some women acquire a special olfactory hyper-æsthesia during pregnancy. Even in old age, as Vaschide's experiments showed, women preserve their olfactory superiority over men. On the whole, it would appear that, as Van de Velde and various other gynæcologists now agree, women are more affected, and more frequently affected, than are men by olfactory impressions.

Since there are chemical resemblances and identities even of odours from widely remote sources, perfumes may have the same sexual effects as are more primitively possessed by the body odours. It seems probable that, as has been emphasized by Iwan Bloch, perfumes were primitively used by women, not as is sometimes the case in civilization, with the idea of disguising any possible natural odour, but with the object of heightening and fortifying the natural odour. If the primitive man was inclined to disparage a woman whose odour was slight or imperceptible—turning away from her with contempt, as the Polynesian turned away from the ladies of Sydney: "They have no smell!"—women would inevitably seek to supplement any natural defects in this respect, and to accentuate their odorous qualities, in the same way as, even in civilization, they have sought to accentuate the sexual prominences of their bodies. In this way, we may, as Bloch suggests, explain the fact that until recent times the favourite odours selected by women have not been the most delicate but the strongest, the most animal, the most sexual: musk, castoreum, civet, and ambergris. The type among these is certainly musk, which, with ambergris, is the chief member of Linnæus's group of *Odores ambrosiacæ*, which in sexual significance, Zwaardemaker remarks, ranks beside the capryl group, and musk is that odour which is most frequently found to resemble the odour of the human body.

The special peculiarity of the olfactory group of sensations in Man is that they manifest the decadence of a sense which in Man's remote ancestors was a chief avenue of sexual allurement. In Man, and even to some degree in the apes, this sense has given place to the predominance of vision. Yet it still bathes us in a more or less constant atmosphere of odours which perpetually move us to sympathy or to antipathy; and in their finer manifestations we still do not neglect but even cultivate them.

(3) Hearing

The chief physiological functions are periodic, and it is not surprising that rhythm is deeply impressed on our organism. The result is that, whatever lends itself to the neuro-muscular rhythmical tendency of the organism, whatever tends still further to heighten and develop that rhythmical tendency, exerts upon us a decidedly stimulating and exciting influence. It is not possible to accept the view of Bücher and Wundt that human song has its chief or exclusive origin in rhythmical vocal accompaniments to systematized work, yet rhythm, whether in its simple form or its more developed form as music, is a powerful stimulant to muscular action. There is considerable ground for the view of the Swedish philologist Sperber that sexuality was the main source from which speech generally was developed. He argues that there are two situations in which an instinctive cry would arise and evoke response: when the hungry infant cries and is fed by the mother; and when the sexually excited male utters a call to which the female responds. The second situation is most likely to have been developed first, and therefore sexuality is probably the first source of speech. This must have occurred, indeed, early in vertebrate development.

Even a single musical note is effective as a physiological stimulus, apart from rhythm, as was well shown by Féré's experiments. But it is the influence of music on muscular work which has been most frequently investigated. Brief efforts with the dynamometer and prolonged work with the ergograph have alike been found to reveal a stimulating influence. With the ergograph Tarchanoff found that lively music, in nervously sensitive persons, will temporarily cause the disappearance of fatigue, though slow music in a minor key had the opposite effect. Féré found that discords were depressing; most, but not all, major keys were stimulating; and most, but not all, minor keys depressing. In states of fatigue, however, the minor keys were more stimulating than the major, an interesting result in harmony with that stimulating influence of various painful emotions in states of organic fatigue which we encounter when investigating sadism. Both the higher and the lower muscular processes, the voluntary and the involuntary, are stimulated by music.

Together with this stimulation of the neuro-muscular system—which may or may not be direct—there is a concomitant influence on the circulation and respiration. Many experiments have been made on man and animals bearing on the effects of music on the heart and lungs, since the Russian physiologist Dogiel found in 1880 that in animals the force and rapidity of the heart were thus increased. Subsequent investigations have shown clearly the influence of music on the circulatory and respiratory systems in man as well as in animals. That music has an apparently direct influence on the circulation of the brain is shown by the observations of Patrizi on a youth who had received a severe wound of the head which had removed a large portion of the skull wall. The stimulus of melody produced an immediate increase in the afflux of blood to the brain.

It is not surprising that music should also, indirectly, influence various viscera and their functions. It affects the skin, increasing the perspiration; it may produce a tendency to tears; it sometimes causes a desire to urinate, or even actual urination. In dogs it has been shown that auditory stimulation increases the consumption of oxygen and the elimination of carbonic acid. Among many animals of various classes, more especially insects and birds, there can be little doubt that the attraction of music is still supported and developed on the basis of sexual attraction, the musical notes of one sex serving as a sexual lure to the other sex. The evidence on this point was investigated by Darwin on a wide basis. It has been questioned, some writers preferring, like Hudson, to adopt the view of Herbert Spencer that the singing of birds is due to "overflow of energy," the relation between courtship and singing being merely "a relation of concomitance." This view is no longer tenable; whatever the precise origin of the musical notes of animals may be, there can now be little doubt that musical sounds, and, among birds, singing, play a large part in courtship. Usually, it would appear, it is the performance of the male that attracts the female; it is only among simple and primitive musicians, like some insects, that the female thus attracts the male. Even the fact that it is nearly always one sex only that is thus musically gifted alone indicates the sexual solution of this problem.

The males of many species of mammals use their vocal powers chiefly, and sometimes exclusively, during the breeding season. Among the higher apes, indeed, the voice is the chief instrument in courting, as well as being a general method of giving vent to excitement. Darwin pointed this out, and, from a different standpoint, Féré, in studying the pathology of the human sexual instinct, stated that he knew of no detailed observations showing the existence of any morbid sexual perversions based on the sense of hearing.

Since not only in the animals nearly related to Man, but in Man himself, the larynx and the voice undergo a marked sexual differentiation at puberty, it is easy to believe that the change has an influence on sexual selection and sexual psychology. At puberty there is rapid development alike of the larynx itself and the vocal cords, which become larger and thicker, while the voice deepens. All these changes are slight in girls, but pronounced in boys, whose voices are said to "break" and then become lower by at least an octave. The feminine larynx at puberty only increases in the proportion of five to seven, but the masculine larynx in the proportion of five to ten. The direct dependence of this change on the general sexual development is shown not merely by its occurrence at puberty, but by the fact that in eunuchs in whom the testicles have been removed before puberty the voice retains its child-like qualities.

Bearing this in mind, we may attach considerable importance to the voice and to music generally as a method of sexual appeal. On this point we may agree with Moll, that "sexual stimulation through the ears is greater than is usually believed," though I consider that it is greater on women than on men, as we should expect, the cause being that, as Robert Müller remarks, a woman's voice retains child-like qualities, and is therefore less specifically feminine than a man's voice is specifically masculine.

Men are, indeed, often able to associate many of their earliest ideas of love in boyhood with women singing or playing; but in these cases it will be found that the fascination was romantic and sentimental, and not specifically erotic, while in adult life the music which often seems to us to be most definitely sexual in its appeal really produces this effect in part from association with the story, and in part from the intellectual realization of the composer's effort to translate passion into æsthetic terms; the actual effect of the music is not sexual, and it can well be believed that the results of experiments as regards the sexual influence of the *Tristan* music on men under the influence of hypnotism have been, as reported, negative. The music of less important composers, however, especially Massenet, has been found to have a definite sexual effect. Helmholtz went too far in stating that the expression of sexual longing in music is identical with that of religious longing.

Féré mentions the case of a young man in hospital with acute arthritis who complained of painful erections whenever he heard through the door the very agreeable voice of the young woman (invisible to him) who superintended the linen. But such phenomena do not appear to be common, or, at all events, very pronounced. So far as my own inquiries go, only a small proportion of men would appear to experience definite sexual feelings on listening to music.

The reasons which make it improbable that men should be sexually attracted through hearing render it probable that women should be so attracted. The change in the voice at puberty renders the deeper masculine voice a characteristic secondary sexual attribute of man, while the fact that, among mammals generally, it is the male that is most vocal—and that chiefly, or even sometimes exclusively, at the rutting season—renders it antecedently likely that among mammals generally, including the human species, there is in the female an actual or latent susceptibility to the sexual significance of the male voice, a susceptibility which, under the conditions of human civilization, may be transferred to music generally. Music is for women, as the Goncourts have expressed it, "la messe de l'amour." It is noteworthy that in novels written by women there is a frequent attentiveness to the qualities of the hero's voice and to its emotional effects on the heroine, while in real life women often fall in love with a man's voice, sometimes even before they have seen him. Vaschide and Vurpas have pointed out that, even in the absence of specific localized sexual effects, the physiological effects of music on women closely resemble those of sexual excitement. Most normal educated women are liable to experience some degree of definite sexual excitement from music, though not always from the same kind of music. In neuropathic subjects the influence may occasionally be more pronounced, and in some morbid subjects (Vaschide and Vurpas remark) sexual relations cannot take place unless aided by music.

It is significant that the evolution of puberty tends to be accompanied by a marked interest in musical and other kinds of art. The majority of young people of educated class, and especially girls, feel an impulse to art about the period of puberty, lasting a few months, or at most a year or two. According to one series of observations, nearly five in six showed an increased and passionate love for music, the curve culminating at the age of fifteen and falling rapidly after sixteen.

(4) Vision

To a large extent vision has slowly superseded the other senses and become the main channel by which we receive our impressions. Its range is practically infinite; it is apt for either abstract or intimate uses. It furnishes the basis on which a number of arts make their appeal, while it is also the sense on which we chiefly rely in exercising the animal function of nutrition. It is not surprising that from the viewpoint of sexual selection vision should be the supreme sense. The love-thoughts of men have always been a perpetual meditation on beauty.

The origin of our ideas of beauty is a question which belongs to æsthetics, not to sexual psychology, and it is a question on which æstheticians are not altogether in agreement. We need not here be concerned to make any definite assertion on the question whether our ideals of sexual beauty have developed under the influence of more general and fundamental laws, or whether sexual ideals themselves underlie our more general conceptions of beauty. Practically, so far as man and his immediate ancestors are concerned, the sexual and the extra-sexual factors of beauty have been interwoven from the first. The sexually beautiful object must have appealed to fundamental physiological aptitudes of reaction ; the generally beautiful object must have shared in the thrill which the specifically sexual object imparted. There has been an inevitable action and reaction throughout. Just as we find that the sexual and non-sexual influences of agreeable odours throughout nature are inextricably mingled, so it is with the motives that make an object beautiful to our eyes. The richly laden word *beauty* is a synthesis of complex impressions obtained through a single sense.

If we survey broadly the ideal of feminine beauty set down by the peoples of comparatively uncivilized lands, it is interesting to note that they all contain many features which appeal to our civilized æsthetic taste, and many of them, indeed, contain no features which obviously clash with our canons. It may even be said that the ideals of some savages affect us more sympathetically than some of the ideals of our own mediæval ancestors. This fact, that the modern European, whose culture may be supposed to have made him especially sensitive to æsthetic beauty, is yet able to find beauty among even the women of savage races, indicates that, whatever modifying influences may have to be admitted, beauty is to a large extent an objective matter. This is confirmed by the fact that the men of the lower races sometimes admire European women more than women of their own race.

It is probably a significant fact, indeed, that we may find a similar element running through the whole animated world. The things that to man are most beautiful throughout Nature are those that are intimately associated with, or dependent upon, the sexual process and the sexual instinct. This is the case in the plant world. It is so throughout most of the animal world, and, as Poulton, in referring to this often unexplained and indeed unnoticed fact, remarks, " the song or plume which excites the mating impulse in the hen is also in a high proportion of cases most pleasing to man himself."

In the constitution of our ideals of masculine and feminine beauty it was inevitable that the sexual characters should from an early period in the history of Man form an important element. From a primitive point of view a sexually desirable and attractive woman is one whose sexual characters are either naturally prominent or artificially rendered so; that is to say, she is the woman obviously best fitted to bear children and to suckle them. Similarly, masculine beauty for a woman embodies the qualities best fitted for an effective mate and protector. To a certain extent the primary sexual characters are thus objects of admiration among savage peoples. In the primitive dances of many peoples, often of sexual significance, the display of the sexual organs on the part of both men and women is sometimes a prominent feature. Even down to mediæval times in Europe the garments of men sometimes emphasized the sexual organs. In some parts of the world, also, the artificial enlargement of the female sexual organs (*labia majora* and *minora* and *clitoris*) is practised, and thus enlarged they are considered an important attraction.

Any insistence on the naked sexual organs as objects of attraction is, however, usually confined to peoples in a low state of culture, though it may be noted that in Japanese erotic pictures the sexual organs of both sexes are often exaggerated. Much more widespread is the attempt to beautify or to disguise the sexual organs by tattooing, by adornment, and by striking peculiarities of clothing. The tendency for beauty of clothing to be accepted as a substitute for beauty of body appears early in the history of mankind, and, as we know, tends to be absolutely accepted in civilization. Hence our realities and our traditional ideals are sometimes hopelessly at variance. Our artists are themselves equally ignorant and confused, and, as Stratz repeatedly showed, they constantly reproduce in all innocence the deformations and pathological characters of defective models.

One of the main primitive purposes of adornment and clothing among savages, however, is not to conceal the body, but to draw attention to it and to render it more attractive. With this we have to recognize the magical influence of both adornment and mutilation as a method of guarding and insulating dangerous bodily functions.

The two motives are largely woven together. The sexual organs begin to become sacred, indeed, and the sexual functions to take on a religious character, at an early period in culture. Generation, the reproductive force in Nature, was realized by primitive man to be a conception of the first magnitude, and among its chief symbols he exalted the sexual organs which thus attained to a solemnity scarcely favourable to purposes of sexual allurement. Phallus-worship may almost be said to be a universal phenomenon ; it is found even among races of high culture, among the Romans of the Empire and the Japanese to-day.

Apart from the religious and magical properties so widely accorded to the primary sexual characters, there are other reasons why they should not often have gained or long retained any great importance as objects of sexual allurement. They are unnecessary and inconvenient for this purpose. Even among animals, it happens with extreme rarity that the primary sexual characters are rendered attractive to the eye of the opposite sex, though they often are to the sense of smell. The sexual regions constitute a peculiarly vulnerable spot, even specially so in Man, and the need for their protection conflicts with the prominent display required for sexual allurement. This end is more effectively attained by concentrating the chief signs of sexual attractiveness on the upper and more conspicuous parts of the body. It is a method already well-nigh universal even among the lower animals.

At the same time, even if not æsthetically beautiful, it is fundamentally necessary that the intromittent organ of the male and the receptive canal of the female should retain their primitive characteristics. They cannot, therefore, be greatly modified by sexual or natural selection, and the primitive character they are thus compelled to retain, however sexually desirable and attractive they may become to the opposite sex under the influence of emotion, cannot easily be regarded as beautiful from the point of view of æsthetic contemplation. Under the influence of art there is a tendency for the sexual organs to be diminished in size, and in our civilization the artist never chooses to give an erect organ to his representations of ideal masculine beauty. It is mainly because the unæsthetic character of a woman's sexual region is almost imperceptible in any ordinary and normal position of the nude body that the feminine form is generally considered a more æsthetically beautiful object of contemplation than the masculine. Apart from this character we are bound, from a strictly æsthetic point of view, to regard the male form as at least equally beautiful. The female form, moreover, often over-passes swiftly the climax of its beauty.

With the growth of culture the very methods which had been adopted to call attention to the sexual organs were retained by a further development for the purpose of concealing them. Even from the first the secondary sexual characters have been a far more widespread method of sexual allurement than the primary sexual characters, and in the most civilized countries to-day they still constitute the most attractive of such methods to the majority of the population. It is the main secondary sexual characters which usually present themselves as beautiful in well-developed persons.

Among these secondary sexual characters most of the indigenous peoples of Europe, Asia, and Africa regard the large hips and buttocks of women as an important feature of beauty. This character represents the most decided structural deviation of the feminine type from the masculine, a deviation demanded by the reproductive function of women, and in the admiration it arouses sexual selection is thus working in a line with natural selection, though, except in a moderate degree, it has not usually been regarded as at the same time in a line with the claims of purely æsthetic beauty. But apart from these high claims, nearly everywhere large hips and buttocks have been regarded as a mark of beauty, and the average man is of this opinion even in the most æsthetic countries. The contrast of this exuberance with the more closely knit male form, the force of association, and the unquestionable fact that such development is the condition needed for healthy motherhood, has served as a basis for an ideal of sexual attractiveness, while broad hips, which involve a large pelvis, are necessarily a characteristic of the highest human races, because the races with the largest heads must be endowed also with the largest pelves.

It can scarcely be an accidental coincidence that it is precisely among people of black race, those with the smallest pelvis, that we find a simulation of the large pelvis of the higher races admired and cultivated in the form of steatopygia. This is an enormously exaggerated development of the subcutaneous layer of fat which normally covers the buttocks and upper parts of the thighs in woman, and in this extreme form constitutes a kind of natural fatty tumour. True steatopygia now only exists among Bushman and Hottentot women, and among the peoples who are by blood connected with them. An unusual development of the buttocks is, however, found among many other African peoples. Sometimes admiration for this characteristic is associated with admiration for marked obesity generally, and it may be noted that a somewhat greater degree of fatness may also be regarded as a feminine secondary sexual character. This admiration is specially marked among several of the black peoples of Africa. An occasional extension of the idea of sexual beauty as associated with developed hips is found in the tendency (which existed at one time in mediæval Europe) to regard the pregnant woman as the physically most beautiful type.

Only second to the attraction of the feminine pelvis, and in civilization usually higher, we must place the breasts. Among Europeans, indeed, the importance of this region is so highly esteemed that even when the general rule against the exposure of the body was most stringent, a European lady in full dress was still allowed more or less to uncover the breasts. Savages, on the contrary, do not usually show any great admiration for this part of the body. Various savage peoples even regard the development of the breasts as ugly and adopt devices for flattening them. The feeling that prompts this practice is not unknown in modern Europe, while in mediæval Europe, indeed, the general ideal of feminine slenderness was opposed to developed breasts, and the garments tended to compress them. But in a high degree of civilization this feeling is unknown, as, indeed, it is unknown to most barbarians. The admiration accorded to developed breasts and pelvis is evidenced by the practice of tightening the waist girth, embodied in the ancient corset. This practice has sometimes been almost universal among peoples of white race and is not unknown among other races.

Another prominent secondary sexual character, belonging to man, and, unlike the breasts and hips, not obviously an index of functional sexual activity, is the beard. This may be regarded as a purely sexual ornament comparable to the somewhat similar growths on the heads of many male animals. The cultivation of the beard varies at different periods of culture, and belongs peculiarly to barbarous peoples who sometimes regard it as sacred. In civilization, it tends to lose this significance, and its value as a sexual ornament is diminished or lost altogether. This was so even in ancient civilizations. Thus in early Rome beards and long hair were worn, but not in later Rome, when epilation of the pubes also became common for women, while beards, considered as indications of gravity and wisdom, were usually reserved for philosophers. In Greek statues the pubes of women is usually hairless, but this does not indicate a general custom in real life, and the vase paintings frequently show pubic hair even for women who were hetairæ, while Helen of Troy, regarded as a type of beauty, is also so represented. The customs of different peoples, and of the same people at different periods, with reference to the estimation of hair (which has been discussed at length by Stoll) differs widely. Sometimes it has been held in the highest honour for men, and as a mark of supreme beauty in women, at other times so far as possible suppressed, and cut, shaved, or epilated.

A main reason for this has been the close association of the hairy system with sex, combined with the realization that, unlike the pelvis and the breasts, the hair no longer has definite biological value. It is thus a field in which likes and dislikes have free play to create their fashions. The ascetic religious elements have notably been an influence unfavourable to hair, even in ancient Egypt, for, as Remy de Gourmont has remarked, " the immorality of the living form resides especially in the pilous system." It was thus inevitable that the influence of Christianity should have been against hair, especially in old days against beards which were denounced by monkish writers, and later against the pudendal hair which in Victorian times it was considered " disgusting " to represent in pictures. Thus religion fostered what were considered the refinements of civilization, and we see at present a widespread tendency to remove the beard in men and in women to epilate the armpits and sometimes the pubes, as well as to minimize the hair generally.

On the whole, however, there is good reason for assuming a certain fundamental tendency whereby the most various peoples of the world, at all events through their most intelligent members, recognize and accept a common ideal of beauty, so that to a certain extent beauty may be said to have an objectively æsthetic basis. This æsthetic human ideal is variously modified in different countries, and even in the same country at different periods, by a tendency, prompted by a sexual impulse which is not necessarily in harmony with æsthetic canons, to emphasize or to repress one or other of the prominent secondary sexual characters.

Another tendency which is apt to an even greater extent to limit the cultivation of the purely æsthetic ideal of beauty is the influence of national or racial type. To the average man of every race the woman who most completely embodies the type of his race is usually the most beautiful, and even mutilations and deformations often have their origin in the effort to accentuate the racial type. Eastern women possess by nature large and conspicuous eyes, and this characteristic they seek still further to heighten by art. The Ainu are the hairiest of races, and there is nothing which they consider so beautiful as hair.

It is difficult to be sexually attracted to persons who are fundamentally unlike ourselves in racial constitution. Thus it frequently happens that this admiration for our own racial characteristics leads to the idealization of features which are far removed from æsthetic beauty. The firm and rounded breast is certainly a feature of beauty, but among many of the black peoples of Africa the breasts fall at an early age, and here we sometimes find that the hanging breast is admired as beautiful.

To make the analysis of sexual beauty fairly complete must be added at least one other factor: the influence of individual taste. Every individual, at all events in civilization, within certain narrow limits builds up a feminine ideal of his own, in part on the basis of his special organization and its demands, in part on the actual accidental attractions he has experienced. It is unnecessary to emphasize the existence of this factor, which has always to be taken into account in every consideration of sexual selection in civilized man. But its variations are numerous, and in impassioned lovers it may even lead to the idealization of features which are in reality the reverse of beautiful. We here approach the field of morbid sexual deviations.

It is thus that we have to recognize another factor in the constitution of the ideal of beauty, one perhaps exclusively found under civilized conditions: the love of the unusual, the remote, the exotic. It is commonly stated that rarity is admired in beauty. This is not strictly true, except as regards combinations and characters which vary only in a slight degree from the generally admired type. "*Jucundum nihil est quod non reficit varietas,*" according to an ancient saying. The greater nervous restlessness and sensitivity of civilization heightens this tendency, which is not infrequently found also among men of artistic genius. In every great centre of civilization the national ideal of beauty tends to be somewhat modified in exotic directions, and foreign ideals, as well as foreign fashions, become preferred to those that are native.

Beauty, if thus the chief, is not the sole, element in the sexual appeal of vision. In all parts of the world this has been well understood, and in courtship, in the effort to arouse tumescence, the appeals to vision have been multiplied and at the same time aided by other secondary appeals.

Thus we have scoptophilia (mixoscopia) or the sexual excitement aroused by the sight of sexual scenes, or even simply of the sexual organs of the opposite sex. To some extent this is entirely normal, its shamefaced manifestations being simply due to the rigid conventional secrecy in which the naked body is held. Many estimable men have in youth sought secret opportunities of watching women in their bedrooms and many estimable women looked through the keyholes of men's bedrooms, though they would not like to acknowledge this. It is indeed a common habit for landladies and servant-girls to fix their eyes at the keyholes of rooms where are couples whom they suspect may be lovers. The persons who cultivate this mixoscopia recklessly are commonly termed "peepers." These manifestations have sometimes attracted the attention of the police, notably in Paris, and women I know have detected men watching them through the skylight at the back of public conveniences in the Tuileries Gardens.

In another form we have the sexual attraction of pictures, not necessarily lascivious in character, of erotic scenes, and the sexual attraction of statues. This is on the one hand the psychological source of what is commonly called pornography (incorrectly since it has no special connection with brothels) and on the other hand of the sexual deviation known as Pygmalionism from the classic story of Pygmalion falling in love with the statue he had himself made. While the interest in erotic scenes and in erotic pictures is natural and normal, when it does not become an absorbing passion, Pygmalionism is morbid because the adored object is an end in itself. Pygmalionism has chiefly been observed in men, but Hirschfeld mentions a lady, moving in the best social circles, who was observed in a museum lifting the fig-leaf from classic statues, and covering the place beneath with kisses. The erotic attraction of pictures is now mainly manifested, and on the widest scale, through the cinema, the influence being the more powerful because of the moving and lifelike nature of the pictures presented. Very many people, especially young women, go evening after evening to the cinema to gaze in a state of sexual excitement at an adored hero, perhaps living thousands of miles away, whom in real life they will never see.

An important secondary appeal to vision associated with movement is that which takes the form of dancing. Here we have what Sadger has called muscle erotism, and Healy describes as muscle and joint pleasure combined with "skin erotism." In dancing there is spectacle combined with muscular action, each becoming under some conditions a sexual stimulus, and the spectacle sometimes more so than the exercise. Among many savage races dancing is often a highly important method of sexual selection, the skilful and athletic dancers rightly warranting feminine choice. The question of the wholesome or unwholesome influence of dancing in civilization has sometimes been debated. Some years ago, Brill investigated this point in New York, among 342 men and women (friends, patients, and others whose answers could be relied on), enthusiasts for the "new" dances, about two-thirds of them men and one-third women. He sent out these questions: (1) Do you ever become sexually excited when dancing the new dances? (2) Do you become excited when watching them? (3) Do you have the same experiences dancing or watching the old dances?

To the first question 14 men and 8 women replied yes; to the second 16 men and 29 women; to the third 11 men and 6 women. Those who said "yes" to the second question included all who replied similarly to the first and third. Relatively to the total number there is a very slight excess of affirmative answers among the women; all of this group were known to Brill and regarded by him as sexually hyperæsthetic. The great majority assert that they are merely conscious of a sense of exhilaration and well-being. The question whether the "new" dances act as gross sexual incitors can be emphatically answered in the negative. Brill justly concludes that both kinds of dances are outlets for sexual tension, only differing in degree, and for nervous and hyperchondriacal women often of great benefit. Even when dancing becomes an epidemic not in itself desirable, it still deserves to be cultivated in so far as it acts as a compromise between the two opposing streams of desire and repression, and serves as a safety valve for high tension.

It must be added finally, that while beauty is primarily a quality of woman, being as such a perpetual meditation of men—and even for women still a feminine quality which they admire—the normal woman experiences no corresponding cult for the beauty of man. The perfection of the body of man is not behind that of woman, but the study of it only appeals to the artist or the æsthetician; it arouses sexual enthusiasm almost exclusively in the male sexual invert. Whatever may be the case among animals, or even among savages, in civilization the man who is most successful with women is not usually the most handsome man, and may be the reverse of handsome. "It is *passion*," Stendhal remarks, "which we demand; beauty only furnishes *probabilities*." Women admire a man's strength, physical or mental, rather than his beauty. The spectacle of force, while it remains within the field of vision, really brings to us, although unconsciously, impressions that are correlated with another sense—that of touch. We instinctively and unconsciously translate visible energy into energy of pressure. In admiring strength we are really admiring a tactile quality which has been made visible. It may therefore be said that, while through vision men are sexually affected mainly by the more purely visual quality of beauty, women are more strongly affected by visual impressions which express qualities belonging to the more fundamentally sexual sense of touch.

In a woman the craving for visual expression of pressure energy is much more pronounced and predominant than in a man. It is not difficult to see why this should be so, even without falling back on the usual explanation that sexual selection implies that the female shall choose the male who will be the most likely father of strong children and the best protector of his family. The more energetic part in physical love belongs to the man, the more passive part to the woman; so that, while energy in a woman is no index to effectiveness in love, energy in a man furnishes a seeming index to the existence of the primary quality of vigour which a woman demands of a man in the sexual embrace. It may be a fallacious index, for muscular strength is not necessarily correlated with sexual vigour and in its extreme degree appears to be more correlated with its absence. But it furnishes "the probability of passion," and in any case it still remains a symbol which cannot be without its effect. We must not, of course, suppose that these considerations are always or often present to the consciousness of the maiden who "blushingly turns from Adonis to Hercules," but the emotional attitude is rooted in more or less unerring instincts. In this way it happens that even in the field of visual attraction sexual selection influences women on the underlying basis of the more primitive sense of touch, the fundamentally sexual sense.

The sexual enjoyment aroused by the spectacle of graceful, skilful, or athletic movement was by Féré termed ergophily, and in a pronounced degree it is specially exhibited by women, and is distinct from the more morbid pleasure occasionally aroused by scenes of horror and cruelty. Féré brought forward a typical case of extreme ergophily in a young married woman who was unable to respond to the affection of her husband though she had no complaint to make of him. She was a delicate child and at the age of four was taken to see a travelling country circus company; she was so impressed and excited by the juggling performance with balls of a little girl scarcely older than herself that she felt strange warm sensations in the genital region followed by a kind of spasm and wetted herself. (When such a spasm occurs in early life detumescence may take the form of urination.) After that the little juggler became a day-dream with her, and sometimes a sleeping dream, followed by the same sensations and micturition. After puberty at fourteen she saw at a circus an elegant and accomplished athlete who produced in her the same effects, and then the little juggler and the athlete alternated in her dream. At sixteen after a mountain excursion and a rich meal she fell asleep and awoke with the vision of the athlete and a powerful orgasm, but, to her satisfaction, no urination (detumescence having ceased to be vesical). She came to live in Paris, and soon all skilful or energetic masculine activities, in theatres, workshops, etc., proved sources of sexual pleasure. Marriage made no difference, though later she came to an explanation with her husband. In minor degree, ergophily may be considered normal.

To sum up, it may be said that beauty is not, as some have supposed, a mere matter of caprice. It rests in part on (1) an objective basis of æsthetic nature which holds all its variations together and leads to a remarkable approximation among the ideals of feminine beauty cherished by the most intelligent men of all races. But beyond this general objective basis we find that (2) the specific characters of the race or nation tend to cause divergence in the ideals of beauty, since beauty is often held to consist in the extreme development of these racial or national anthropological features; and it would, indeed, appear that the full development of racial characters indicates at the same time the full development of health and vigour. We have further to consider that (3) in most countries an important and usually essential element of beauty lies in the emphasis of the secondary and tertiary sexual characters; the special characters of the hair on woman, her breasts, her hips, and innumerable other qualities of minor saliency, but all apt to be of significance from the point of view of sexual selection. In addition we have (4) the factor of individual taste, constituted by the special organization and the peculiar experiences of the individual and inevitably affecting his ideal of beauty. Often this individual factor is merged into collective shapes, and in this way are constituted passing fashions in the matter of beauty, certain influences which normally affect only the individual having become potent enough to affect many individuals. Finally, in states of high civilization and in individuals of that restless and nervous temperament which is common in civilization, we have (5) a tendency to the appearance of an exotic element in the ideal of beauty, and in place of admiring that kind of beauty which most closely approximates to the type of their own race men begin to be agreeably affected by types which more or less deviate from that with which they are most familiar.

The question is still further complicated by the fact that sexual selection in the human species is not merely the choice of the woman by the man, but also the choice of the man by the woman. And when we come to consider this we find that the standard is altogether different, that many of the elements of beauty as it exists in woman for man have here fallen away altogether, while a new and preponderant element has to be recognized in the shape of a regard for strength and vigour. This is not purely a visual character, but a tactile pressure character translated into visual terms.

To state the sexual ideal is not, however, by any means to state the complete problem of human sexual selection. The ideal that is desired and sought is, in a large measure, not the outcome of experience; it is not even necessarily the expression of the individual's temperament and idiosyncrasy. It may be largely the result of fortuitous circumstances, of slight chance attractions in childhood, of accepted traditions consecrated by romance. In the actual contacts of life the individual may find that his sexual impulse is stirred by sensory stimuli which are other than those of the ideal he had cherished and may even be the reverse of them.

Beyond this also, we have reason for believing that factors of a still more fundamentally biological character, to some extent deeper even than all these psychic elements, enter into the problem of sexual selection. Certain individuals, apart altogether from the question of whether they are ideally or practically the most fit mates, display a greater energy and achieve a greater success than others in securing partners. These individuals possess a greater constitutional vigour, physical or mental, which conduces to their success in practical affairs generally, and probably also heightens their specifically philogamic activities.

Thus, the problem of human sexual selection is in the highest degree complicated. When we gather together such scanty data of precise nature as are at present available, we realize that, while generally harmonizing with the results which the evidence not of a quantitative nature would lead us to accept, their precise significance is not at present altogether clear. It would appear on the whole that in choosing a mate we tend to seek parity of racial and anthropological characters together with disparity of secondary sexual characters and complementary psychic characters.

It is a variation, but a slight variation, that we seek.

BIBLIOGRAPHY

DARWIN, *Descent of Man.*

LEONARD DARWIN, *Eugenic Reform,* Chapter XX, "Sexual Selection."

PYCRAFT, *The Courtship of Animals.*

HAVELOCK ELLIS, *Man and Woman; Studies in the Psychology of Sex,* Vol. IV, "Sexual Selection in Man."

WESTERMARCK, *The History of Human Marriage,* Vol. I.

CRAWLEY, *The Mystic Rose,* edited by Besterman.

ALEXANDER STONE, *The Study of Phallicism.*

A. A. BRILL, "The Psychopathology of the New Dances," *New York Medical Journal,* April 25th, 1914.

CHAPTER III

THE SEXUAL IMPULSE IN YOUTH

The First Appearance of the Sexual Impulse

It used to be believed that in childhood the sex impulse had no existence at all. That belief was not so common as some have supposed. But if it is possible to maintain that the sex impulse has no normal existence in early life, then every manifestation of it at that period must be "perverse," and even Freud, who regards infantile sexuality as normal, also regards it as "perverse," as he phrases it, "polymorph-perverse." In any discussion of the matter, however brief, it is essential to clear up this confusion.

It must be said at the outset that what may fairly be termed manifestations of the sexual impulse—even when we do not adopt a wide extension of the term "sexual"—are undoubtedly much more frequent than was formerly supposed. There is also a much greater range in their force, their precocity, and their nature than has been commonly suspected.

Even in the primary and initial aptitude of the genital organs for sexual stimulation there is a fundamental range of variation. The aptitude of some infants at an early age to manifest genital reactions, which were usually regarded as reflex signs of irritation, was long ago a familiar observation. Such manifestations do not persist in memory, so that we have no direct evidence as to whether or not they are pleasurable, but many persons of both sexes can recall agreeable sensations connected with the genital organs in childhood; they are not (as is sometimes imagined) repressed; what is repressed, and usually indeed not experienced, is the impulse to mention them to grown-up persons, and they are commonly not mentioned to anyone. But they tend to persist in memory because they stand out of relation to ordinary experience and in striking contrast tc it.

Definite sexual self-excitement has long been known to occur at an early age. Early in the nineteenth century various authors in France and elsewhere—Marc, Fonssagrives, Perez, etc.—gave cases of children of both sexes who masturbated from the age of three or four. Robie found that in boys the first sex feelings occur between the ages of five and fourteen, in girls between eight and nineteen; in both boys and girls these first manifestations more frequently appear during the later than the earlier years. Hamilton, in his more carefully detailed inquiry, has found that 20 per cent. males and 14 per cent. females find pleasure in their sex organs before the age of six. Katharine Davis, comparing groups of men and women, found that 20·9 per cent. boys began to masturbate up to and including the age of eleven, and 49·1 per cent. girls, though during the next three years the percentage of boys was much in excess of the girls. It is a mistake to suppose that all children experience, or are capable of experiencing, genital excitement or pleasurable sexual sensations. Crucial cases occur in which the child, innocently led away by another child who gives assurance that friction will favour the development of the penis in size, will in this innocence sedulously try to procure the supposed benefit but without attaining in any degree either genital reaction or sensory pleasure, although in due course at puberty, if not before, the organ becomes fully excitable. There is thus a wide range of genital and sexual aptitude in childhood. How far the differences are due to definitely different hereditary antecedents it is not always easy to say. On the whole it would appear, as we should expect, that the child of sound and solid ancestry is less sexually excitable in childhood, and the child of more unsound heredity or of hypersexual parents more precociously excitable. Dr. Hamilton's inquiries indicate that the later sex life begins the more satisfactory marriage turns out.

The subject becomes more complex when we go beyond localized genital phenomena of sex. And here we encounter the *libido* of the psycho-analysts. In early days that met with violent opposition when applied to infancy and childhood, nor can it be said that the opposition has been entirely overcome. It is now recognized, however, that much depends on the way in which we define the term *libido*. Like many Freudian terms, it was not happily chosen, and it is not easy to dissociate it from the English term " libidinous." Jung, one of the most distinguished analysts outside the Freudian school, dissociates libido, indeed, from any special connection with sex and takes it in a wide sense as " psychic energy " corresponding to the " élan vital " of Bergson, or, in English, " vital urge," which is the term some people would like to use, for there is no doubt that we cannot dissociate the term *libido* from definite sex energy. Freud has wavered in his view of *libido* and its development. As he remarks in his illuminating essay on the " Infantile Organization of the Libido " (1923), at one time he emphasized its early pre-genital organization, though later he came to accept a close approximation of the sexuality of childhood to adult sexuality. But the infantile genital organization, he goes on to say, really involves the primacy of the phallus, which he regards as the only genital organ recognized in childhood. At the same time he speaks of a " pre-genital " phase and asserts that " not until puberty does the polarity of sexuality coincide with *male* and *female*." Some have detected here an undue tendency to theoretic generalization in a world which consists of individuals, each with a different heredity, and naturally also with a different mode of reaction to the external world. But the main point is that, for Freud, sexual polarity is only attained at puberty. Therefore, since for the ordinary person " libidinousness " mainly rests on sexual polarity, the Freudian *libido* scarcely seems to call for any excessive horror. It is the Freudian terminology which is at fault. We may agree with Ernest Jones that if we divide sex activity into two phases of " initial pleasures " and " end pleasures," " the manifestations before puberty are almost entirely confined to the former group." We must, however, admit exceptions.

Freud's conception of the *libido* would have met with less

opposition if he had at the outset taken up the position which at last he took in 1925 (*Das Ich und das Es*) when, more or less discarding *libido*, he set forth the relationship of the *ego* to the *id* (the term by which *es* has been ingeniously translated), the *id* being the more or less unconscious and primitive self with its passions, and the *ego* the more conscious and reasonable self, in closer reaction with the outer world, which gradually develops out of the *id* and separates itself off from it. As Freud himself remarks, this conception fairly well corresponds with popular and generally accepted ideas.

When we survey widely the activities of children it would not seem that it is generally " the primacy of the phallus " which we find most striking (most of those familiar with babies would say that it is the primacy of the thumb and toes), and so far as it is, it is often (as indeed Freud remarks) essentially an impulse of curiosity, which some mothers unfortunately repress and so drive in and unduly emphasize. Here are the most " curious " parts of the body, the parts (with fingers and toes) that for a child are most like playthings. This interest may lead on to pleasurable sensation, but for most children it would appear that what may be regarded as sexual sensation is outside the genital sphere, being sexual sensation of the threshold, that is to say sensation of a kind that would in an adult lie on the threshold of the sexual sphere and lead up to it (thus legitimately belonging to the art of love). The difference is that such sensations in the child, while pleasurable, do not usually pass over the threshold of the actual sexual sensation.

Such phenomena are in the first place most usually in the oral region. This we should expect, as the most acute pleasure of the infant could scarcely fail to be derived from the sensitive lips of the mouth in contact with the milk-yielding nipple of the mother. Since the mouth is an erogenic or sexually stimulating zone in adult life we cannot be surprised that it should be a pleasure-centre on the sexual threshold even in infancy. Thumb-sucking sometimes becomes a substitute for nipple-sucking when it is unattainable or outgrown ; it is held by some—although the opinion is disputed by numerous authorities—that in predisposed children this may be a kind of masturbation and later lead on to ordinary masturbation. It is a practice found among a considerable and varying proportion of young children of both sexes and may even begin immediately after birth.

Only second to the emergence of the oral centre is probably the anal centre. As long as the motions are passed automatically and without restraint there is little opportunity for the anal region to become a pleasure centre. But as soon as any restraint is imposed gratification in the discharges is certain to be felt and the pleasurable sensitivity of the anus is liable to become developed; it is often in later years an erogenic zone, though not so often or so profoundly as the oral region. It is held by some psychoanalysts that at an early age there is in some subjects a tendency to retain the fæces with a pleasure aim, and that such a tendency is significant for later psychic development; this, however, has been denied by others as not easy to prove. Much the same may be said of the urinary discharge, though here the pleasure, alike in the infant and the adult, is more exclusively in the discharge itself, and some observers note that the infant may find pleasure in bestowing this discharge on a specially preferred person, though it is quite likely that this is often a misinterpretation of the facts, and that the discharge of urine in the infant under the influence of pleasurable emotion may be no more intentional than it is in the adult woman in whom it occasionally occurs by reflex action, and to her great vexation, during the sexual orgasm. Hamilton found that 21 per cent. men and 16 per cent. women admit being interested in urine or playing with it in early life, and exactly the same percentage as regards fæces.

On the psychic side there is even less doubt of the liability of children to experience emotions which may fairly be called sexual than there is on the physical side. Many years ago Sanford Bell showed, on a collective basis, the frequency of these manifestations, which all have had occasions to observe sometimes. His report may still be read with profit. He had studied the question for fifteen years, both in and out of schools, and personally observed 800 cases, while he had obtained records of 1,700 other cases (thus 2,500 in all) from 360 other observers of whom only five could recall no experience of that kind from their own childhood, a fact which indicates that it is a mistake to suppose that repression of such early experiences is common; when repression occurs it is evidently abnormal and probably due to inborn peculiarities. Bell found that emotion of this kind may be witnessed as early as the middle of the third year, and that in the nature of its manifestations there tend to be several stages of which the first usually continues to the age of eight, and the second to the age of fourteen. In the first stage the boy is usually more modest and less aggressive than the girl. The emotion is detected by a number of little signs which it is difficult to avoid assigning to a sex origin. A tendency to hug and kiss is common, but does not always occur, and there is frequently a desire to conceal the emotion from its object and from anyone else. While some form of touch contact is frequently sought, it is not in general specifically sexual, and when it is Bell was inclined to regard the case as precocious. The erethism, as he well remarks, is not usually (though it may be) manifested in the sex organs, but it is distributed throughout the entire body, especially the vascular and nervous systems. Spring is the period of the year when these manifestations are most likely to occur.

Students of childhood, psycho-analytic and others, have since confirmed and elaborated these observations. Freud has again and again dealt with the matter, and Oskar Pfister, in his extensive and discursive work on love in children and its defects of development, comes to the conclusion that there is an amazing and unsuspected multiplicity of manifestations in the love sentiments of children.

It is, as already indicated, characteristic of the sexual or pseudo-sexual interests of children that they should mainly fall outside the sphere which for the adult is that of sex proper, partly because on the physical side the genital centres are still undeveloped and partly because on the psychic side the opposite sex has not yet usually acquired the definite significance which after puberty sooner or later it possesses.

An interesting and often overlooked trait of childish sexuality is algolagnia, or a pleasurable interest in pain, this including pleasure in the witnessing of pain, the inflicting of pain, or the experiencing of it. Various adult names are commonly applied to these manifestations, such as "cruelty," "sadism," "masochism," etc., and this is probably inevitable because it is only so that adults can explain to themselves these manifestations of the childish psyche. But they are misleading and unfortunate, for they are far away from the aims of childhood. The child has not, for instance, yet formulated the humanely adult notion of "cruelty," and when we remember that even for many adults it has no clear existence we cannot be surprised that it is alien to the children who amiably and pleasantly witness the sufferings of the lower animals and often themselves increase or cause them. Children are at work—or, if you wish, at play—in the exercise-ground of inquisitive reason and as yet undifferentiated emotion: the fossilized rules of adult morality are here misplaced. It is the function of education, in the proper sense of that term (for the fallacy that education means *putting in* and not *bringing out* is still common among the ignorant), to help the child to educe in due course the activities of later life, and to make clear to him, as soon as his comprehension permits, that his own early unrestrained impulses do not work in the adult world. The fact that we are here primarily concerned with exercises in the field of emotion, only incidentally liable to reach the threshold of pain, is shown in the child's equal or greater liking to suffer its infliction. Games of "punishment" with much reciprocal smacking have always been privately popular among children of both sexes, perhaps especially girls, the hair-brush often being used for this purpose. Self-flagellation is also sometimes practised, and even after puberty, when the genital centres are fully active, it may be adopted by either sex to heighten the solitary pleasure of the sexual impulse in the absence of a person of the opposite sex. Day-dreams of torture are a not uncommon source of pleasure even among young children, and at a rather later age one has heard of Foxe's *Book of Martyrs* proving a source of thrilling delight. Sometimes the child experiences an irresistible impulse to inflict pain on himself and often on his penis, which indicates that, even if not a source of sexual excitement in the adult sense, the penis is already a centre of emotional interest. Such facts recall the castration-complex to which some psycho-analysts attach enormous importance. A string may be strongly tied round the penis; or it may even be violently struck; and the case has lately been recorded of a girl of nine who tied a thread round her clitoris and was unable to remove it, so that surgical interference became necessary. Sensation and emotion are still in a comparatively diffused and as it were uncrystallized form. As the realization of pain is so early necessary in life for self-preservation it is inevitable that painful emotions should be those in which the still vague pleasure impulses tend to take shape. Hamilton found that among his subjects, who may all be said to be of high character and culture, only 49 per cent. men and 68 per cent. women never experienced pleasure in inflicting pain; while nearly 30 per cent. of both men and women had had pleasure in experiencing pain.

How far we are here from adult developments is shown by the now well recognized fact that neither similarity of sex nor closeness of blood relationship provides any bar to these manifestations. The adult who succeeds in discerning the occurrence of such manifestations begins to talk solemnly and pedantically of "homosexuality" and "incest" and the "Œdipus complex," without realizing the absurdity he is perpetrating. He would indeed be speaking quite rationally if he were dealing with the like phenomena in his own grown-up world. There can be no homosexuality when there is yet no conception of sexuality, and no incest before the barriers of relationship are known. As a distinguished psycho-analyst, Dr. Jelliffe, has said of this manner of labelling the impulsive activity of childhood, "expressing it in terms of conscious adult activity is nonsense." Even apart from sex, the best psychologists of childhood (like Stern in his *Psychology of Early Childhood*) are trying to make clear that we must not measure children by our adult psychic powers, but learn to understand their different natures. Until we have realized this, until we have cleared away the elaborate structure of childhood sexuality erected on the adult pattern by adults who seem to have lost all memory of youth, we shall wander among vain shadows in this field. Here certainly is a kingdom of knowledge into which only those can enter who become as little children.

At this point it is necessary to refer to a psychological trait to which psycho-analysts, above all Freud, who first called attention to it, have in the past, and to some extent still, attached supreme importance: the so-called Œdipus complex. It is not, on the surface, quite happily so called, for what we hereby mean psychologically is simply an attraction of love (a "wish to marry") the parent of opposite sex, on the part of the young child, with a corresponding jealousy of the parent of the same sex. Whereas in the myth Œdipus experienced no such feelings, but was compelled by the oracle and the gods to marry his mother and kill his father unwittingly, in spite of all his own struggles to avoid these crimes; but this opposition Freud explains away by saying that oracle and gods were a glorified embodiment of the Unconscious. Freud's Œdipus complex, when he first put it forward some thirty years ago—certainly in an incautious way and with a misapplied use of the word "incest"—was, as he frequently stated, greeted with horror and execration. That attitude, to one of his strong and combative temperament, merely aroused a more emphatic assertion of the doctrine. In some degree, in some form or another, even an inverted form, the Œdipus complex, Freud declared, "is a regular and very important factor in the mental life of the child." He went on to find that "it does not seem impossible" that the Œdipus complex is the source of all perversions and also "the actual nucleus of the neuroses." Rank, at the time closely associated with him, showed with the help of his wide literary culture how frequently and variously this motive had entered dramatic poetry. Finally in 1913, in *Totem and Taboo*, Freud developed a conception of the Œdipus complex as lying at the root of primitive morality, furnishing that sense of guilt which to Freud seems " the ultimate source of religion and morality," the earliest form of Kant's categorical imperative, and the first embodiment of the great cosmic figures, which, beginning as Parents, became God, Fate, Nature, what we will.

But the psycho-analysts who have thus placed the Œdipus complex at the foundation of a large part of human culture have failed to realize that that complex can only be associated, if at all, with a particular family constitution, and that the family, far from having only one single form of constitution, has varied widely. A patriarchal family, such as we have had during historical times in the parts of Europe best known to us, is essential for an Œdipus complex. But that is not a kind of family always and everywhere known. The substance of the family is biological but its forms are socially moulded. This is made clear by Malinowski (who started with a bias favourable to psycho-analysis) in his book *Sex and Repression in Savage Society*. The complexes which are supposed to mould culture could only have arisen under culture, and cultures are of various kinds. Nor can we accept a " primeval horde equipped with all the bias, maladjustments and ill-tempers of a middle-class European family and then let loose in a prehistoric jungle." Every type of civilization cannot but have a special type of complex as its necessary by-product.

The Œdipus complex, further, rests on the belief that there is a strong natural human tendency, appearing at the earliest age, to experience sex love to near relations which can only be overcome by stern laws and severe repressions. It is agreed by all authorities that the free exercise of incestuous impulses is incompatible with a family order, and that on such a basis no developed culture would be likely to arise. But authorities differ as to the natural or unnatural character of incestuous impulses. Westermarck held originally that there is a definite natural instinct averse in incest ; Freud holds that there is from infancy a strong natural instinct to incest ; Malinowski does not accept the aversion to incest as natural but as introduced by culture, "a complex scheme of cultural reactions." The position I have long held largely harmonizes these opposing views. There is a sexual attraction towards persons with whom there is close contact, such persons being often relations, and the attraction being therefore termed "incestuous." Hamilton found that 14 per cent. men had had incestuous impulses in childhood; they aroused no feeling of fear; 10 per cent. had flashes of sex feeling towards mother and 28 per cent. towards sister; seven women towards father and five towards brother. The recollection sometimes aroused a little embarrassment, but evidently no serious sense of guilt. This is a weak attraction under normal circumstances (there are always exceptions) and is quickly overcome when a fascinating new object of desire from outside his own circle strikes the young beholder. There is no anti-incestuous instinct, no natural aversion; but a deep stirring of the sexual impulse needs a strong excitement, and for this a new object is required, not one that has become commonplace by familiarity. This is a view to which Westermarck shows himself favourable in the later edition of his great work on marriage, and it had previously been accepted by Crawley, as well as by Heape. It is clear to anyone who grasps the physiology of the sexual process and the psychology of courtship. A typical illustration may be quoted from Restif de la Bretonne's autobiography, *Monsieur Nicolas*, a precious document for erotic psychology. We here learn how an extremely precocious child was from the age of four in some degree sexually excitable by his female companions and playmates, though he received their caresses with much shyness. It was not till the age of eleven that he became highly aroused, even to the extent of attaining coitus, and losing all his early shyness, and this was with *a girl who was a stranger* and belonging to another village. Many bad theories might have been avoided had this psychological fact been clearly understood. There is no "aversion to incest," but under natural conditions a deep sexual attraction requires a powerful stimulus, and this cannot normally arise out of familiarity. It is noteworthy that the most pronounced cases of incestuous love occur between brother and sister who have not been brought up together, so that the influence of familiarity is absent.

Various objections have been brought against my statement of the psychological basis of exogamy, but they are due to misunderstandings and also a failure to allow for many highly relevant considerations. Some critics have been misled by too exclusively thinking of the conditions among civilized man and domesticated animals. Some have failed to see that there is no question of absolute indifference to the sexual stimulus of familiar persons, which may easily exist and sometimes indeed is peculiarly strong. Others have rightly insisted that incest is unlikely to produce the best offspring or to result in domestic peace, and that exogamy is a highly important factor in social evolution. These influences may very well be responsible for the incest-taboo and remain responsible for maintaining it. But they could hardly have arisen except upon the foundation, and by the support, of the undoubted psychic tendency to which I have called attention. Social institutions are never unnatural in origin; they can only arise on a natural basis. In primitive life, moreover, we find, as Crawley points out, a naïve desire to assist Nature, as it were, by adding to what is normal the categorical imperative of custom and law.

To-day we may look back serenely on the Œdipus complex and the ferocious reactions it seems to have evoked. When the facts are viewed directly and simply, without any attempt to make them look either terrifying or grandiloquent, or to generalize them into universal doctrines, it is easy to discover the very natural fact that the young boy is attracted to his mother (the corresponding phenomenon is the attachment of the young girl to her father) and is jealous at first of what distracts his mother's attention away from him. Jealousy is an entirely natural primitive emotion; every dog is inclined to growl at a seeming attempt to share his bone; any cat may be displeased at the effort of a strange cat to share her plate. Many of us—even the most normal and least neurotic—can recall, or have been told, that in early childhood we disapprove at first of the appearance of a baby brother or sister. But we can also recall that in a very short time we were completely reconciled to the new phenomenon and were even proud to assist in lovingly tending it. Any feeling of hostility to the father seldom, under normal conditions, entered at any stage. The reason is fairly obvious. The baby is new and arouses new feelings; the father has been there from the first; nothing occurs to change the attitude towards him; he is accepted as a matter of course.

But, we see also, the situation is undoubtedly favourable to morbid and emotional developments in constitutionally neurotic subjects, especially under the influence of injudicious parental behaviour, such as favouritism or careless neglect. We may then have the whole chain of manifestations described by psycho-analysts. It is necessary to be alive to these possibilities, and prepared to unravel such a case fearlessly, for the path of psychology cannot be followed except with courage. But it is not necessary to generalize from a single case or even from many cases. And it is fatal to all sound conclusions to set out with a predetermined pattern and to attempt to fit every case on to it.

All this is now becoming clearer and is beginning to be admitted even by psycho-analysts. Thus Rank, who was so active in developing the conception of the Œdipus complex in its early stages, twenty years later, in his suggestive work on *Modern Education*, remarks that "the Œdipus complex, as the attraction to the parent of the opposite sex and jealousy of the parent of the same sex, is not so clearly found in practice as mythology represents it and as Freud at first believed," adding that it has not been easily possible even for psycho-analysts to maintain it. Elsewhere Rank observes that the famous "mother-complex" is not so much a real fixation of the child on the mother as merely a sign of the prevalence to-day of the belief in the influence of the mother in the child's education.

The castration-complex is associated by psycho-analysts with the Œdipus complex, Freud regarding it as primarily a reaction to intimidation in the field of sex, and any restraint on infantile activity being ultimately ascribed to the father. It sometimes happens that mothers and nurses, seeing the young child handling his penis, playfully threaten to cut it off, and the child may possibly take the threat seriously, especially if he observes that his sister has no penis; while the little girl may feel it a deprivation to lack an organ her brother possesses. It is not easy to assert that these feelings count for much in ordinary children. Freud in 1923, while asserting its "invariable presence," found it difficult to believe it due to chance threats which may never occur, and was driven to assume that the child constructed the dogma for himself. But his opinion has varied, and in 1928 he stated that "no male human being is spared the shock of threatened castration." He claims, not only that the castration-complex may play a large part in the formation of neuroses, but even in the formation of character in the healthy child. That the castration-complex is influential in some neurotic persons there can be no doubt. Some persons of keen intelligence but neurotic disposition, when able to review their early development, have found much significance in the influence upon them of foolish nurses in arousing a castration-complex.

The definite manifestation that has always most prominently attracted attention in connection with this aspect of early life is that which from old time has been termed "masturbation." Here it is convenient and possibly legitimate to speak of *sexuality*, although it is not strictly correct for we are concerned with an act which may, and often does, begin in a merely generalized and instinctive search for pleasurable sensations. But since it is an act that is not confined to early life but may occur at any age, often in connection with the most developed ideas of sex, it would be hyper-critical to attempt to draw a line of distinction.

The ancient and common name of the act indicates the excitation of the sexual zone in either sex by means of the hand. But commonly and quite inevitably, the word is employed to cover all methods by which friction can be employed to produce pleasurable sensations in the genital sphere. No doubt the hand is the most frequent instrument and that which, in the absence of mental inhibitions and physical impediments, is most naturally employed. But there are many other ways: in boys, games, sports, gymnastics, even the accidental pressure of the clothes may suffice, especially under condition of general erethism, to produce erection and even orgasm, frequently to the surprise, and sometimes the alarm or the horror, of the subject to whom this experience comes; states of tension and apprehension, and spectacles arousing emotions of horror or of pleasure, may produce the same results, as well as actual experience of a similar kind, such as the punishment of whipping, the classical example of this being the experience of young Rousseau at the hands of his governess, which had, as he believed, a permanent influence on his highly sensitive psychic disposition. In girls, the action of the hands, though as in boys it is the most common method, is even less essential; a casual contact of the sexual parts may prove pleasurable even in the first childhood and be one of a girl's earliest memories; later, contact and friction with external objects may be instinctively sought; small girls will, without concealment, rub themselves against the corner of a chair, or the handle of a chest of drawers; young women will develop and continue a similar habit and even be able to excite themselves against the leg of a table at public restaurants. Without any extraneous help at all, it is sometimes possible for a girl to obtain excitement and orgasm by rubbing the thighs together, or, when in a favourable emotional state, by pressing them tightly together. And, as in boys, the same results may occur almost or quite spontaneously, under the influence of exciting spectacles or seductive thoughts. This, we see, is hardly distinguishable from what may happen, in a normal manner, between two lovers.

In boys who have had no earlier spontaneous impulses of sexual activity and no initiation from companions, the first orgasm usually occurs at puberty during sleep, with or without dreams, sometimes causing the boy much anxiety or shame, until in the course of years he learns to accept it as the almost inevitable accompaniment of adult life when it is being lived continently. In girls, however, it is not inevitable under similar conditions. It is rare (as I have frequently pointed out though the statement has not always been accepted) for girls to have their *first* experience of sexual excitement (with or without orgasm) in sleep, and the supposition that they commonly do is due to ignorance. The boy awakes sexually in sleep, spontaneously. The girl must be actively awakened, by others or herself, though after that, even if it may not occur until long after she has reached adult age, she will be liable to experience the most vivid erotic dreams. We probably have here an interesting psychic sexual difference, the greater sexual activity of the male, the greater sexual quiescence of the female, which does not, however, mean superior sexuality of the male, or inferior sexual needs of the female; it may be indeed the reason why the girl is more liable to hysterical and other nervous symptoms, if we regard these as manifestations of latent sexual energy.

Robie, in America, among a large number of persons of both sexes found few or none who had not had experience of masturbation or other form of auto-erotic activity at some period of their lives and often before the age of eight. His observations were not always very precise. Dr. Katharine Davis, who gave special attention to this point, found, among 1,000 American college women above the age of twenty-two, that 60 per cent. gave definite histories of masturbation. She investigated the whole question, perhaps with more thoroughness and in greater detail than any other worker. Among unmarried college women graduates she found that 43·6 per cent. began the practice from the third to the tenth years inclusive; 20·2 per cent. from 11 to 15 inclusive; 13·9 per cent. from 16 to 22 inclusive; 15·5 per cent. from 23 to 29 inclusive. Comparing her results with those of other investigators dealing with men the results are as follows:—

	Men	*Women*
Up to and including 11 years .	20·9	49·1
Up to and including 12–14 years .	44·3	14·6
Up to and including 15–17 years .	30·3	6·2
Up to 18 years and over . .	4·5	30·1

These results carry weight because the groups include about 500 men to about 900 women. They show, to an unexpected degree, that girls masturbate early more often than boys, and that during adolescence it is the boys who largely predominate, while after adult age is reached, as we should anticipate, women are in a large majority.

Dr. Hamilton, in his careful study of 100 married men and 100 married women of good social standing, found that 97 per cent. of the men and 74 per cent. of the women had at some period masturbated. These results are fairly in accordance with the more general conclusion of Moll, whose work on *The Sexual Life of the Child* (1908) was the earliest comprehensive study of the subject and is still among the most judicious. Moll remarks, however, that masturbation is not as common as is sometimes supposed in Germany, and I may add that it seems not so common in England, or even in France, as the American percentage might lead us to anticipate.

It will be seen that these manifestations extend far beyond the classic conception of "masturbation" in its literal and commonly accepted sense, which cannot really be said to constitute a separate group, for it blends with the larger group without definite frontiers.

When we thus view this group of manifestations as a whole it is seen why we cannot properly term them "perverse." They are natural; they are the inevitable result of the action of the sexual impulse when working in the absence of the object of sexual desire, occurring, under such conditions, even in some of the lower animals; and they are emphatically natural when they occur before adult age. It is natural also that they should occur in adult age when the sexual urge seems irresistible and when normal sexual approaches are undesired or undesirable, although, it must be added, it is equally natural when, under such circumstances, they are inhibited or repressed by other considerations which may seem of a superior order.

It is instructive to explore the attitude towards prepubertal and youthful sexuality in different stages of culture and different periods of history. When we are concerned with an impulse so primitive and fundamental as that of sex we cannot decide what is " natural " and what is " perverse " merely by the standard set up in accordance with shifting fashions of thought, the religious or social customs of one particular age. Least of all can it be said that the age we are ourselves emerging from, with its peculiar and highly coloured views of sex, furnishes any universal standard.

Let us, for instance, turn to a race of a culture outside our own traditions, which has been studied with scientific care, the Trobrianders of New Guinea, as represented in Malinowski's *Sexual Life of Savages.* Children in the Trobriand Islands possess a freedom and independence which extends to sexual matters. No special precautions are taken, or would easily be possible, to prevent children seeing their parents in sexual intercourse or from hearing discussion of sexual matters, though their elders think highly of children who do not repeat what they may thus hear or see. On fishing expeditions, when girls follow their fathers, it is usual for the men to remove the pubic fig-leaf, so that the shape of the male body is never a mystery for the girls. Both boys and girls receive instruction in sexual matters from slightly older companions, and from an early age play at sex games, which enable them to gain some knowledge of these matters and to gratify natural curiosity, even to obtain a certain amount of pleasure ; the hand and the mouth are commonly used for genital manipulations in these games. Little girls usually begin to play at sex at four or five years, and real sex life may begin from between the age of six or eight, while for the boys it begins between ten and twelve. The ordinary round games played by boys and girls in the centre of the village have at times a strong flavour of sex. The grown-ups regard all these manifestations as natural, and see no reason to scold or interfere. No harm comes of it, not even illegitimate children, though how this is prevented remains a mystery. The young Trobrianders palliate crude sexuality by the help of a poetic instinct, and show indeed, Malinowski remarks, " a great sense of the singular and the romantic in their games."

There are, however, widely different attitudes towards sex even in the same part of the world and among peoples not very widely separated in culture and race. Margaret Mead, in *Growing up in New Guinea*, describes the Manus people of the Admiralty Islands to the north of New Guinea as extremely puritanic. They regard sex with aversion and excretions with disgust, repressing and avoiding their manifestations and seeking the maximum of secrecy. The children, though carefully trained in physical respects, are otherwise treated with extreme indulgence and left free; but sexual manifestations, including masturbation, are slight and infrequent, because there are few opportunities for isolation. There seemed to be much sexual frigidity, and the married women do not admit pleasure in married life and seek to avoid sexual intercourse, nor are there any signs of romantic affection.

Another picture of youthful sex life outside our own culture, though this time not untouched by our civilization, is presented by Margaret Mead in *Coming of Age in Samoa*. Here our civilization has had a considerable dissolving influence on the old Samoan culture, so that what might seem a new and artificial culture has grown up and with considerable rapidity. Yet it has grown up naturally on what is evidently the foundation of the old Samoan culture, deprived of all but the minimum of its taboos and restrictions, and it seems to work beneficially. Small boys and girls tend to avoid each other, not by external command but by custom and instinct; yet from the earliest age, owing to the general absence of privacy, they begin to be familiar with the essential facts of life and death, including the details of sex and sexual intercourse. They also have an individual sex life from childhood; nearly every little girl masturbates from the age of six or seven, more or less in secret, the boys also, but more usually in groups, and casual homosexual practices are common; on the part of growing girls or women working together such casual relationships are regarded as "a pleasant and natural diversion, just tinged with the salacious." Such "perversions" are neither banned nor cultivated into institutions;

they are simply the sign of the recognition of a wide range of normality, and public opinion, while viewing attention to the details of sex as unseemly, does not regard them as wrong. It is claimed by Margaret Mead that the Samoans by this system " legislate a whole field of neurotic possibility out of existence " ; there is no neurosis, no frigidity, no impotence. Facility of divorce makes unnecessary an unhappy marriage (though adultery does not necessarily destroy marriage), and economic independence of the wife places her on the same level as the husband.

When we turn to the European tradition, and to the sources of our modern civilization, the earliest references to these manifestations show no clearly implied disapproval, or at the most an occasional touch of contempt, and there is even in Greek literature an association of masturbation with gods. In historical times we find that admired philosophers of the Cynic school boasted of the advantages of satisfying sexual needs in a solitary manner. In Rome there appears to have been a considerable amount of indifference to these matters, and even in the Christian Church, for over a thousand years, there were so many extravagant sexual excesses to combat that the spontaneous solitary manifestations of sex scarcely attracted attention. It was not till the Reformation and at first mainly in Protestant countries, though the movement quickly spread to France and other Catholic countries, that moralists and physicians began to be much troubled about masturbation. This was marked in the eighteenth century. At the same time opportunity was furnished to quacks to offer more or less fantastic remedies for the evils which were beginning to be attributed to " self-abuse." Even until the end of the last century serious physicians frequently took for granted that some grave result or other might be induced by masturbation.

It was during the second half of the nineteenth century, when a new biological conception under the inspiration of Darwin was slowly permeating medicine, that the idea of infantile and youthful " perversion " began to be undermined ; on the one hand the new scientific study of sex, started by the pioneering work of Krafft-Ebing at the end of the third quarter of the century, showed how common are such so-called " perversions " in early life, while, on the other hand, the conception of evolution began to make it clear that we must not apply developed adult standards to undeveloped creatures, what is natural at one stage not necessarily being natural at the previous stage.

An early representative of these influences was the Italian psychiatrist Silvio Venturi, who belonged to the Positivist school which sought in Italy to fertilize medicine with the new biological and social conceptions ; he published in 1892 his elaborate study, *Le Degenerazioni Psicosessuali*, as exhibited in the individual and in social history, a work wherein various large and fruitful conceptions were thrown out. Venturi regarded sexual development as a slow process, not properly to be termed " sexual " until puberty, yet made up of separate factors which began at the beginning of life their separate development (infantile erections being such a factor and the later erotic sensibility of the lips being similarly developed in early life by non-erotic exercise) before they combine, after puberty, to constitute what may properly be termed sexuality, or, as Venturi insisting on the psychic element termed it, *amore.* Masturbation (onanism, as Venturi always terms it) is regarded as " the germ of what later will be love." It appears in early youth, having its rudimentary roots in infancy, simply as a physical pleasure, without erotic imagery, as the satisfaction of an unknown and indeterminate organic need, certainly of sexual nature, but appearing to consciousness more like the action of scratching a sensory surface that itches, though the psychic condiment of forbidden fruit may be added to its enjoyment. The act is gradually complicated by psychic elements and genuinely erotic stimuli, which slowly approximate it to an act of coitus with a hallucinatory mate, and it thus passes almost insensibly into adult sexual love, so disappearing, or else is retarded in ways which vary with the individual. Its elements, however, such as those that are fetishistic, may be retained, by arrest of development, as Venturi states (following Lombroso and in accordance with the views of to-day), to constitute what in adult age, when carried so far as to replace the normal aim of sex, are described as "perversions." As Freud subsequently expressed it: "Perverted sexuality is nothing but infantile sexuality"; that is to say what is normal in the child may become abnormal when it occurs in the adult. Masturbation, thus, Venturi concluded, far from being the vice combated by teachers and moralists, is "the natural passage by which is reached the warm and generous love of youth and later the calm and positive matrimonial love of maturity."

BIBLIOGRAPHY

A. Moll, *The Sexual Life of the Child.*

Sanford Bell, "The Emotion of Love between the Sexes," *American Journal of Psychology*, July, 1902.

Oskar Pfister, *Love in Children.*

Katharine B. Davis, *Factors in the Sex Life of Twenty-two Hundred Women.*

G. V. Hamilton, *A Research in Marriage.*

Malinowski, *Sexual Life of Savages.*

Margaret Mead, *Growing Up in New Guinea; Coming of Age in Samoa.*

Freud, *Introductory Lectures on Psycho-analysis.*

Ernest Jones, *Papers on Psycho-analysis.*

Auto-erotism

In considering even the earliest phenomena of childhood we have already reached the manifestations covered by the term auto-erotism. I devised this term, "auto-erotism" in 1898 for those spontaneous solitary sexual phenomena of which genital excitement during sleep may be said to be the type. The term is now generally used, though not always in the exact sense in which I defined it, but sometimes only to connote sexual activity directed towards the self. That is unduly to narrow the term down, and it is not in accordance with the usual sense of the auto-group of terms; thus *automatic* action does not mean action *towards*, but *by*, the self, without direct external impulse. If we narrow the term *auto-erotic* we have no term left to indicate the whole group.

By "auto-erotism," therefore, I mean the phenomena of spontaneous sexual emotion generated in the absence of an external stimulus proceeding directly or indirectly from another person. In a wide sense, which cannot be wholly ignored here, auto-erotism may be said to include those transformations of repressed sexual activity which are a factor of some morbid conditions (as probably in hysteria) as well as of the normal manifestations of art and poetry, which more or less colour the whole of life.

Auto-erotism in the largest sense, says Dickinson, includes any self-love in any self-expression, not merely the victims of sexual deviation, but the scientist, the explorer, the sportsman, the mountain-climber.

Such a definition excludes the normal sexual excitement aroused by the presence of a beloved person of the opposite sex ; it also excludes the deviated sexuality associated with an attraction to a person of the same sex ; it further excludes the manifold forms of erotic fetishism, in which the normal focus of sexual attraction is displaced, and voluptuous emotions are aroused by some object which to the ordinary lover is only of subordinate importance. The auto-erotic field remains extensive ; it more especially includes (1) *erotic day-dreaming ;* (2) *erotic dreams in sleep ;* (3) *narcissism,*[1] in which erotic emotion is generated by self-contemplation ; and (4) *masturbation*, including not only self-excitement by the hand but by a great variety of methods exerting a direct influence on the sexual organs and other erogenous centres, even methods which are initiated centrally.

BIBLIOGRAPHY

HAVELOCK ELLIS, *Studies in the Psychology of Sex*, Vol. I, " Auto-erotism."

Erotic Day-dreaming

This (which is also termed phantasy) is a very common and important form of auto-erotism, besides being some-

[1] Some of Freud's followers (though not Freud himself) would confine the use of the term " auto-erotism " to this particular form. I regard this as illegitimate. In all forms of auto-erotism the subject finds satisfaction in his own self-excitement, without the presence of another person being necessary, but his sexual impulse is by no means necessarily directed *towards himself*.

times the early stage of masturbation. The day-dream was long since studied in its chief form, in the "continued story," by Mabel Learoyd, of Wellesley College. The continued story is an imagined narrative, more or less peculiar to the individual, by whom it is cherished with fondness, and regarded as an especially sacred mental possession, to be shared only, if at all, with very sympathizing friends. It is commoner among girls and young women than among boys and young men: among 352 persons of both sexes, 47 per cent. among the women and only 14 per cent. among the men, had any continued story. The starting-point is an incident from a book, or, more usually, some actual experience, which the subject develops; the subject is nearly always the hero or the heroine of the story. The growth of the story is favoured by solitude, and lying in bed before going to sleep is the time specially sacred for its cultivation. G. E. Partridge well described the physical accompaniments of day-dreaming, especially in Normal School girls between sixteen and twenty-two. Pick recorded more or less morbid cases of day-dreaming, usually with an erotic basis, in apparently hysterical men. Among nearly 1,500 young people (more than two-thirds girls and women) studied by Theodate Smith, continued stories were found to be rare—only 1 per cent. Healthy boys, before fifteen, had day-dreams in which sports, athletics, and adventure had a large part; girls put themselves in the place of their favourite heroines in novels. After seventeen, and earlier in the case of girls, day-dreams of love and marriage were found to be frequent. Though by no means easy to detect, these elaborate and more or less erotic day-dreams are everywhere not uncommon in young men and especially in young women. Each individual has his own particular dream, which is always varying and developing, but, except in very imaginative persons, to no great extent. Such a day-dream is often founded on a basis of pleasurable personal experience, and develops on that basis. It may involve an element of perversity, even though that element finds no expression in real life. It is, of course, fostered by sexual abstinence. Most usually there is little attempt to realize it. It does not necessarily lead to masturbation, though it sometimes causes some sexual congestion or even spontaneous sexual orgasm.

The day-dream is a strictly private and intimate experience, not only from its very nature, but also because it occurs in images which the subject finds great difficulty in translating into language, even when willing to do so. In other cases it is elaborately dramatic or romantic in character, the hero or heroine passing through many experiences before attaining the erotic climax of the story. This climax tends to develop in harmony with the subject's growing knowledge or experience ; at first merely a kiss, it may develop into any refinement of voluptuous gratification. The day-dream may occur alike in normal and abnormal persons. Rousseau, in his *Confessions*, describes such dreams, in his case combined with masochism and masturbation. Raffalovich refers to the process by which in sexual inverts the vision of a person of the same sex, perhaps seen in the street or the theatre, is evoked in solitary reveries, producing a kind of " psychic onanism," whether or not it leads on to physical manifestations.

Although day-dreaming of this kind has until recent times been little studied, since it loves secrecy and solitude, and has seldom been counted of sufficient interest for scientific inquisition, it is really a process of considerable importance, and occupies a large part of the auto-erotic field. It is frequently cultivated by refined and imaginative young men and women who lead a chaste life and would often be repelled by masturbation. In such persons, under such circumstances, it must be considered as strictly normal, the inevitable outcome of the play of the sexual impulse. No doubt it may often become morbid, and is never a healthy process when indulged in to excess, as it is liable to be by refined young people with artistic impulses, to whom it is in the highest degree seductive and insidious. Though the day-dream is far from always coloured by sexual emotion, yet it is a significant indication of its really sexual origin that, as I have been informed by persons of both sexes, even in these apparently non-sexual cases it frequently ceases on marriage.

The importance of sex day-dreams is well brought out by Hamilton's careful inquiries. He found that 27 per cent. men and 25 per cent. women were able to say positively that they had sexual day-dreams before knowing anything about sex matters; many others were uncertain, while 28 per cent. men and 25 per cent. women had sex day-dreams before puberty. Only 1 per cent. men and 2 per cent. women had no sex day-dreams after puberty, and 57 per cent. men and 51 per cent. women said that after eighteen and before marriage sex day-dreams occupied the mind a good deal; 26 per cent. men and 19 per cent. women (all married) still find sex day-dreams sufficiently absorbing to interfere with work.

Day-dreaming often plays an important part in the lives and activities of persons constitutionally predisposed to become artists, and especially, as is easy to understand, novelists, so that while in ordinary persons too absorbed a concentration in phantasy carried on into adult-life is undoubtedly unwholesome, because it leads away from real life, in these persons it finds as it were a way back to reality in the creation of art forms. Freud has suggested that the artist may be constitutionally endowed with a specially strong capacity for sublimation, and aptitude for repression, so that he can bring his phantasy into so strong a stream of pleasure that, for a time at least, repressions are outbalanced and dispelled.

BIBLIOGRAPHY

G. E. Partridge, " Reverie," *Pedagogical Seminary*, April, 1898.

Theodate Smith, " The Psychology of Day Dreams," *American Journal of Psychology*, October, 1904.

Havelock Ellis, *The World of Dreams*; *Studies in the Psychology of Sex*, Vol. VII, " The History of Florrie."

S. Freud, *Introductory Lectures on Psycho-Analysis.*

W. McDougall, *Outline of Abnormal Psychology.*

J. Varendonck, *The Psychology of Day Dreams.*

Erotic Dreams in Sleep

The psychological significance of dreams has always been recognized, however variously it has been understood and interpreted. In the early traditions of mankind we find dreams treated seriously, as having a magical, religious, or prophetic bearing; they retain this in civilized folklore, while among many savage races of to-day dreaming is regarded as highly significant. With the rise of modern scientific psychology dreaming speedily came under consideration for more or less serious study and from various viewpoints.[1] In recent times this study has become more elaborate, and in psycho-analysis, as we know, the phenomena of dreaming are regarded as carrying great weight.

While the general prevalence of dreaming is accepted, there has not always, however, been complete agreement that it is a normal and constant and therefore completely healthy and natural phenomenon, Freud even regarding it as at once both neurotic and healthy. It seems most reasonable to regard it as entirely natural. Animals dream, and we may sometimes note that a sleeping dog imitates the movements of running; savage races dream, and while there are a great number of people who are not conscious of dreaming, they often find traces of dreams when they begin to give attention to the matter; we may well believe that their mental activity during sleep is usually at so low an ebb that it leaves no memory on awakening.

There has been the same difference of opinion regarding erotic dreams, accompanied or not by orgasm, as regarding dreams generally. That under conditions of sexual abstinence in healthy individuals there tend to be some auto-erotic manifestations during waking-life, both theory and a careful study of the facts lead us to believe. There can be no doubt, however, that, under the same conditions, the occurrence of the complete orgasm during sleep with, in men, seminal emissions, is altogether normal. In many parts of the world, indeed, such manifestations are attributed to the excitation of demons. The Catholic Church has attributed serious importance to the impurity of what it

[1] Freud, who does not however claim a scholarly knowledge of the literature, has under-rated the amount of psychological attention given to dreaming, and even speaks as though it had been a common belief that "dreaming is not a mental but a somatic phenomenon," a statement which is meaningless.

termed *pollutio*, while Luther also seems to have regarded erotic dreams as a kind of disease demanding at once the medicine of marriage. Even some distinguished medical authorities (notably Moll and Eulenburg) have put nocturnal seminal emissions on the same level as the nocturnal emission of urine or as vomiting, and it cannot be denied that under primitively natural conditions there is justification for this view.

Since, however, some degree of sexual abstinence is more or less inevitable under our social conditions, most authorities are inclined to regard the nocturnal phenomena which result from that abstinence as fairly normal ; they are only concerned as to its frequency.

Paget declared that he had never known celibate men who had not such emissions from once or twice a week to every three months, both extremes being within the limits of good health, while Brunton regarded once a fortnight or once a month as about the usual frequency, at these periods the emissions often following two nights in succession, and Rohleder stated that they may normally occur for several nights in succession. Hammond considered also that they occur about once a fortnight. This was also found the most usual frequency among over 2,000 Moscow students investigated by Tchlenoff. Ribbing regarded ten to fourteen days as the normal interval, and Hamilton found from a week to a fortnight the most frequent interval (19 per cent. cases). Löwenfeld put the normal frequency at about once a week ; this seems near the truth as regards many fairly healthy young men and it corresponds with the exact records of several healthy young adults which I have obtained. It occasionally happens, however, that nocturnal emissions are entirely absent (Tchlenoff's investigations seem to show their absence in about 10 per cent., but Hamilton in only 2 per cent.). In other fairly healthy young men they seldom occur except at times of intellectual activity or of anxiety and worry.

Nocturnal emissions are usually, though not invariably, accompanied by dreams of a voluptuous character in which the dreamer becomes conscious in a more or less fantastic manner of the more or less intimate presence or contact of a person of usually the opposite sex. It would seem, as a general rule, that the more vivid and voluptuous the dream, the greater is the physical excitement and the greater also the relief experienced on awakening. Sometimes the erotic dream occurs without any emission, and not infrequently the emission takes place after the dreamer has awakened. Occasionally the approaching orgasm is repressed in the half waking state; this is termed by Näcke *pollutio interrupta.*

A wide and comprehensive investigation of erotic dreams was carried out by Gualino, in Northern Italy, based on inquiries among 100 normal men—doctors, teachers, lawyers, etc.—who had all had experience of the phenomena. Gualino shows that erotic dreams, with emissions (whether or not seminal), begin somewhat earlier than the period of physical development as ascertained by Marro for youths of the same part of Northern Italy. Gualino found that all his cases had had erotic dreams at the age of seventeen; Marro found 8 per cent. of youths still sexually undeveloped at that age, and while sexual development began at thirteen years, erotic dreams began at twelve. Their appearance was preceded, in most cases for some months, by erections. In 37 per cent. of the cases there had been no actual sexual experiences (either masturbation or intercourse); in 23 per cent. there had been masturbation; in the rest, some form of sexual contact. The dreams are mainly visual, tactual elements coming second, and the *dramatis persona* is usually either an unknown woman (27 per cent. cases), or one only known by sight (56 per cent.), and in the majority is, at all events in the beginning, an ugly or fantastic figure, becoming more attractive later in life, but never identical with the woman loved during waking life. This, as Gualino, Löwenfeld, and others have pointed out, accords with the general tendency for the emotions of the day to be latent in sleep. The emotional state in the pubertal stage, apart from pleasure, was anxiety (37 per cent.), desire (17 per cent.), fear (14 per cent.). In the adult stage, anxiety and fear receded to 7 per cent. and 6 per cent. respectively. Thirty-three of the subjects, as a result of sexual or general disturbances, had had nocturnal emissions without dreams; these were always found exhausting. In more than 90 per cent. erotic dreams were the most vivid of all dreams. In 34 per cent. of cases they tended to occur very soon after sexual intercourse. In numerous cases they were peculiarly frequent (even three in one night) during courtship, when the young man was in the habit of kissing and caressing his betrothed, but they ceased after marriage. It was not noted that position in bed or a full bladder exerted any marked influence in the occurrence of erotic dreams; repletion of the seminal vesicles is regarded as the main factor.

It has been noted by many (Löwenfeld, etc.) that people seldom dream erotically of the persons whom they are in love with, even after falling asleep thinking of the beloved. This has been attributed, no doubt rightly, to the exhaustion and repose of the acute emotion during sleep; it is well known, also, that we seldom dream of the griefs of the day though very often of its trivial details. It has also been noted by many (Stanley Hall, etc.) that in erotic dreams, not only individuals who are quite indifferent to the dreamer when awake, but very trifling personal details, or imagined contacts, will suffice to produce orgasm.

The diagnostic value of sexual dreams, as an indication of the sexual nature of the subject when awake, has been emphasized by various writers (Moll, Näcke, etc.). Sexual dreams tend to reproduce, and even to accentuate, those characteristics which make the strongest sexual appeal to the subject when awake. At the same time, this general statement has to be qualified, more especially as regards inverted dreams. In the first place, a young man, however normal, who is not familiar with the feminine body when awake, is not likely to see it when asleep, even in dreams of women; in the second place, the confusions and combinations of dream imagery often tend to obliterate sexual distinctions, however free from perversion the subject may be. It thus sometimes happens that people who are perfectly normal may have abnormal dreams, and in a few cases the erotic dreams of normal persons are habitually abnormal without the existence of any ground for believing that this is due to a real or even latent deviation. It is sometimes important to bear this in mind.

There seem to be, generally speaking, certain differences in the manifestations of auto-erotism during sleep in men and women which are probably not without psychological significance. In men the phenomenon is fairly simple; it usually appears about puberty, continues at intervals of varying duration during sexual life provided the individual is living chastely; and is generally, though not always, accompanied by erotic dreams which lead up to the climax, its occurrence being, to some extent, influenced by a variety of circumstances: physical, mental, or emotional excitement, alcohol taken before retiring, position in bed (as lying on the back), the state of the bladder, sometimes the mere fact of being in a strange bed, and to some extent apparently by the existence of monthly and yearly rhythms. On the whole, it is a fairly definite and regular phenomenon which usually leaves little conscious trace on awakening, beyond in some cases a sense of fatigue and, occasionally, a headache. In women, however, the phenomena of auto-erotism during sleep seem to be much more irregular, varied, and diffused. It seems to be the exception for girls to experience definitely erotic dreams about the period of puberty or adolescence. While it is the rule in a chaste youth for the orgasm thus to manifest itself (Hamilton found it to begin in 51 per cent. between twelve and fifteen), it is the exception in a chaste girl. As pointed out when dealing with early manifestations of sex, it is not until the orgasm has been definitely produced in the waking state—under whatever conditions it may have been produced—that in women it begins to occur during sleep, and even in a strongly sexual woman living a repressed life it is often infrequent or absent (in 60 per cent. according to Hamilton). In women who have become accustomed to sexual intercourse, erotic dreams of fully developed character occur, with complete orgasm and accompanying relief, as may also occasionally be the case in women who are not acquainted with actual intercourse; some women, however, even when familiar with actual coitus, find that sexual dreams, though accompanied by emissions, are only the symptom of desire and do not produce relief.

One of the most interesting and important characters by which the erotic dreams of women—and, indeed, their dreams generally—differ from those of men is in the tendency to evoke a repercussion on the waking life, a tendency more rarely noted in men's erotic dreams, and then only to a minor extent. This is common, even in healthy and normal women, and is exaggerated in neurotic subjects, by whom the dream may even be interpreted as a reality, and so declared on oath, a fact of practical importance, since it may lead to unfounded accusations of assault under anæsthesia.

The tendency of the auto-erotic phenomena of sleep to be manifested with such energy as to flow over into the waking life, and influence conscious emotion and action, is especially seen in hysterical women, in whom it has, therefore, chiefly been studied. Sante de Sanctis, Gilles de la Tourette, etc., have emphasized the influence of dreams on the waking life of the hysterical, and the special influence of erotic dreams, to which, doubtless, we must refer those conceptions of *incubi* and *succubi* which played so important a part in the demonology of the Middle Ages. Such erotic dreams of the hysterical are by no means always, or even usually, of a pleasurable character. In some cases the illusion of sexual intercourse even provokes acute pain. This was affirmed by the witches of old and is also found to-day. Sometimes this is largely the result of a conflict in consciousness with a merely physical impulse which is strong enough to assert itself in spite of the emotional and intellectual abhorrence of the subject. It is thus but an extreme form of the disgust which all sexual physical manifestations tend to inspire in a person who is not inclined to respond to them. Somewhat similar psychic disgust and physical pain are produced in the attempts to stimulate the sexual emotions and organs when these are exhausted by exercise. It is quite probable, however, that there is a physiological, as well as a psychic, factor in this phenomenon, and Sollier, in his elaborate study of the nature and genesis of hysteria, by insisting on the capital importance of the disturbance of sensibility in hysteria, and the definite character of the phenomena produced in the passage between anæsthesia and normal sensation, sought to reveal the mechanism of this feature of auto-erotic excitement in the hysterical.

No doubt there has been a tendency to exaggerate the unpleasant character of the auto-erotic phenomena of hysteria. That tendency was an inevitable reaction against an earlier view, according to which hysteria was little more than an unconscious expression of the sexual emotions, and as such was unscientifically dismissed without any careful investigation. We may agree with Freud that the sexual needs of the hysterical are just as individual and various as those of normal women, but that they suffer from them more, largely through a moral struggle with their own instincts, and the attempt to put them into the background of consciousness. In many hysterical and psychically abnormal women, auto-erotic phenomena, and sexual phenomena generally, may be highly pleasurable, though such persons are often quite innocent of any knowledge of the erotic character of the experience.

BIBLIOGRAPHY

Havelock Ellis, "Auto-erotism" and "The Phenomena of Sexual Periodicity" in *Studies in the Psychology of Sex*, Vol. I, and "The Synthesis of Dreams" in Vol. VII; also *The World of Dreams*.

Stanley Hall, *Adolescence*.

S. Freud, *The Interpretation of Dreams*.

Masturbation

Masturbation, which has already been discussed in dealing with the sexual phenomena of childhood, means, in the strict sense, the use of the hand to procure sexual excitement on the subject himself. In a wider sense, it is applied to all forms of self-excitation adopted for this end, and it is even possible to speak illogically of "psychic masturbation" in which the excitation is brought about by thought unaided by any physical act. The term "onanism" is sometimes applied in the same sense, but without justification, since the device of Onan was not in any sense an act of masturbation, but simply *coitus interruptus*. Hirschfeld has devised the term "ipsation," distinguishing it from "auto-erotism," as being gratification on the individual's own body as a physical object, and not as a psychic object.

Masturbation, in the wider sense, is a widespread phenomenon among animals and man in all parts of the world. It is so widespread that we cannot, strictly, speak of it as "abnormal." It is a phenomenon which lies on the borderland between the normal and the abnormal, and is liable to occur whenever any restraint is placed on the natural exercise of the sexual function.

Among animals in the domesticated and isolated state—and sometimes also in the wild state, though this is less easy to observe—various forms of spontaneous solitary excitement occur, both in males and females, sometimes by flapping the penis against the abdominal walls, and frequently (especially in females) by rubbing the sexual parts against external objects.

In the human species, similar phenomena are by no means found in civilization alone. They have doubtless been highly developed under the conditions of civilization, but it is by no means true that (as Mantegazza thought) masturbation is one of the moral characteristics of Europeans. It is found among peoples of nearly every race of which we have intimate knowledge, however natural the conditions they live under, and among some it is practised with frequency, and is by both sexes generally recognized as a custom in early life. We may even find among peoples of a somewhat low state of culture the use by the women of refinements for masturbation, notably the artificial phallus, which is also used in Europe to-day, though not among the general population.

On the other hand, the use, or rather abuse, of the ordinary objects and implements of daily life in obtaining auto-erotic satisfaction, among the ordinary population in civilized modern lands, has reached an extent and variety which can only be feebly estimated by the occasional resulting mischances which reach the surgeon's hands. Thus vegetables and fruits (especially the banana) are frequently used by women, but they are unlikely to lead to any dangerous results and so their use remains undetected. A vast number of objects have, however, been removed from the vagina and urethra by surgical interference; among the commonest may specially be named pencils, sealing wax, cotton reels, hairpins, glass stoppers, candles, corks, and tumblers. Nine-tenths of the foreign bodies found in the female vagina and urethra are due to masturbation. The age at which they are found is chiefly between seventeen and thirty. Hairpins have been found in the female bladder with special frequency, because the urethra is normally a highly erogenous sexual centre and tends to "swallow" what is introduced into it, while the shape of the hairpin (which used to be the implement most easily available to a woman in bed) specially lends itself to disappearance in this way.

Another class of objects used for masturbation does not come under the surgeon's notice: the external objects with which the sexual region may be brought in contact. The garments worn, chairs, tables, and other articles of furniture come under this head. Reference may also be made to the sexual excitement which may occur, accidentally or intentionally, in the gymnasium (as in climbing poles), or when riding, or cycling, or using the treadle sewing-machine, or by the influence of tight-lacing. None of these sources of exercise or compression, it must be added, is necessarily a cause of sexual excitement.

This group of forms of auto-erotic excitement merges into the form of thigh-friction, by which the more or less voluntary pressure or friction of the thighs is brought to bear on the sexual region. This is sometimes practised by men and is fairly common among women. It is even found in female infants. It is a widespread practice, and in some countries (as Sweden) it is stated to be the commonest form of masturbation in women.

Masturbation may also be exercised by applying friction

or other stimulation to outlying erogenous zones, as by flagellation or urtication of the nates, or rubbing the breasts and nipples. Almost every part of the body may indeed, in exceptional cases, become erogenous and be manipulated for the sake of the voluptuous sensations aroused.

There is yet another class of auto-erotic cases in which sexual excitement occurs spontaneously when the thoughts are turned to voluptuous subjects, or even non-voluptuous subjects of an emotional nature, or when sexual excitement is deliberately aroused (Hammond's "psychic coitus") by directing the imagination on the act of sexual intercourse with an attractive person of the opposite sex. These auto-erotic manifestations merge into the erotic day-dreaming which has already been considered. Dr. Davis found that reading books that suggest sexual thought is a most frequent cause of masturbation, spooning to a much smaller extent, and dancing still less.

If we proceed to investigate precisely the exact extent, degree, and significance of the auto-erotic phenomena of which masturbation is the type, we are met by many difficulties and considerable differences of opinion.

With regard to their occurrence among males, the balance of reliable opinion is in favour of masturbation having been practised at some time in life—though in many cases very rarely or for a very brief period—by over 90 per cent. individuals. Thus, in England, Dukes, the physician to Rugby School, stated that from 90 to 95 per cent. of all boys at boarding school masturbate. In Germany, Julian Marcuse, on the basis of his experience, concludes that 92 per cent. male individuals have masturbated in youth, and Rohleder puts the proportion somewhat higher. In America, Seerly found that among 125 academic students only about 6 per cent. assured him that they had never masturbated, and Brockman, even among theological students, found that 56 per cent. stated, without being asked, that they practised masturbation. Tchlenoff, among Moscow students, found that 60 per cent. acknowledged spontaneously that they had masturbated. Such spontaneously offered information necessarily indicates a really much greater frequency, since many individuals are far too ashamed of the practice to acknowledge it.

As to whether masturbation is more common in one sex than the other opinion formerly varied, and the chief authorities were about equally divided, though among the general public it was usually considered more common in boys than in girls. The question may now, however, be considered in the light of definite data, to which reference has already been made in discussing the first appearance of the sexual impulse. The sexual distribution of masturbation has been somewhat obscured by the tendency to concentrate attention on a particular set of auto-erotic phenomena. We must group and divide our facts rationally if we wish to command them. If we confine our attention to very young children, the evidence shows that the practice is more common in females, and such a result is in harmony with the fact that precocious puberty is most often found in female children, which is, in many cases, associated with precocity in sexual habits. In puberty and adolescence occasional or frequent masturbation is common in both boys and girls, though, I believe, less common than is sometimes supposed. It is difficult to say whether it is more prevalent among boys or girls; one is inclined to conclude that it prevails more widely among boys. It is true that boys' traditions and their more active life keep the tendency in abeyance, while in girls there is much less frequently any restraining influence of corresponding character; but, on the other hand, the sexual impulse, and consequently the tendency to masturbation, tend to be aroused later, and less easily, in girls than in boys. After adolescence there can be little doubt that masturbation is more common in women than in men. Men have, by this time, mostly adopted some method of sexual gratification with the opposite sex; women are to a larger extent shut out from such gratification; moreover, while in rare cases women are sexually precocious, it more often happens that their sexual impulses only gain strength and self-consciousness after adolescence has passed. In many cases masturbation is occasionally (especially about the period of menstruation) practised by active, intelligent, and healthy women, who otherwise lead a continent life. This is specially the case as regards young and healthy women who, after having normal sexual relationships, have been compelled for some reason or other to break them off and lead a lonely life. But we have to remember that there are some women, evidently with a considerable degree of congenital sexual hypo-æsthesia (no doubt, in some respect or another, below the standard of normal health), in whom the sexual instinct has never been aroused, and who not only do not masturbate, but do not show any desire for normal gratification ; while in a large proportion of other cases the impulse is gratified passively in other ways. The auto-erotic phenomena which take place spontaneously, by yielding to reverie, with little or no active interference, certainly occur much more frequently in women than in men.

Until recent years there has been a wide difference of opinion as to the results of masturbation. While a few authorities considered that it had no special evil results beyond such as might equally follow from excessive coitus, the great majority attributed to masturbation, even when not excessive, an enormous variety of serious morbid conditions from insanity downwards. A more temperate view now prevails. It is generally believed that masturbation may, in special cases, lead on to various undesirable results, but it is no longer held that, even when practised to excess, it can, in healthy and sane individuals (supposing that such are likely to practise it to excess), produce the highly morbid states once supposed to be a common consequence.

It appears to have been largely due to Griesinger, in the middle of the last century, that we owe the first authoritative appearance of a saner, more discriminating view regarding the results of masturbation. Although still to some extent fettered by the traditions prevalent in his day, Griesinger saw that it was not so much masturbation itself as the feelings aroused in sensitive minds by the social attitude towards masturbation which produced evil effects, and a hidden strife between shame, repentance, good intentions, and the irritation which impels to the act. He added that there are no specific signs of masturbation, and concluded that it is oftener a symptom than a cause. The general progress of educated opinions since that date has confirmed and carried forward the results cautiously stated by Griesinger. This distinguished alienist thought that, when practised in childhood, masturbation might lead to insanity. Berkhan, in his investigation of the psychoses of childhood, found that in no single case was masturbation a cause. Vogel, Uffelmann, Emminghaus, and Moll, in the course of similar studies, all came to almost similar conclusions. It is only on a congenitally morbid nervous system, Emminghaus insisted, that masturbation can produce any serious results. Kiernan stated that the supposed results of masturbation are due to either hebephrenia or hysteria in which an effect is taken for the cause. Christian, during twenty years' experience in hospitals, asylums, and private practice in town and country, found no seriously evil effects from masturbation. He thought, indeed, that it may be a more serious evil in women than in men. But Yellowlees considers that in women " it is possibly less exhausting and injurious than in the other sex," which was also the opinion of Hammond, as well as of Guttceit, though he found that women pushed the practice much further than men, and Näcke, who gave special attention to this point, could not find that masturbation is a definite cause of insanity in women in a single case. Koch also reached a similar conclusion as regards both sexes, though he admitted that masturbation may cause some degree of psychopathic deterioration. Even in this respect, however, he pointed out that when practised in moderation it is not injurious in the certain and exceptionless way in which it is believed to be in many circles, while it is the people whose nervous systems are already injured who masturbate most easily and practise it more immoderately than others ; the chief source of the evil is self-reproach and the struggle with the impulse. Maudsley, Marro, Spitzka, and Schüle still recognized a specific " masturbatory insanity," but Krafft-Ebing long since rejected it, and Näcke decidedly opposed it. Kraepelin stated that excessive masturbation can only occur in a dangerous degree in predisposed subjects; so, also, Forel and Löwenfeld, as at an earlier period Trousseau. Recent authorities may, indeed, be said to be almost unanimous in rejecting masturbation as a cause of insanity.

The testimony of expert witnesses with regard to the influence of masturbation in producing other forms of psychoses and neuroses is becoming equally decisive. Since West, many years ago, it is generally accepted that among children idiocy, convulsions, epilepsy, hysteria, etc., are not due to masturbation, as an efficient cause, though it has been believed by a few that hysteria and epilepsy might be thus induced. Leyden, among the causes of diseases of the spinal cord, included no form of sexual excess. "In moderation," Erb remarked, "masturbation is not more dangerous to the spinal cord than natural coitus, and has no bad effects; it makes no difference whether the orgasm is effected normally or in solitude." This is also the opinion of Toulouse, of Fürbringer, of Curschmann, and most other authorities.

It is, however, perhaps going too far to assert that masturbation has no more injurious effect than coitus. If the sexual orgasm were a purely physiological phenomenon this position would be sound. But the sexual orgasm is normally bound up with a mass of powerful emotions aroused by a person of the opposite sex. It is in the joy caused by the play of these emotions, as well as in the discharge of the sexual orgasm, that the satisfaction of coitus resides. In the absence of the desired partner the orgasm, whatever relief it may give, must be followed by a sense of dissatisfaction, perhaps of depression, even of exhaustion, often of shame and remorse. Practically, also, there is more probability of excess in masturbation than in coitus, though whether, as some have asserted, masturbation involves a greater nervous effort than coitus is more doubtful. It thus seems somewhat misleading to assert that masturbation has no more injurious effect than coitus. But in a moderate form it is, as Forel held, much on the same level as sexual excitement in sleep.

Reviewing the general question of the supposed grave

symptoms and signs of masturbation, and its pernicious results, we may reach the conclusion that in the case of moderate masturbation in healthy, well-born individuals no seriously pernicious results necessarily follow. With regard to the general signs of masturbation, of which a vast number have been alleged, we may agree that there are none which can be regarded as reliable.

We may conclude finally that the opposing views on the subject may be simply explained by the fact that the writers on both sides have ignored or insufficiently recognized the influence of heredity and temperament. They have done precisely what many unscientific writers on inebriety have continued to do unto the present day, when describing the terrible results of alcohol without pointing out that the chief factor in such cases has not been the alcohol, but the organization on which the alcohol acted.

While we may thus dismiss the extravagant views, widely held during the past century, concerning the awful results of masturbation as due to ignorance and false tradition, aided by the efforts of quacks, it must be pointed out that, even in healthy or moderately healthy individuals, any excess in solitary self-excitement may still produce results which, though slight, are yet harmful. The skin, digestion, and circulation may all be disordered; headache and neuralgia may occur; and, as in normal sexual excess or in undue frequency of sexual excitement during sleep, there is a certain general lowering of nervous tone. Probably the most important of the comparatively frequent associated conditions—this also arising usually on a morbid soil—is what used to be termed "neurasthenia" with its manifold symptoms.

In some cases it would seem that masturbation, when practised in excess, especially if begun before the age of puberty, may lead to inaptitude for coitus, as well as to indifference to it, and sometimes to undue sexual irritability, involving premature emission and practical impotence. Dickinson states that the most consistently "frigid" women are the auto-erotic. This is, however, the exception, especially if the practice has not been begun until after puberty. In such cases some peripheral irritation or abnormal mental stimulus trains the physical orgasm to respond to an appeal which has nothing whatever to do with the fascination normally exerted by the opposite sex. At puberty, however, the claim of passion and the real charm of sex begin to be felt, but, owing to the physical sexual feelings having been trained into an abnormal channel, these new and more normal sex associations remain of a purely ideal and emotional character, without the strong sensual impulses with which under healthy conditions they tend to be more and more associated as puberty passes on into adolescence or mature adult life. In this way, in some women, often highly intellectual women, a precocious excess in masturbation has been a main cause, not necessarily the sole efficient cause, in producing a divorce in later life between the physical sensuous impulses and the ideal emotions. If early masturbation is ever a factor in developing sexual inversion, it may operate in this manner, the repulsion for normal coitus helping to furnish a soil on which the inverted impulse may develop unimpeded. It is important to realize that the possible evil results are exceptional. Dr. Katharine Davis, in her extensive investigation, which is the most elaborate and valuable study of masturbation in women we possess, found, when comparing the group of happily married women with the group of the unhappily married, that the number in each group of those who before marriage had engaged in masturbation or other similar sex play (not including sexual intercourse) was almost identical.

On the psychic side the most frequent and the most characteristic result of persistent and excessive masturbation seems to be a morbid heightening of self-consciousness without any co-ordinated heightening of self-esteem. The man or woman who is kissed by a desirable and desired person of the opposite sex feels a satisfying sense of pride and elation, which is absent from the manifestations of auto-erotic activity. This must be so, even apart from the masturbator's consciousness of the general social attitude toward his practices and his dread of detection, for that may also exist as regards normal coitus without any corresponding psychic effect. The masturbator, if his practice is habitual, is thus compelled to cultivate an artificial consciousness of self-esteem, and may show a tendency to mental arrogance. Self-righteousness and religiosity constitute, as it were, a protection against the tendency to remorse. A morbid mental soil is, of course, required for the full development of these characteristics. The habitual male masturbator, it must be remembered, is often a shy and solitary person; individuals of this temperament are especially predisposed to excesses in all the manifestations of auto-erotism, while the yielding to such tendencies increases the reserve and the horror of society, at the same time producing a certain suspicion of others. In some extreme cases there may, as Kraepelin believed, be some decrease of psychic capacity, an inability to grasp and co-ordinate external impressions, weakness of memory, deadening of emotions, or else the general phenomena of increased nervous irritability.

In either sex auto-erotic excesses during adolescence in young men and women of intelligence—whatever absence of gross injury there may be—still often encourage a certain degree of psychic abnormality, and tend to foster false and high-strung ideals of life. Kraepelin referred to the frequency of exalted enthusiasms in masturbation, and Anstie long ago remarked on the connection between masturbation and premature false work in literature and art. It may be added that excess in masturbation has sometimes occurred in men and women whose work in literature and art cannot be described as premature and false.

It must always be remembered, however, that, while the practice of masturbation may be harmful in its consequences, it is also, in the absence of normal sexual relationships, frequently not without good results. In the medical literature of the last hundred years a number of cases have been incidentally recorded in which the patients found masturbation beneficial, and such cases might certainly have been enormously increased if there had been any open-eyed desire to discover them. We must recognize that masturbation is, in the main, practised for its sedative effect on the nervous system. In normal persons, well past the age of puberty, and otherwise leading a chaste life, masturbation would be little practised except for the physical and mental relief it brings.

These considerations led the late Dr. Robie, on the strength of considerable clinical experience in the United States, to go beyond the simple recognition of the substantial harmlessness of active auto-erotic practices, and in his *Rational Sex Ethics* (1916) and later books actually to recommend them, especially to women, as of therapeutic value in nervous conditions and salutary to health, much on the same level as normal sexual intercourse. This doctrine needs much qualification. In its extreme form it is far too simple-minded a solution of the difficulties involved. Such a recommendation may be just as undesirable as the old-fashioned recommendations of prostitution or of continence. The self-gratification of shut-in solitude may not be an improvement on the eager and active desires of the unsatisfied. The physician's attitude should be one of sympathetic comprehension, but only the individual himself can decide what course of action best suits his temperament and circumstances.

More reasonable, therefore, than the attitude of Robie is that of Wolbarst who, while holding that masturbation should not be actually encouraged, considers that a point may be reached when the impulse should not be restrained, and quotes a Chinese proverb, that " It is better to satisfy the body than to discolour the mind." We should avoid any harsh condemnation of the practice when it is admitted, especially when there is self-condemnation. At the same time, he properly adds, it is not possible to commend those " moralists " who approve of masturbation as a method of preserving an imaginary " virtue." There is more real virtue in cherishing the natural impulse to sexual love and in adventurously facing the natural desires born of that impulse.

We have to recognize that we are concerned with a

manifestation which belongs to a vast group of auto-erotic phenomena, and that, in some form or another, such manifestations are inevitable. It is our wisest course to recognize this inevitableness of sexual and transmuted sexual manifestations under the perpetual restraints of civilized life, and, while avoiding any attitude of excessive indulgence or indifference, to avoid also any attitude of horror, for our horror not only leads to the facts being effectually veiled from our sight, but itself serves to manufacture artificially evils that may be greater.

BIBLIOGRAPHY

HAVELOCK ELLIS, " Auto-erotism " in *Studies in the Psychology of Sex*, Vol. I.
A. MOLL, *The Sexual Life of the Child.*
STANLEY HALL, *Adolescence.*
FREUD, *Three Contributions to Sexual Theory.*
KATHARINE DAVIS, *Factors in the Sex Life of Twenty-two Hundred Women.*
G. V. HAMILTON, *A Research in Marriage.*
NORTHCOTE, *Christianity and Sex Problems.*
WOLBARST, *Children of Adam.*

Narcissism

This condition may best be regarded as a form of auto-erotism, as indeed its extreme and most highly developed form. It is a conception which has assumed rather different shapes at the hands of different psychologists of sex, so that a brief sketch of its history may be desirable. Forty years ago it had no definite existence for science, though long clearly traceable in fiction and poetry, while its central situation was symbolized in classic Greek days by the figure of Narcissus. Here and there, indeed, psychiatrists noted such a condition as a symptom in individual cases, but in 1898, when first putting forward a sketch (in the *Alienist and Neurologist*) of auto-erotism, I concluded by describing, with a case, as its extreme form, the Narcissus-like tendency sometimes found, more especially perhaps in women, for the sexual emotions to be absorbed, and often entirely lost, in self-admiration. This paper was at once summarized in

Germany by Dr. Näcke, who translated my " Narcissus-like tendency " as " Narcismus," expressing his agreement, and calling this " the most classical form " of what I termed auto-erotism, though, he added (which I had not done), that there would be actual sexual orgasm accompanying the Narcissism ; this cannot be accepted Rohleder observed in men some pronounced cases of this condition which he called " automonosexualism," which is also the term used by Hirschfeld. Then in 1910 Freud adopted from Näcke the name and conception of Narcissism, regarding it, however, simply as a stage in the development of masculine sexual inversion, the subject being supposed to identify himself with a woman (usually his mother) and so to acquire self-love. In 1911 Otto Rank, taking up the matter from my treatment of it, developed it on generally Freudian lines, tending also to show, not merely that it was, as I had included it, within the normal range of variation, but a fairly ordinary stage of sexual development. Rank's study evidently impressed Freud, who in 1914 accepted and emphasized Rank's view, stating positively that there is a primary Narcissism in every individual, the libidinal complement to the egoism of the instinct of self-preservation, and that it may sometimes dominate object-choice, various alternatives then arising, according as a person loves (*a*) what he is himself ; (*b*) what he once was ; (*c*) what he wanted to be ; or (*d*) someone who was once part of himself. It is at this point that the conception of Narcissism remains most suitable for ordinary use.

Freud himself has at some points modified his view and at others further extended it, while numerous analysts, both of the Freudian and other schools, have carried it to an extreme point, considering religions and philosophies as expressions of Narcissism. Finally it has been suggested (by Ferenczi) that Nature herself in the process of evolution is guided by Narcissistic motives. Evidence for Narcissism has also been found (as by Róheim) among savages and in folk-lore ; the work of Sir James Frazer, as Rank first pointed out, here furnishing much material for psychological use.

BIBLIOGRAPHY

HAVELOCK ELLIS, *Studies in the Psychology of Sex*, Vols. I. and VII.

S. FREUD, *Three Contributions to Sexual Theory*, and *Collected Papers*, Vol. IV.

J. HARNIK, "The Developments of Narcissism in Man and Woman," *Int. Jour. Psycho-analysis*, January, 1924.

Education in Sex

When we survey the manifestations of infancy and childhood, we see that in relation to sex they may sometimes be apparently non-existent, when present are usually vague, and when definite are frequently not to be explained in the way they would be explained if occurring in an adult.

The result has been, as we know, that—putting aside those persons, now growing few in number, who were once horrified at the suggestion of anything sexual in the infantile psyche—even good observers have varied in their attitude and policy with regard to sex in early life. There are those who feel unable to recognize any genuine sexual manifestations, at an early age, in healthy normal children; there are those who recognize it all the time, alike in sound and in neurotic children, though finding that its manifestations vary and change; there are those, it may perhaps be added, who, even admitting the presence of sexual signs, regard them as not normal for the stage of childhood. That, at all events, is the later opinion of Rank in his work on *Modern Education*. "Sexuality is not natural to the child," he observes; "it might rather be conceived of as the individual's natural enemy, against which he defends himself, from the beginning, with his whole personality." Such a view at all events harmonizes with a common attitude in culture, even in primitive culture, whether or not we are entitled to push it back to childhood.

The proper attitude towards sexuality in the child is, therefore, one of watchful hygiene, which must always be unobtrusive. The childish erotic impulses are often unconscious, and nothing is gained by rendering them conscious or by concentrating attention on them. It is necessary to guard against the child doing any manifest injury to himself or others. It also seems desirable in some cases to warn the mother not only against too great an anxiety to punish a child exhibiting these manifestations, but also against any excess of physical tenderness which may unduly arouse the emotions of susceptible children. It is above all necessary to cultivate an understanding of the child's nature. Adults are prone to attribute their own feelings to children. Many acts of children, which to adults appear to reveal vicious sexual motives, often have no sexual motive at all, but spring merely from the play impulse or from the desire for knowledge. This fallacy has doubtless been favoured in recent years by unguarded adherents of psycho-analytic doctrines.

It is unfortunate that the students of childhood have often been people who have gained their knowledge from the study of neurotic subjects. "All the *general* conclusions derived from the study of the present-day type of neurotic," Otto Rank remarks in his *Modern Education*, "must be received with great caution, for under other conditions Man reacts differently." He adds that the present-day child cannot be compared with primitive Man and that it may perhaps be best that education should not be too definite.

It is now held by the best authorities that the sexual guidance of children should begin, so far as its elements are concerned, at a very early age, and that a wise and tender mother is the ideal person to perform this really maternal duty. It may, indeed, be added that only a mother can perform it rightly, and the training of mothers is an essential condition for the wholesome development of children. There is danger, it is sometimes said, that children's minds will be artificially concentrated on sexual subjects, of which otherwise they might remain blissfully unconscious. It is important, however, to remember the natural operations of a child's mind. A child's desire to know where babies come from is not a symptom of sexual consciousness, it is a natural desire to discover an important scientific fact. Again, at a little later age, the desire to know and see how the bodies of persons of the opposite sex are made is equally innocent and natural. It is the forced and unreasoned suppression of these natural curiosities, and not their gratification, which favours an unhealthy sexual consciousness. The child secretly concentrates himself on the solution of these mysteries only because any open attempt to solve them is on every hand rebuffed.

There should be nothing formal or special about the knowledge of sex imparted by the mother to her child. When the relation between mother and child is natural and intimate every function must from time to time come up for consideration, and the sensible mother will deal with each as it arises, though without carrying her information further than the child's curiosity at the time demands. Sex and excretion will be dealt with as simply as anything else, and neither with the slightest sign of repulsion or of disgust. Servants and nursemaids have frequently been apt not only to treat sex with reprehension but excretion with disgust. The wholesome mother feels no disgust for her child's excretions, and that attitude is important, for as the organs of sex and of excretion are on the surface so closely adjoined any attitude of disgust towards one is likely to embrace the other. It is sometimes said that the right attitude to inculcate is that both sets of organs alike are neither "disgusting" nor "sacred." But, in one way or another, it has soon to be made clear that, while both sets of organs are natural and neither disgusting, there is an immense difference in their ultimate significance, and that what proceeds from sex may be so tragic for the individual and so fateful for the race that, even if we reject the word "sacred" for sex, we must find some other word of equal poignancy.

The value of early sex-instruction for after-life is shown by Dr. Katharine Davis's extensive investigation among married women. When divided into two groups, according as they regarded themselves as happily or unhappily married, it was found that 57 per cent. of the happy group had received some general sex instruction in early life, but only 44 per cent. of the unhappy group. Dr. G. V. Hamilton's results, which are based on much smaller data, do not entirely agree, but he found the significant fact that the best source of early sex instruction for girls was the mother; 65 per cent. of married women who received such instruction were in the group whose sexual relations are "adequate," but less than 35 per cent. in the "inadequate" group; when the early information came from contemporaries or obscene talk, the percentage for the adequate group fell to 54, and the married life of the small group who had received instruction from father or brother was unsatisfactory.

The points to be attained are that the child's simple and natural questions should be answered simply and naturally when they first begin to be asked, so that his thoughts may not be arrested, and emotion generated, by the creation of a mystery. It is by waiting too late that mischief is liable to be caused. There is the added difficulty that nearly every parent is too shy or too awkward to begin talking about sex to the child who is emerging from childhood. Before then it is easy. As regards the naked body, similarly, much morbid curiosity may be aroused in the child who is growing up without ever seeing the naked bodies of children of the opposite sex, and the sudden casual sight of naked adults, for the first time, may sometimes produce a painful shock. It is desirable that children should be familiar with the sight of each other's naked bodies, and some parents also adopt the plan of themselves bathing naked with their children when the latter are still very young. Various risks are thus avoided, while such simplicity and openness tend to delay the development of sexual consciousness, and to inhibit the development of undesirable curiosities. It may even happen, and not infrequently, that the little boy or girl who is brought up familiarly with a sister or brother in bathing, never even so much as discovers that there is any sexual difference of physical conformation. All the influences that delay precocious sexual consciousness are of good augury for future development; the wise sexual hygienist realizes that this end cannot be attained by the artificial creation of mysteries.

But we must always bear in mind that the attitude

towards the child which is now becoming recognized as wisest is not yet firmly established. If it is true, as has been lately said, that the child has to create his parents in accordance with his own needs, it is also true that the situation thus presented is not easy to adjust on the basis of our ancient traditions of which the existence must always be recognized, so that the child's position is far less simple than it used to be. It is indeed to-day peculiarly difficult. He is no longer subjected to a generally accepted and rigidly fixed collective method of education, while he is still too undeveloped to assume the self-discipline of the adult. "The child of to-day," Rank remarks, "has to pass through a more critical childhood than perhaps the child of any earlier period in the history of Man."

We must not, therefore, be surprised if, even under generally improved conditions, we still encounter the "difficult" or "problem" child. Both heredity and environment still tend to the occasional production of such children. The more enlightened views now beginning to prevail will often prove a sufficient guide in dealing with these cases without resort to special expert assistance, but not always. We may, therefore, view with satisfaction the growing tendency to view such "problem children" not, as formerly, merely as "naughty" or "vicious," but as proper subjects for the combined attentions of the physician, the psychologist, the psychiatrist, and the social worker. The desirability of special Child Guidance Clinics with this end in view is becoming constantly more recognized since, in 1909, with the aid of the inspiration and public-spirited generosity of Mrs. W. F. Dummer, the Juvenile Psychopathic Institute, with Dr. William Healy as Director, was instituted in Chicago, becoming established in 1914 as a department of the Juvenile Court. This may be said to be the origin of the movement in favour of Child Guidance Clinics. As they have since developed they consist essentially of a team of three persons, psychiatrist, psychologist, and social worker. It may sometimes happen that a doctor with a special personal equipment for such cases may, more simply and conveniently, combine these three functions in himself, but the requirements are seldom combined, nor can the ordinary doctor often find time for such special work. It is probable, therefore, that these clinics will continue to develop, though not in connection with any special school of thought or practice, which would be undesirable. The New York Institute for Child Guidance has been planned on a large scale. The London Child Guidance Clinic was established in 1930.

The investigations involved by Child Guidance may lead us to a deeper knowledge of human types. What is now called "Constitutionology"—the study of the special psycho-physical types into which human beings tend to fall—proved attractive to physicians at an early period, for such a study is obviously of high importance both for medicine and for life. It is only in recent years, however, that the data have come into existence for placing such a study on a sound basis. It may indeed be said that it was only with the publication in 1921 of the epoch-marking book of Professor Kretschmer, *Physique and Character*, that constitutionology has been placed on a genuinely scientific foundation, though it is still at an early stage and continuously developing.

Looked at broadly, sexual enlightenment and education possess to-day a deeper significance than they have ever possessed before. Sexual initiation at puberty has always had a well-recognized racial importance. In Central Africa, as we know, and in many other parts of the world among the peoples we choose to regard, more or less inaccurately, as "primitive," such initiation is at once a sacred rite and a practical preparation for adult life. The child may be, and often is, already familiar with sex as play, and the grown-up people often treat such play with indulgence. But at puberty it becomes a more serious matter. The claims of the community and the race have to be considered; the youth or girl has to be fitted into his or her social place in the group, and for this what may be termed a moral education is necessary. It is often short and sharp, perhaps with some physical mutilation or severe abstinence or isolation, while the elders impart instruction in the duties of life and reveal the sacred mysteries of the tribe. Thereafter the child becomes a man or a woman, and takes on new privileges, new duties, new responsibilities. It is an admirable system: nothing better could well be devised under more or less primitive conditions of life. It has been unfortunate that in Christendom the relics of such systems had so far decayed as to become insignificant, or for the most part to disappear.

To-day we are waking up to that loss and striving to repair it. But we can no longer build up any system on the same lines, and before building at all we have to consider the nature of the phase of civilization out of which we are passing.

In that phase the insistence was all on the intellect and the methods of teaching which carried weight, or acquired wide popularity, were methods of educating the intelligence. But the sexual impulse—which yet is the main foundation of social as well as personal life—is not easily brought into the sphere of intelligence. So it has come about that our educational systems have, even up to the present, almost completely excluded the irrational element of sex; they have had little in common with those admirable, and, so far as the conditions allowed, complete schemes of initiation which prevailed in earlier ages of the world, the ages in which Man learned to become Man. Education with us has not been an education for life, but only for a part of life, especially the money-earning part.

This has been associated with—in various stages and degrees—an indifference, dislike, even contempt for that part of life which is based on the sexual impulse, since it failed to come into the sphere of intelligence with which our educational activities were concerned. It is a familiar fact that, among the products of our educational system, the more clever individuals—that is to say those whose narrow abilities are concentrated on the cultivation of intelligence—often adopt a sneering or cynical attitude where matters of love and sex are concerned. That is the natural outcome of their school training, although it was not a designed outcome. It was certainly not the usual outcome of the ancient methods of initiation into life. In building up our new system we have, therefore, to avoid the perils of the systems from which we immediately proceed.

But there is another point and one at which we must avoid the example of primitive societies: that is to say in delaying sexual initiation to puberty. The work of the psycho-analysts has made widely known the fact, which though previously known was not fully grasped in its full significance, that sexuality is far from beginning only at puberty. The racial bearing of sexuality begins at puberty, but its personal bearing—which is indirectly racial—may and often does begin much earlier, even in infancy.

A practical result of this fact is that the first initiation in sex, since it is called for in early childhood, is taken out of the hands of the community which of old conducted the puberty initiations, and placed in the hands of the parents. Under these conditions it is not a formal and conscious initiation, but a slow, natural, and almost imperceptible process under the guidance of a parent, usually the mother, who is freed from the taboos and inhibitions which formerly made it difficult for adults to recognize the existence of the phenomena of sex where their children were concerned, or to speak of them naturally.

In the schools, concomitantly and as the child develops, we may reasonably expect to see an elementary training in biology, covering the main facts of human life—including, though with no undue insistence, sex—given to all boys and girls. As a distinguished biologist, Ruggles Gates, has said: "Every schoolboy and girl should, as an essential part of their education, receive some instruction regarding the nature, structure, and action of plant and animal organisms, as well as their relationships and reactions upon each other. They should know something of heredity, and realize that every organism inherits and transmits its genetic peculiarities, down to the finest details of difference."

That education, as it develops, leads up to a racial initiation corresponding to the rites of more primitive peoples. It is along these biological lines that we reach the modern conception of that aspect of sex which the ancients regarded as sacred, for we must not, I would say once more, accept the notion of those foolish though well-meaning people who wish to bring up children to regard sexuality as commonplace, on the same level as nutrition and excretion. Along the line of biology it is easy to understand that sex is much more than that; it is not merely the channel along which the race is maintained and built up, it is the foundation on which all dreams of the future world must be erected. There are other and more personal ends to which the sexual impulse may be directed, but there is always this solid central fact.

The other ends also remain important. The indifference and even contempt with which our educational systems have treated the impulse of sex have blunted the far-spreading motive powers of that impulse. Yet they have at the same time rendered more urgent the need to cherish and develop the energies that reside in the impulse of sex. Intelligence alone, indispensable as it always remains, is sterile; it has no vital and penetrating influence in the organism. But amid the sterilizing tendencies of our life the impulse of sex still remains unimpaired, however concealed or despised. It is even, perhaps, as Otto Rank has termed it, "the last emotional resource which the exaggerated rationalization of our education has left us." Here, alike in its natural manifestations and in its sublimations—for the two go together and neither can flourish with the complete suppression of the other—we possess a great hope for our future civilization.

BIBLIOGRAPHY

A. Moll, *The Sexual Life of the Child.*

Havelock Ellis, *Studies in the Psychology of Sex*, especially Vols. I. and VI.; also "The New Mother" in *More Essays of Love and Virtue.*

Stanley Hall, *Adolescence.*

Rev. T. W. Pym, "Need of Education in Questions of Sex," *British Medical Journal*, August 1st, 1931.

Mary Chadwick, *Difficulties in Child Development* (dealing especially with the mistakes of parents in bringing up their children).

OTTO RANK, *Modern Education: A Critique of its Fundamental Ideas*, 1932.
W. HEALY, *The Individual Delinquent*, 1915.
BERNARD HART, "Work of a Child Guidance Clinic," *British Medical Journal*, September 19th, 1931.
KRETSCHMER, *Physique and Character*.
WINIFRED DE KOK, *New Babes for Old*.
K. DE SCHWEINITZ, *How a Baby is Born: What Every Child Should Know*.

CHAPTER IV

SEXUAL DEVIATION AND THE EROTIC SYMBOLISMS

Sexual Deviations

It was formerly taken for granted by all writers on the life of sex that there is but one pattern for that life, and that any straying from that one pattern was not " normal." This was assumed and never discussed. There seemed even to be no need to define precisely what this single pattern was ; every one was supposed to know instinctively. As soon as we begin to inquire into the actual and intimate facts of the sexual life, however, we see that this ancient and traditional assumption was mistaken. So far from there being only one pattern of sex-life, it would be nearer the truth to say that there are as many patterns as there are individuals. At the least there are a number of types of pattern to one or other of which the individual tends more or less, never exactly, to approximate. This has been visible to me ever since I began to study sexual psychology, and I have sought to make clear that here, as elsewhere in nature, we have to admit a wide limit of variation within the normal range. To-day this is gradually being recognized by experienced observers. To quote but one distinguished gynæcologist, Dickinson expresses " a growing scepticism about a fixed pattern of sex."

In order to remain within the normal range, all variations must at some point include the procreative end for which sex exists. To exclude procreation is perfectly legitimate, and under some circumstances morally imperative. But sexual activities entirely and by preference outside the range in which procreation is possible may fairly be considered abnormal ; they are deviations.

Sexual deviations were formerly called " perversions." That word arose at a time when sexual anomalies were universally regarded as sins or crimes, at the least as vices. It is still used by those whose ideas are rooted in traditions of the past which they cannot outgrow. In earlier years I have myself used it, though under protest, and with explanation of what I thereby meant. I now realize that (as Dickinson also has pointed out) the time has come to avoid the word, so far as possible, altogether. Even in the original Latin, *perversus* sometimes conveys a moral judgment; it dates from days anterior to the scientific and medical approach to sexual matters, which is concerned to understand sexual anomalies, and if necessary to treat them, but not to condemn them. To retain here a word which belongs to a totally different order introduces scientific confusion, even apart from the undoubted and highly important practical fact that it has unfortunate results on those persons who are told that they have been guilty of "perversion." The term is completely antiquated and mischievous, and should be avoided.

The term "displacement" has sometimes been used to indicate an unusual fixation of the sexual impulse. Such a term has the advantage of being morally neutral, but as it involves a static conception of the sexual impulse, which is really dynamic and living and liable to change, it is less satisfactory than "deviation" which is a term retaining dynamic force.

For a long time past I have used the term "symbolism" for many, or most, sexual deviations. By "erotic symbolism" (or more narrowly, erotic fetishism [1]) is meant a condition in which the psychological sexual process is either abridged or deviated in such a way that some special part of the process, or some object or action normally on its margin or even outside it altogether, becomes, often at an early age, the chief focus of attention. What is to the normal lover of secondary importance, or even indifferent, thus becomes of primary importance, and may properly be said to be the symbol of the whole sexual process.

[1] The term "erotic fetish" was originally confined to articles of clothing, but since Binet's classic essay on the subject in 1888 this limitation has been discarded.

Looked at broadly, all the sexual deviations are examples of erotic symbolism, for in every case it will be found that some object or act that for the normal human being has little or no erotic value has assumed such value ; that is to say, it has become a *symbol* of normal love. Moreover, erotic symbolism comes into play even in the more refined forms of normal love, for these involve a tendency to concentrate amorous attention on some special points in the beloved person, such points being themselves unimportant but acquiring a symbolic value.

When we thus use the term " symbolism " in its more ancient sense and apply it in the erotic field to deviations which were formerly called indiscriminately " perversions," it is seen to go beyond the more narrow significance assigned to it in psycho-analytic literature. The psycho-analyst, when using the term, mainly has in view a certain psychological mechanism which is often undoubtedly operative. " The essential function of all forms of symbolism," says Ernest Jones, " is to overcome the inhibition that is hindering the free expression of a given feeling-idea." That is undoubtedly one way, and an interesting way, in which a symbol may function ; but we must not incautiously attribute it to all forms of symbolism. To take a highly typical symbol : the flag is for the patriot the symbol of his country, but his devotion to it is not the conquest of an inhibition, and when in old days the sailor nailed the flag to the mast in battle it was certainly not because he feared to give free expression to his love for his country. A fundamental significance of the symbol is (as this example indicates) that it gives concrete shape to a more abstract feeling-idea. When a lover concentrates his attention on some special feature of his mistress or her belongings—her hair or her hand or her shoe—he is not overcoming an inhibition ; he is bringing to a more manageable concrete focus the diffused emotion which he feels for the beloved's whole personality. There is nevertheless a special class of symbols by which an indirect representation replaces something hidden which is the real motive force, because it has characteristics in common with it and can thus give a satisfaction which is really imparted by the hidden thing it represents. Even if psycho-analysts have sometimes exaggerated the range of this class of symbolisms, it exists and must not be overlooked.

The extent of erotic symbolism is seen when we attempt to group and classify the phenomena which may be brought under this head. Such phenomena may be conveniently arranged in three great classes, on the basis of the objects which arouse them.

1. PARTS OF THE BODY.—(A) *Normal:* Hand, foot, breasts, nates, hair, secretions and excretions, odours (ophresiolagnia). (B) *Abnormal:* Lameness, squinting, pitting of smallpox, etc., Paidophilia, or the sexual love of children,[1] presbyophilia, or the love of the aged, and necrophilia, or the attraction for corpses, may be included under this head, as well as the excitement caused by animals (erotic zoophilia).

2. INANIMATE OBJECTS.—(A) *Garments:* Gloves, shoes and stockings and garters, aprons, handkerchiefs, underlinen. (B) *Impersonal objects:* Here may be included all the various objects that may accidentally acquire the power of exciting sexual feeling in auto-erotism. Pygmalionism (iconolagnia) or the sexual attraction of statues may also be included.

3. ACTS AND ATTITUDES.—(A) *Active:* Whipping, cruelty, exhibitionism, mutilation and murder. (B) *Passive:* Being whipped, experiencing cruelty. Personal odours and the sound of the voice may also be included under this head. (C) *Scoptophilia or mixoscopia or voyeurism:* including objects and scenes found to be sexually stimulating; the vision of climbing, swinging, etc.; the acts of urination and

[1] Paidophilia is sometimes regarded as a separate deviation. Medico-legally it is convenient so to regard it. I am, however, inclined to agree with Leppmann, who has carefully studied sexual outrages on children, that, psychologically, there is no definite deviation on a congenital basis involving an exclusive sexual attraction to unripe girls. It may easily be associated with impotent senility. Otherwise it occurs either as an occasional luxurious speciality of a few over-refined persons, or, more commonly, as part of a general indiscriminating sexual tendency in the weak-minded. So far as it has any psychological definition, it may best be regarded as resembling the symbolisms.

defæcation (urolagnia and coprolagnia); the coitus of animals.

It will be seen that there is a vast range of kind and degree in these deviations of the sexual impulse. At one end we find the innocent and amiable attraction which his mistress's glove or slipper may possess for the lover—an attraction which has been felt by the finest and sanest minds—and at the other end the murderous outrages of a Jack the Ripper. But we have to remember that there is at no point any definite frontier, and that by insensible gradations the systematic arrangement of sexual deviations can be seen to pass from the harmless mania to the murderous outrage. So that even when we are not dealing with the criminal or medico-legal field, but are mainly concerned with the psychology of the normal sex-life, we cannot avoid the consideration of deviations, for at one end they all come within the normal range.

The extreme forms of symbolism are chiefly found in men. They are so rare in women that Krafft-Ebing stated, even in the late editions of his *Psychopathia Sexualis*, that he knew of no cases of erotic fetishism in women. They do, however, occur occasionally, even in well-marked forms. In its normal form erotic symbolism is undoubtedly quite common in women, and, as Moll points out, even the general fascination exerted on women by the soldier's uniform is probably due to the action of a symbolism of courage. But it also occurs in abnormal forms. There is indeed one form of erotic fetishism—kleptolagnia or erotic kleptomania—which in its typical form occurs almost exclusively in women.

BIBLIOGRAPHY

Havelock Ellis, *Studies in the Psychology of Sex*, especially Vols. III. and V.
G. V. Hamilton, *A Research in Marriage.*
R. W. Dickinson and Lura Beam, *A Thousand Marriages.*
Krafft-Ebing, *Psychopathia Sexualis.*
Thoinot and Weysse, *Medico-Legal Aspects of Moral Offences.*
Ernest Jones, "The Theory of Symbolism," *Papers on Psycho-Analysis*, Chap. VIII.
S. Herbert, *The Unconscious in Life and Art.*

Sexual Deviations in Childhood

When we took a wide survey of the sexual phenomena of childhood and adolescence we saw that it is not easy, once we have put aside our religious, ethical, or social pre-judgments, to introduce the idea of "perversion." Biologically, many things are natural that are outside our conventions, while ethnographically and historically there is no uniformity in conventions. I find it quite impossible, therefore, and even mischievous, to describe the child in the term that was once frequently employed by Freud as "polymorph-perverse," though the term has since been more or less supplanted, as Jelliffe points out, by "auto-erotic," or, as some would prefer, "pre-genital." For, as Freud himself has more recently seen, the barriers gradually built up by development and education do not yet exist for children. There cannot therefore be any question of "perversion," for that would be to judge them precisely in the way in which Freud himself says they should not be judged—"by the moral and legal codes of mature and fully responsible persons." The impression of "polymorphous perversity" is merely superficial; it is (as I have frequently had occasion to point out) the kind of "perversity" which an ignorant observer might find in the twisted fronds of young ferns. The conditions of life demand that twisted shape in the young growing things, and the real "perversity" would be if the young thing were to exhibit the shape of that which is fully grown.

It is necessary to emphasize this point, for even would-be pioneers and pedagogues of what is sometimes called "sexology" are often entangled in the meshes of the past. The extravagant horror of "perversity," the mania for finding and dwelling on "perversions" in the young, is itself the most perverse of perversions. It is seldom found, so far as is yet known, among any people living a sane and reasonably natural life, whether we turn to the savages of to-day or to the races of the classic civilization in which we have our own roots. We may indeed say as much of the same tendency when directed against adults. The so-called "perversions" of childhood persist—in some form or other and in some varying degree—when the child is grown up, for, as Jelliffe remarks, "very few people are really grown up." The difference is that there is now super-added the adult act of intercourse adequate to insure, if necessary, the consummating union of sperm-cell and germ-cell. But the "perversions" of childhood and adolescence may remain in due subordination as part of the play-function of sex, a legitimate and even desirable part of the art of love and the technique of impregnation. They are within the legitimate range of variation. It is only, if ever, allowable to call them *perversions* when so magnified as to replace the desire for the central act of sex-union and when they have diminished or abolished the ability to effect it.

It thus comes about that we have specially to avoid speaking about "perversions" in early life. The child's mind does not work in quite the same way as the adult mind; what is "natural" in one phase is not necessarily so at an earlier phase of development. So that it is not always easy either for the child to understand the operations of the adult's mind, or the adult the child's. It is unfortunate that adults do not more vividly realize what they were themselves as children. Many of us, however, can recall how misunderstood we sometimes were, and how unjustly we were in consequence treated. That is liable to happen even in matters where children and adults have much in common and is, therefore, still more likely to happen in the field of sex where they have so little in common.

Yet we must not conclude that sexual anomalies do not occur in early life. It is, however, much more a question of quantity than of quality, a question of degree rather than of kind. Whether of kind or of degree we can rarely err in attributing them, at all events in part, to an unsound heredity. When the child exhibits latent transformations of sexual impulse, likely to be harmful to himself or others—such as algolagnia carried to the point of bloodshed or that form of theft I term kleptolagnia—we cannot be concerned with a child of sound heredity, and all our care is demanded in devising appropriate conditions for dealing with the case, either therapeutic or hygienic. For we must always remember that, in approaching such conditions, there are some persons who, by a peculiar twist of mind, seem incapable of appreciating the hereditary factors of human actions, while others, by an equally peculiar but opposed twist of mind, seem incapable of appreciating the acquired factors of human action. Both these kinds of people do useful work in the direction along which their line of vision extends. But each alone is incapable of reaching a sane and balanced picture of the whole mechanism of life. We need to combine their two lines of vision in order really to see the object, and so be enabled to seek the cure for an anomaly in so far as it is acquired, and to secure the right conditions for it in so far as it is inborn and constitutional.

There are two kinds of anomaly we may often find in the early sex life, but with a tendency, under unfavourable conditions, to persist in adult life: the tendency to defect and the tendency to excess—hypo-conditions and hyper-conditions. Both kinds of anomaly are specially liable to occur in a civilization like our own, where the stimulations to sexual activity and the restrictions on that activity—both external and internal—are alike so powerful. The anomalies by defect (the hypo-æsthesias and hypo-excitabilities) are less serious in early life than those by excess (the hyper-æsthesias and hyper-excitabilities), for they may simply indicate a development which is slow but quite likely to proceed vigorously when adult life is reached. It may even be more likely to turn out happily, perhaps vigorously, when it is late. This is significantly suggested by Hamilton's inquiries: he found that the later sexual curiosity arises the more satisfactory (as shown by adequate orgasm, which he regards as the most convenient test) married life is likely to be. It is thus that we may probably explain one of the most curious and unexpected of Hamilton's results: the women who were shocked or frightened when they first learned the facts of sex show a decidedly more satisfactory married sex-life (nearly 65 per cent., with adequate orgasm) than those who were pleased, interested, or gratified when they first learned the facts of sex. The children who were gratified were, we may assume, those with an already developed sex life, the children who were shocked, those with an undeveloped sex life. So that this result, far from being really anomalous, is in line with the result that the children with no early sex curiosity have eventually the most satisfactory married life. Sexual precocity, while by no means necessarily of evil omen, is less promising for future welfare than its absence. It may be added that Dr. Katharine Davis did not find any markedly greater proportion of later happiness in girls who had not masturbated or had sexual play in childhood, as compared to those who had had such early sex experience. Dickinson and Pearson state that there is a real difference in the way of better health among those women who keep on with the habit of masturbation than with those who drop it after early life; this might be considered due to greater health and vigour in those who continue the habit, and it is a common experience for women to find that improved health means increased or resumed auto-erotic activity. They also state that there is no appreciable difference in health between those who begin to masturbate early and those who start after eighteen, which is not a conclusion we can unreservedly accept.

As regards the treatment of defects and excesses of sexuality in the young, the question of the defects is in any case simple. The evidence seems, as we have seen, to indicate that it is more likely than not to be a satisfactory state in the years before puberty, provided always that it occurs naturally, and has not been produced artificially, or merely superficially, by unwholesome external conditions, whether physical or psychic. The anomalies by excess are so numerous and often so complex that each has to be considered by itself. A wise physician is here required, familiar with children and their difficulties. In former days such physicians can scarcely be said to have had any existence; they are very far indeed from being numerous to-day; but there is good reason to hope that, along the lines of child-study and child-guidance that are now being developed, the wise treatment of sexual anomalies of childhood and youth will no longer be so rarely found.

But for the main part it is in the home that child guidance must begin and, for most children, end. And it is the mother—though there is an important place for the father even in the guidance of girls—who is the naturally elect child guide. Nowadays motherhood is a serious vocation, to which not all women are called. It is a discipline which makes many demands, and women may be thankful if, in a world rapidly becoming over-filled, it is really true that the Napoleons of the fûture will no longer clamour so loudly at the marriage bed for cannon fodder. It is few mothers, but the best, that humanity now needs. That, we may be sure, will eventually mean a revolution in our sex life, a revolution beginning, as any such revolution must begin, in infancy.[1]

The mothers of the immediate past, from this point of view, may roughly be divided into two classes: a majority who, from ignorance or timidity, almost altogether ignored sex in their children—an attitude which often turned out well—and a minority who suffered from the evils of half-knowledge and displayed a nervous anxiety and apprehension over this matter which by no means always proved beneficial. To-day the new mother, living in a world in which a more wholesome atmosphere begins to prevail in relation to sex, is learning by herself to assume an attitude towards her children which is different from that of either of these two classes. She is alert and informed, but at the same time not over-eager to interfere even with those manifestations concerning the nature and tendency of which she may not feel fully assured. She is realizing—sometimes almost instinctively—that her child has various phases to pass through before reaching full development, that too great an anxiety to interfere even with activities that seem undesirable may

[1] This is not the place to insist that it will not end there or be confined to sex. Dr. Grace Pailthorpe, in her *Studies in the Psychology of Delinquency*, finds that defective social sentiments are more prevalent and more significant in young criminals than defective intelligence, and these are directly traceable to the early home. The new mother will be an important agent in transforming society by helping to eliminate criminality.

be yet more mischievous than the activities themselves, and that the main thing is to understand the child, to win his confidence, and so to become a trusted adviser in his difficulties. This intuition, it may be remarked, is sound. Those who are intimately acquainted with children and infants are aware that, for instance, confirmed masturbation prolonged into adult life may occur in subjects whose mothers have from the first been energetically attempting to combat the habit, or that thumb-sucking, which some regard as tending to pass into masturbation, may be practised with obvious enjoyment from earliest infancy and later slowly disappear, if not interfered with, without being replaced by more definitely sexual modes of enjoyment.

When we turn from the home to the school difficulties are increased, since the school, in which many children are miscellaneously crowded together away from the guidance of those who know and love them best, is necessarily an unnatural state of life in which the possibilities of evil are multiplied. Elizabeth Goldsmith (in *Sex in Civilization*) tells of a school where " we have come to the conclusion that it is desirable not to curb the young child in his masturbatory activity, to study the whole child's adjustment and put the emphasis on his being a healthy, outgoing active child, satisfied in his relationships and activities." That " emphasis " is urgent and we are not told the results of this policy. No doubt it is still too early to speak definitely; we must wait until the adult can look back on his own early life. It is hardly a policy that can be carried out auspiciously without a considerable degree of well-informed awareness.

The usual policy in schools has been, as we know, to cultivate blindness, and when, by chance, a culprit is discovered to " make an example of him." (This is illustrated in Hugh de Sélincourt's novel, *One Little Boy*, in which the whole question is admirably presented.) While the auto-erotic practices of girls, though widely varied, are usually carried on very secretly, and often more or less unconsciously, boys are inclined to be less secretive; in large schools are sometimes found masturbation clubs, secret societies of which of course the teachers rarely suspect the existence. In such centres there are usually exceptional boys of congenital hyper-sexual temperament—of the kind who, when they become conspicuous, are now termed "problem children." As their morbidity is often associated with force of character they tend to exert an undue influence on companions who are of more normal temperament but still at an impressionable age. When many children are brought together, careful elimination of the problem cases is an essential condition if freedom for natural development is to be allowed. The results of experimental attempts have shown that otherwise all sorts of bad habits, hygienic and other, quite apart from the sphere of sex, are encouraged, and the strong are able to exert their youthful impulses of cruelty, natural or morbid, in persecuting the weak. Thus those who cultivate the ideal of allowing the child to pass unimpeded through his own natural stages of development encounter the difficulty that they must not only restrain their own impulse of interference, but that they must be careful to remove other influences which impede or distort natural development. The treatment, which sometimes involves the segregation of these "problem children," must always be highly individualized, since cases endlessly vary, and call for a high degree of specialized skill; while in such children an abnormal sex element is frequently to be detected, their peculiarities of behaviour, which are often of an anti-social character, extend far beyond the sexual sphere.

For ordinary children, however, it remains true that the responsibility must inevitably rest in the first place on the parents and especially the mother. That is why motherhood can no longer be regarded as a merely animal function, but has become a vocation demanding enlightened and trained intelligence, and not to be exercised by women who are not called to it by natural aptitude of mind as well as of body. The evil influence of incompetent, careless, or foolish parents is now becoming generally recognized. Even parents who would object to be classed under any of these heads are constantly liable, when absorbed in their own occupations or carried away by varying moods of the moment, to alternate between unreasonable severity and equally unreasonable indulgence, and so to call out highly critical reactions in their children who sit in judgment over them, for children are hypercritical of their parents, in an egoistic anxiety that *their* parents should be models of perfection.

"The people who best disciplined children and taught them self-control," Professor Winifred Cullis remarked at a meeting of the Parents' Association in London, "were other children." This is a wise observation so long as it is taken in connection with the considerations here brought forward. Life must be lived with our equals and we cannot live without discipline and control.[1] There must always be repression in life, in the sense of an inhibition of impulses and a subordination of some natural possibilities. There is no room in social life for unrestrained licence; as Freud well says, in the admirable twenty-seventh lecture of his *Lectures on Psycho-Analysis*, "free living is itself a repression," for it crushes the half of our impulses and the most human half, in which ultimately our happiness must mainly lie. It is better that elders should not be the imposers of discipline and control, but rather the guides and referees when difficulties arise. From the earliest age there begins

[1] It is interesting to observe that even when we are dealing with abnormal youth of delinquent tendency the principle of self-discipline among equals will still work. In Dr. Pailthorpe's report of *Studies in the Psychology of Delinquency* an account is given of the homes for difficult and neglected children successfully carried out under the charge of Aichhorn, a distinguished educational authority of Vienna. The most difficult group was segregated and allowed to do exactly as they liked, so long as no gross injury took place, the staff not to interfere, though so far as possible to share the life of the boys. "At first pandemonium ensued. The lads smashed crockery and windows, hit each other about, threw their food about, and even went so far as to urinate and defæcate anywhere they chose. At the end of a month the inside of these barracks was indescribable and the staff completely worn out. The doctor now asked for other barracks, and he started again. The boys themselves seemed exhausted and tired, and when taken into new barracks wished now to behave decently. Gradually they became interested, wanted to learn, sought things to do, and a spirit of friendly rivalry came into being. With this came the commencement of the idea of self-government. Pressure was gradually brought to bear by members of the community on those others who did not so readily fall in with the unwritten laws of the group." The success of the movement has been recognised and the City Council has placed more and more groups under the director's supervision.

the formation of self-discipline and self-control, and it may most naturally and most wholesomely arise in that life among equals for which all education that is worth anything is the training ground.

BIBLIOGRAPHY

A. Moll, *The Sexual Life of the Child.*
S. Freud, *Three Contributions to Sexual Theory.*
Stanley Hall, *Adolescence.*
Havelock Ellis, " Sexual Education," *Studies in the Psychology of Sex*, Vol. VI.
William and Dorothy Thomas, *The Child in America : Behaviour Problems and Programs.*
O. Rank, *Modern Education.*

Urolagnia and Coprolagnia

The most usual erotic symbolisms in childhood are those of the scatologic group, the significance of which has often been emphasized by Freud and others. The channels of urination and defæcation are so close to the sexual centres that the intimate connection, physical and psychic, between the two groups is easily understood. Urination and defæcation are processes which in any case could not fail to interest the youthful mind, for they gratify the childish impulse to make things, and are thus a rudimentary form of the artistic impulse, at the same time a manifestation of power. Hamilton found that 21 per cent. of his married men and 16 per cent. of his married women had in childhood had fæcal and urinary interests, and scatological fancies or play. These functions also appear to absorb something of the nervous energy which later goes into the sexual channel ; in young girls, and occasionally in women, when tumescence has occurred, detumescence may take the form of a spasmodic and involuntary emission of urine. There is probably a connection between nocturnal enuresis and sexual activity, sometimes masturbation. Freud believes that retention of the contents of the bowels for the sake of pleasurable sexual sensations may occur in childhood ; and it is certain that even in later life the contents of the bladder are sometimes retained for the same reason. Children not unusually believe that the sexual acts of their elders have some connection with urination or defæcation, and the mystery with which the excretory acts are surrounded helps to support this theory. An interest in these functions is not uncommonly prolonged beyond the age of puberty, especially in girls, but it tends to die out, sometimes with a feeling of shame at the attention bestowed on it, as the interest in sex matters develops. Occasionally it persists in the adult sexual impulse; more commonly perhaps, there is a more or less forced repression of the infantile scatologic interests which may then play the part attributed to them by Freud. But before puberty, scatologic interests may be regarded as normal; at this age the child has still much in common with the primitive mind, which, as mythology and folk-lore show, attributes great importance to the excretory functions. We may regard these interests as merely a phase in normal development. In so far as they persist in adult life they remain normally in the background, with a certain range of variation, and still able to exercise, at all events as regards urination, a legitimate part in the play-function of sex.

Extreme cases have been described, notably of the coprolagnic or coprophilic tendency. In such a case (one was recorded in full detail by Moll) an interest in the whole process of defæcation and its product may be so developed that it replaces all normal sexual interests. In minor degrees of this tendency, we have anal erotism (supposed to be associated with early constipation or the impulse to restrain evacuation to procure pleasure); it has specially been explored by psycho-analysts, who regard it as based on a primary tendency of childhood, which, after in childhood it is repressed, may lead to psychic traits of orderliness, frugality, even stinginess; and when not repressed lead to other psychic traits the reverse of these. This is a matter for further investigations. Hamilton took it into consideration, and found ten persons (nine women and one man) who denied early anal erotism but had early constipation and showed in an unusually large proportion stinginess, orderliness, sadism, masochism, hoarding, and extravagance ; but these results were too confused and contradictory to support speculations as to the precise relationship of early constipation to adult psychic traits.

After childhood coprolagnia is not usually associated with urolagnia, although the association may be found in slight forms. The extreme forms of coprolagnia are in men, but urolagnia, while more frequent in both sexes, is specially frequent, though often only in a slight degree, in women. It is doubtless encouraged by the close and obvious connection of the urinary function with the sexual organs, as well as by actual nerve connections. Young girls and women will sometimes seek to rival the attitude of the other sex in urination, a rivalry possible for many who are still young and have not borne children, as maternity usually enfeebles the expulsive muscular force. There is no necessary homosexual tendency here involved.

Considerable importance has sometimes been attached to what Sadger has termed " urethral erotism," or urinary erotism, using the term widely, to cover not only the urethra and the urine, but the whole peripheral urinary apparatus from the bladder to the urethral orifice. It is claimed that this kind of erotism in early life may present the type of the later sexual life when by what may seem a natural transition erotism is transferred to the more strictly sexual sphere and its secretion ; and, correspondingly, urinary irregularities may become seminal irregularities. It has further been argued that such urethral erotism may extend to the highest psychic sphere, since it is in regulation of the urinary as well as bowel functions that *duty* first appears to the infant.

A tendency for bed-wetting to be associated with sexuality has long been noted. Enuresis and urethral erotism have by Freud and some other psycho-analysts been associated with psychic traits of ambition and aggressiveness. This supposition may have started in the fact that a special urinary interest in girls can manifest itself as rivalry with the urinary function in boys. There seems, however, no real and frequent association of urinary erotism with such rivalry which, also, is common enough in those completely devoid of such erotism.

I have been accustomed to apply the term Undinism to the frequent presence of an early interest in water in general, and the urinary function in particular, persisting in later life. This interest, not amounting to a definite deviation of the sexual impulse, or becoming a substitute for it, is common, especially in women, among whom its presence may be accounted for by various circumstances of their life, perhaps now becoming less prevalent by changed social conditions, but there always remains a closer association between sexual emotion and urination in women than in men, in whom the seminal and urinary functions of expulsion are in general mutually exclusive. The love of water generally is also associated with a greater tendency in women than in men to find pleasure in tactile associations.

BIBLIOGRAPHY

Havelock Ellis, *Studies in the Psychology of Sex*, Vol. V.; also " Undinism," *Studies in the Psychology of Sex*, Vol. VII.

Ernest Jones, *Papers on Psycho-Analysis*, " Anal Eroticism," Chapters XXX. and XL.

Erotic Fetishism

The most typical of the erotic symbolisms is constituted by erotic fetishism, a term devised by Binet in 1888. Even an erotic symbolism such as exhibitionism may be fetishistic, and every fetish is a symbol. The number of objects—not only parts of the body but inanimate things—which may acquire special erotic significance is practically infinite. There is indeed nothing that may not take on such significance. That is why the legal attempt to suppress " obscenity," regarded (according to the judicially recognized definition) as a tendency to " deprave and corrupt those whose minds are open to such immoral influences," is completely unworkable. Thus Dr. Jelliffe's patient, Zenia X., wrote that sex symbols became insistent at the age of thirteen and fourteen : " From this time on, though more fully in later years since the struggle has been more consciously sexual and thus more violent, I have been surrounded by symbols, particularly of the phallus: a garden hose in use or a jet of water, pears particularly or other elongated fruits, long pendant catkins, the pistil in the centre of a flower, a stick or stick-shaped object thrust into a round hole, the lobe of the ear with which I have toyed since birth, my teeth, and my tongue which I have nervously pressed against them until weary, a finger which seemingly in order to suppress a sudden sexual thought I have many times pointed before me and then in quick correction have drawn in and folded within the others, the thumb which again involuntarily in a repressive effort is folded close within the fingers, certain letters of the alphabet. These are some of the symbols which have beset me on every hand, thrusting themselves continually before me, to remind me of the phallus or of the actual contact of the organs male and female."

The manifold complexity of sexual symbols is again brought out in a case described by Marcinowski, a highly intelligent married woman of twenty-seven, who was neurotic with slight germs of morbid deviation. The symbols were apt to occur in her dreams which she was skilful in interpreting: ships in haven were often the symbol of coitus, as was sailing in a ship; water was the symbol of the mother's body (connected with early ideas that the bladder was associated with coitus); to die (being self-abandonment) is to be in love; a knife is a phallic symbol; worms and snakes are small masculine organs; the horse and the dog are sexual symbols (she had once kissed a dog's penis), as are doves; a railway engine (attractive to her from childhood) is a symbol of the penis, as is also a tree and a banana; to kill equals coitus (she had sometimes had sadistic fancies); many fish are symbols of coitus; rain, urine, and tears are symbols of semen; wanting to urinate is for her a form of sexual excitement.

Most of these symbols are liable to occur anywhere and to anyone. The necessary conditions for a symbol to become a fetish seems to be a special predisposition, no doubt usually of neuropathic nature, though this is by no means always obvious, and a strong impression by which the object is poignantly presented to consciousness at a moment of strong sexual excitement, this event often occurring before or about puberty. The accidental association without the predisposition will scarcely suffice to evoke a fetish (except in slight degree), for such accidental associations are constantly occurring. Hirschfeld has argued that a fetish is frequently the real expression of the individual's special temperament. The soldier's red coat acts like a fetish on the servant girl because it is a symbol of the martial and virile character which appeals to her, and it may well be that in many less obvious cases the fetish really expresses ideals based on individual idiosyncrasy. But in most cases this cannot be proved, and is often indeed scarcely susceptible of proof on account of the neutral character of the fetish. A boy admires a woman who one day urinates in his presence so that he catches a glimpse of her abundant pubic hair, and such hair henceforth becomes an almost indispensable fetish to him ; a youth is lying on the floor when a charming girl playfully places her foot on him, continuing to play with him thus until sexual excitement occurs, and he becomes a lifelong foot-fetishist.

Such fetishisms are, in a slight degree, entirely normal. Every lover becomes specially attracted to some individual feature of the beloved or to some of the various articles that come in contact with her. But this tendency becomes abnormal when it is exclusive or generalized, and it becomes a definite deviation when the fetish itself, even in the absence of the person, becomes completely adequate not only to arouse tumescence, but to evoke detumescence, so that there is no desire at all for sexual intercourse.

In milder though definitely abnormal cases, the subject himself devises the appropriate treatment by taking care that his fetish is set, as it were, in the ante-chamber to courtship, so that it shall not cause any arrest or deviation of the emotion it arouses. In more serious cases the fetishist often derives so much gratification from his perversion, and finds this gratification so easy, that he has no wish to become normal. In some cases fetishism leads to various anti-social offences, especially to the theft of the desired fetish, such as shoes, handkerchiefs, or wearing apparel. Without leading to criminal actions it may prove annoying from the undue sexual excitement caused, as in the case of a young woman for whom eyeglasses or spectacles were a fetish, and who experienced excitement whenever she saw them worn, even by a woman. In such cases hypnotism was formerly resorted to, sometimes with success.

There are certain forms of erotic fetishism which are apt to be complicated in their psychological bearings. This is notably the case as regards foot-fetishism, which, under the conditions of civilization whereby the foot is usually seen clothed, becomes shoe-fetishism. There would seem to be an almost natural basis for foot-fetishism in the tendency to a world-wide association of the foot with the sexual organs. Even among the Jews the "foot" was used as a euphemism for the sexual organs, and we read, for instance, in Isaiah of "the hair of the feet," meaning the pubic hair. In widely separated parts of the world, moreover, the foot has been a centre of modesty. It was so even in Spain, and Peyron noted in 1777 that the feminine custom of concealing the feet was only then passing out of fashion, and "a woman who shows her feet is no longer ready to give her favours," as, it may be added, she was also in classic Rome. Even for the normal lover the foot is one of the most attractive parts of the body. Stanley Hall found that among the parts specified as most admired in the other sex by young men and women who answered a *questionnaire*, the feet came fourth (after the eyes, hair, stature and size). Other observers, however, like Hirschfeld, have found the hand a much more frequent fetish than the foot. Infants are peculiarly interested in the foot, primarily in their own. Moreover, in many parts of the world, notably China, some parts of Siberia, as well as ancient Rome and mediæval Spain, a certain degree of foot-fetishism has been recognized.

It is not usual for the normal lover, in most civilized countries to-day, to attach primary importance to the foot, such as he frequently attaches to the eyes. In a small but not inconsiderable minority of persons, however, the foot or the shoe becomes the most attractive part of a woman, and in some morbid cases the woman herself is regarded as a comparatively unimportant appendage to her foot or her shoes. Restif de la Bretonne furnishes an interesting example of foot-fetishism in a writer of considerable importance; in his case the fetishism was well marked, but it was never extreme, and the shoe, however attractive, was not an adequate substitute for the woman.

Eccentric as foot-fetishism may appear, it is thus simply the re-emergence, by a pseudo-atavism or arrest of development, of a mental or emotional impulse which was probably experienced by our forefathers, and is often traceable among young children to-day. The occasional reappearance of this bygone impulse and the stability which it may acquire are thus conditioned by the sensitive reaction of an abnormally nervous and usually precocious organism to influences which, among the average and ordinary population of Europe to-day, are either never felt, or quickly outgrown, or strictly subordinated in the highly complex crystallizations which the course of love and the process of tumescence create within us. An interesting case was elaborately psychoanalysed by L. Binswanger: Gerda, as a child, had acquired the habit of sitting on her heels with her shoe pressed against the vulva and anus. This would cause excitement in these erogenic zones and she would find pleasure in urinating (perhaps as a form of detumescence). The shoe became her friend and lover and darling, to be carefully protected and guarded from the eyes of others. The foot, and especially the shod foot, became blended with all her sexual ideas, the representative of the phallus, and even, as among primitive peoples, the symbol of all fertility. On this foundation phobias and other symptoms in time developed, to some extent overlying and diminishing the original manifestations.

It may be added that this is by no means true of foot-fetishism only. In some other fetishisms a seemingly congenital predisposition is even more marked. This is not only the case as regards hair-fetishism, fur-fetishism, etc. In many cases of fetishisms of all kinds not only is there no record of any commencement in a definite episode (an absence which may be accounted for by the supposition that the original incident has been forgotten), but it would seem in some cases that the fetishism developed very slowly. In this sense, although we cannot speak of foot-fetishism as strictly atavism, it may be seen to arise on a congenital basis. We may, with Garnier, regard the congenital element as essential.

This congenital element of erotic symbolism is worth noting because more than any other form of sexual deviation the fetishisms are those which are least clearly conditioned by inborn states of the organism and most frequently aroused by seemingly accidental associations or shocks in early life. Inversion is sometimes so fundamentally ingrained in the individual's constitution that it arises and develops in spite of the strongest influences in a contrary direction. But a fetishism, while it may possibly tend to occur in sensitive, nervous, timid, precocious individuals—that is to say, individuals of more or less neuropathic heredity—can usually, though not always, be traced to a definite starting point in the shock of some sexually emotional episode in early life.

Associations of this kind may occur in the early experiences of the most normal persons. The degree to which they will influence the subsequent life and thought and feeling depends on the degree of the individual's emotional receptivity, or the extent to which he is hereditarily susceptible of abnormal deviation. Precocity is undoubtedly a condition which favours such deviation; a child who is precociously and abnormally sensitive to persons of the opposite sex before puberty has established the normal channels of sexual desire, is peculiarly liable to become the prey of a chance symbolism. All degrees of such symbolism are possible. While the average insensitive person may fail to perceive them at all, for the more alert and imaginative lover they are a fascinating part of the highly charged crystallization of passion. A more nervously exceptional person, when once such a symbolism has become firmly implanted, may find it an absolutely essential element in the charm of a beloved and charming person. Finally, for the individual who is thoroughly unsound the symbol becomes generalized ; a person is no longer desired at all, being merely regarded as an appendage of the symbol, or being dispensed with altogether ; the symbol is alone desired, and is fully adequate to impart by itself complete sexual gratification. While it may be considered a morbid state to demand a symbol as an almost essential part of the charm of a desired person, it is only in the final condition, in which the symbol becomes all-sufficing, that we have a completely morbid variation. In the less complete forms of symbolism it is still the woman who is desired, and the ends of procreation may be served ; when the woman is ignored and the mere symbol is an adequate and even preferred stimulus to detumescence the pathological condition becomes complete.

Krafft-Ebing regarded shoe-fetishism as, in large measure, a more or less latent form of masochism, the foot or the shoe being the symbol of the subjection and the humiliation which the masochist feels in the presence of the beloved object. Moll, more correctly, states that the connection is " very frequent." This was also the opinion of Garnier, who was, however, careful to point out that there are many cases in which no such connection can be traced.

While we may properly admit the frequency of the connection, we must be cautious in making any general attempt to amalgamate masochism and foot-fetishism. In the broad sense in which erotic symbolism is here understood, both masochism and foot-fetishism may be co-ordinated as symbolisms ; for the masochist his self-humiliating impulses are the symbol of ecstatic adoration ; for the foot-fetishist his mistress's foot or shoe is the concentrated symbol of all that is most beautiful and elegant and feminine in her personality. But if in this sense they are co-ordinated, they often remain entirely distinct. Masochism, indeed, merely simulates foot-fetishism ; for the masochist the shoe is not strictly a symbol, it is only an instrument which enables him to carry out his impulse ; the true sexual symbol for him is not the shoe, but the emotion of self-subjection. For the foot-fetishist, on the other hand, the foot or the shoe is not a mere instrument, but a true symbol, the focus of his worship, an idealized object which he is content to contemplate or reverently touch. He himself usually has no impulse to any self-degrading action, nor the slightest emotion of subjection. It may be noted that in the typical case of foot-fetishism which is presented to us in the person of Restif de la Bretonne he repeatedly speaks of "subjugating" the woman for whom he feels this fetishistic adoration, and mentions that even when still a child he especially admired a delicate and fairy-like girl in this respect because she seemed to him easier to subdue. His attitude throughout life was active and masculine, not masochistic.

In determining whether we are concerned with a case of fetishism or of masochism, it is necessary to take the subject's whole mental and emotional attitude into consideration. The same act may have a different significance in different persons. Krafft-Ebing believed that the desire to be trodden on is absolutely symptomatic of masochism. That is not the case. The desire to be trodden on may be found as an erotic symbolism, associated with foot-fetishism, and not involving any desire to be subjugated. That was clearly seen in a pronounced case I have recorded in a man, now dead, whom I knew, a man of masterful and enterprising disposition and with no desire for subjugation. In a rather similar case more recently recorded by Marchand and Fuller they point out that there were no indications of masochism. Even when a masochistic tendency appears, that may be merely secondary, a parasitic growth on the symbolism.

This desire to be trodden on sometimes experienced by foot-fetishists is itself interesting, because it shows how the narrower attraction of fetishes tends to be merged in the wider attraction of erotic symbols; the foot is more than a mere material object to be idolized when it belongs to a beloved person. It is a centre of force, an agent for exerting pressure; and thus it furnishes a point of departure not only for the static erotic fetish, but for the dynamic erotic symbolization. The energy of its movements becomes a substitute for the energy of the sexual organs themselves. Here we have a symbolism which is altogether different from that fetishism which is adoration of a definite object ; it is a dynamic symbolism finding its gratification in the spectacle of movements which ideally recall the fundamental rhythm and pressure reactions of the sexual process. The same tendency is well illustrated by a case observed by Charcot and Magnan, in which a foot-fetishist was specially excited by the act of hammering a nail into a woman's shoe—evidently a symbol of coitus.

Before leaving the general discussion of erotic fetishism, some reference may be made to anti-fetishism. This term was introduced by Lombroso in 1897 to cover cases of strong aversion to definite features or objects which might be possible erotic fetishes. Lombroso specially associated the anti-fetish with disgust at sexual phenomena presented at or before puberty. The term has been adopted by Hirschfeld, who attaches importance to this antipathy. L. Binswanger prefers the term negative fetish.

BIBLIOGRAPHY

FREUD, *Three Contributions to Sexual Theory.*
HAVELOCK ELLIS, *Studies in the Psychology of Sex,* Vols. III and V.

Stuff-Fetishism and Erotic Zoophilia

It is now necessary, without entirely leaving the field of fetishism, to touch on a special group of sexual symbols in which the association of contiguity with the human body is usually absent : the various methods by which animals, or animal products, or the sight of animal copulation, may arouse sexual desire in human persons. Here we encounter a symbolism mainly founded on association by resemblance ; the animal sexual act recalls the human sexual act ; the animal becomes the symbol of the human being.

The group of phenomena we are here concerned with includes several sub-divisions. There is, first, the more or less sexual pleasure sometimes experienced, especially by young persons, in the sight of copulating animals. This has been termed *Mixoscopic zoophilia;* it falls within the range of normal variation. Then we have the cases in which the contact of animals, stroking, etc., produces sexual excitement or gratification; this is a sexual fetishism in the narrow sense, and is by Krafft-Ebing termed *Zoophilia erotica.* We have, further, the class of cases in which a real or simulated sexual intercourse with animals is desired. Such cases do not involve fetishism in the narrow sense, but they come within the sphere of erotic symbolism, as here understood. This class falls into two divisions: one in which the individual is fairly normal, but belongs to a low grade of culture; the other in which he may belong to a more refined social class, but a psychopathic condition is present. In the first case we may properly apply the simple term bestiality (it is called sodomy in some countries, but this is incorrect as well as confusing, and to be avoided), in the second case it may perhaps be better to use the term *Zooerastia,* proposed by Krafft-Ebing.

Among children, both boys and girls, it is common to find that the copulation of animals is a mysteriously fascinating spectacle. It is inevitable that this should be so, for the spectacle is more or less clearly felt to be the revelation of a secret which has been concealed from them. It is, moreover, a secret of which they feel intimate reverberations within themselves, and even in perfectly innocent and ignorant children the sight may produce an obscure sexual excitement. It would seem that this occurs more frequently in girls than in boys. Even in adult age, it may be added, women are liable to experience the same kind of emotion in the presence of such spectacles. In the sixteenth century, both in England and France, the ladies of royal and aristocratic circles would almost openly go to enjoy such spectacles. In more modern times such sights are regarded as both prurient and morbid, and for ill-balanced minds no doubt are so.

While the contemplation of animal coitus is an easily intelligible and in early life, perhaps, an almost normal symbol of sexual emotion, there is another sub-division of this group of animal fetishisms which forms a natural transition from the fetishisms which have their centre in the human body : the *stuff-fetishisms* or the sexual attraction exerted by various tissues, perhaps always of animal origin. Here we are in the presence of a somewhat complicated phenomenon. In part we have, in a considerable number of cases, the sexual attraction of feminine garments, for all such tissues are liable to enter into the dress. In part, also, we have a sexual deviation of tactile sensibility, for in a considerable proportion of these cases it is the touch sensations which are potent in arousing the erotic impulse. But in part, also, it would seem, we have here the conscious or sub-conscious presence of an animal fetish, and it is notable that perhaps all these stuffs, and especially fur, which is by far the commonest of the groups, are distinctively animal products. We may perhaps regard the fetish of feminine hair—a much more important and common fetish, indeed, than any of the stuff-fetishisms—as a link of transition. Hair is at once an animal and a human product, while it may be separated from the body and possesses the qualities of a stuff. Krafft-Ebing remarks that the senses of touch, smell, and hearing, as well as sight, seem to enter into the attraction exerted by hair.

As a sexual fetish hair belongs strictly to the group of parts of the body ; but since it can be removed from the body and is sexually effective as a fetish in the absence of the person to whom it belongs, it is on a level with the garments which may serve in a similar way, with shoes or handkerchiefs or gloves. Psychologically, hair-fetishism presents no special problem, but the wide attraction of hair—it is sexually the most generally noted part of the feminine body after the eyes—and the peculiar facility with which when plaited it may be removed have sometimes rendered hair-fetishism a condition of special medico-legal interest.

The hair-despoiler (*Coupeur des nattes* or *Zopfabschneider*), however modern fashions may have diminished his activities, might formerly have been found in any civilized country, though the most carefully studied cases occurred in Paris. Such persons are usually of nervous temperament and bad heredity; the attraction of hair occasionally develops in early life; sometimes the morbid impulse only appears in later life after fever. The fetish may be either flowing hair or braided hair, but is usually one or the other, and not both. Sexual excitement and ejaculation may be produced in the act of touching or cutting off the hair, which is subsequently, in many cases, used for masturbation. As a rule, the hair-despoiler is a pure fetishist, no element of sadistic pleasure entering into his feelings.

The stuff-fetishes are most usually fur and velvet; feathers, silk, and leather also sometimes exert this influence; these are all, it will be noted, animal substances. The most interesting is probably fur, the attraction of which is not uncommon in association with passive algolagnia. As Stanley Hall showed, the fear of fur, as well as the love of it, is by no means uncommon in childhood; it may appear in infancy and in children who have never come in contact with animals. It is noteworthy that in most cases of uncomplicated stuff-fetishism the attraction apparently arises on a congenital basis, as it appears in persons of nervous or sensitive temperament at an early age and without being attached to any definite or causative incident. The sexual excitation is nearly always produced by touch rather than by sight. If the specific sexual sensations may be regarded as a special modification of ticklishness, the erotic symbolism in the case of these stuff-fetishisms would seem to be a more or less congenital deviation of ticklishness in relation to specific animal contacts.

A further degree of deviation in this direction is reached in erotic *zoophilia*, as exemplified in a case recorded by Krafft-Ebing. In this case a congenital neuropath, of good intelligence but delicate and anæmic, with feeble sexual powers, had a great love of domestic animals, especially dogs and cats, from an early age; when petting them he experienced sexual emotions, although he was innocent in sexual matters. At puberty he realized the nature of his feelings and tried to break himself of his habits. He succeeded, but then began erotic dreams accompanied by images of animals, and these led to masturbation associated with ideas of a similar kind. At the same time he had no wish for any sort of intimate intercourse with animals, and was indifferent as to the sex of the animals which attracted him ; his sexual ideas were normal. Such a case seems to be one of fetishism on a tactile basis, and thus forms a transition between the stuff-fetishisms and the complete perversion of sexual attraction towards animals.

Krafft-Ebing considered that this is radically distinct from erotic *zoophilia.* This view cannot be accepted. Bestiality and *zooerastia* merely present in a more marked form a further degree of the same phenomenon which we meet with in erotic *zoophilia ;* the difference is that they occur either in more insensitive or in more markedly psychopathic persons. It is, however, somewhat doubtful whether we can always or even usually distinguish between *zooerastia* and bestiality, for it seems probable that in most cases of ordinary bestiality some slight traces of mental anomaly might be found, if such cases always were, as they should be, properly investigated. As Moll remarks, it is often hardly possible to draw a sharp line between vice and disease.

We here reach the grossest and most frequent perversion in the group : bestiality or the impulse to attain sexual gratification by intercourse, or other close contact, with animals. In seeking to comprehend this deviation it is necessary to divest ourselves of the attitude toward animals which is the inevitable outcome of refined civilization and urban life. Most sexual deviations, if not in large measure the actual outcome of civilized life, easily adjust themselves to it. Bestiality (except in one form to be noted later) is, on the other hand, the sexual anomaly of dull, insensitive, and unfastidious peasants. It flourishes among primitive peoples and rural communities. It is the vice of the clod-hopper who is unattractive to women or inapt to court them. In some stages of culture it is not a vice at all. Thus, when in Sweden at the end of the thirteenth century it was first made an offence by the Swedish pagan provincial laws, it was still only as an offence against the owner of the animal, who was entitled to compensation. Among still simpler peoples, such as the Salish of British Columbia, animals are regarded as no lower in the scale of life than human beings, and in some respects superior, so that there is no place for our conception of "bestiality."

Three conditions have favoured the extreme prevalence of bestiality: (1) primitive conceptions of life which built up no great barrier between man and the other animals; (2) the extreme familiarity which necessarily exists between the peasant and his beasts, often combined with separation from women; (3) various folk-lore beliefs such as the efficacy of intercourse with animals as a cure for venereal disease, etc.

Bestiality in the country is far from infrequent. For the peasant, whose sensibilities are uncultivated and who makes but the most elementary demands from a woman, the difference between an animal and a human being in this respect scarcely seems to be very great. "My wife was away too long," a German peasant explained to the magistrate, "and so I went with my sow." It is an explanation that to the peasant, ignorant of theological and juridical conceptions, may seem natural and sufficient. Bestiality thus resembles masturbation and other manifestations of the sexual impulse which may be practiced merely *faute de mieux*, and not as, in the strict sense, deviations of the impulse. In this way it is found among soldiers at the front compelled to live an abstinent life, and the goat has been mentioned in this connection both in mediæval and earlier days and among the troops of the Great War.

But it is by no means only their dulled sensibilities, or the absence of women, which accounts for the frequency of bestiality among peasants. A highly important factor is their constant familiarity with animals. It is scarcely surprising that peasants should sometimes regard animals as being not only as near to them as their fellow human beings, but even nearer.

A large number of animals have been recorded as employed in the gratification of sexual desire at some period or in some country, by men and sometimes by women. Domestic animals are naturally those which most frequently come into question, and there are few if any of these which can altogether be excepted. The sow is one of the animals most frequently abused in this manner. Cases in which mares, cows, and donkeys figure constantly occur, as well as goats and sheep. Dogs, cats, and rabbits are heard of from time to time. Hens, ducks, and especially in China, geese are not uncommonly employed. The Roman ladies were said to have had an abnormal affection for snakes. The bear and the crocodile are also mentioned.

The social and legal attitude towards bestiality has reflected in part the frequency with which it has been practiced, and in part the disgust mixed with mystical and sacrilegious horror which it has aroused. It has sometimes been met merely by a fine, and sometimes the offender and his innocent partner have been burnt together. In the Middle Ages and later its frequency is attested by the fact that it formed a favourite topic with preachers even of the fifteenth and sixteenth centuries. It is significant that it was thought necessary to fix the periods of penance which should be undergone respectively by bishops, priests, and deacons who might be guilty of bestiality.

The extreme severity which was frequently exercised toward those guilty of this offence was doubtless in large measure due to the fact that bestiality was regarded as a kind of sodomy, an offence which was viewed with a mystical horror, apart altogether from any actual social or personal injury it caused. The Jews seem to have felt this horror; it was ordered that the sinner and his victim should both be put to death. In the Middle Ages, especially in France, the same rule often prevailed. Men and sows, men and cows, men and donkeys were burnt together. At Toulouse a woman was burnt for having intercourse with a dog. Even in the seventeenth century a learned French lawyer justified such sentences. It seems probable that even to-day, in the social and legal attitude towards bestiality, sufficient regard is not paid to the fact that this offence is usually committed either by persons who are morbidly abnormal or who are of so low a degree of intelligence that they border on feeble-mindedness. Moreover, it has to be remembered that, except in the occasional cases which involve cruelty to animals, or are united with sadism, bestiality is not a directly anti-social act at all; so long as there is no cruelty, it is, Forel remarks, " one of the most harmless of the pathological aberrations of the sexual impulse."

BIBLIOGRAPHY

KRAFFT-EBING, *Psychopathia Sexualis.*
W. HOWARD, " Sexual Perversion," *Alienist and Neurologist,* January, 1896.
FOREL, *The Sexual Question.*
THOINOT and WEYSSE, *Medico-Legal Moral Offences.*

Kleptolagnia

The ancient term (it dates from the eighteenth century) " kleptomania," originally put forward as a " monomania," has never been generally accepted in medicine and has usually been denied altogether in law. When used it was generally meant to indicate simply a more or less irresistible impulse to theft, an obsession for which there is no conscious motive and which the subject (usually a woman) struggles against; it was regarded as most nearly allied with manic-depressive insanity. The tendency now is to allow it to drop out of use. When a " morbid impulse " is brought forward in court as a defence for theft it is too easy for the magistrate to retort: " That is what I am here to cure." But there is a fairly definite condition, not a vague obsession, but due to precise and traceable causes, which cannot so be dismissed, and comes before us here as within the sphere of sex psychology. This is the so-called " erotic kleptomania " for which the best name is probably " kleptolagnia." That name (to indicate the association of theft with sexual feeling, in analogy with " algolagnia ") was devised by the psychiatrist Kiernan, of Chicago, about 1917. I adopted it at once, and have ever since regarded it as the most suitable name for this condition. (Similarly " pyrolagnia " may be used for the rare condition of "erotic pyromania.") The condition itself seems to have been first recorded by Lacassagne, of Lyons, in 1896.

Kleptolagnia may be said to arise on the wide basis of algolagnia, that is to say, the association of pain, here in the form of anxiety, with sexual emotion. It had been vaguely touched on by various observers, who had not clearly understood it before French psychiatrists (such as Depouy in 1905) described definite cases. They showed that the mental process involved was really the process of sexual tumescence and detumescence symbolically transformed into an obsessive impulse, an impulse accompanied by resistance and struggle, to seize secretly some more or less worthless object —frequently a piece of silk or other stuff which could be, as the subject already knew, used to secure sexual excitement —culminating in an act of theft which corresponded to, and was sometimes actually accompanied by, sexual detumescence and emotional relief. No further value was attached to the stolen object, which was concealed or thrown away by the subject, usually a woman and often in good circumstances. She may not be clearly aware of the sexual source of her behaviour, and, if conscious, would not as a rule spontaneously avow it. We see that kleptolagnia is not truly a form of kleptomania though it used to be confused with it, for kleptomania is theoretically regarded as motiveless and irresistible, while in kleptolagnia there is a definite motive, whether or not conscious,—though that motive is not really theft,—and the act is not irresistible but carried out with reasonable precaution at a suitable moment. The subject, though often or always neurotic, is not necessarily highly psychopathic. We are not in the presence of insanity, and kleptolagnia is not to be put with the now almost extinct "kleptomania," but under sexual psychology; it may be regarded as a morbid form of erotic fetishism.

There are other less common combinations of sexual impulse with theft which, though allied, must be distinguished from kleptolagnia as here understood. One such condition was specially described by Stekel in 1908. The theft here is not erotic, that is, it is not a method of sexual gratification, and is not the theft of a fetish, but of any object appearing to offer sexual suggestion. It is a substitute for sexual gratification, occurring especially in women with repressed emotions due to the impotency of their husbands. Stekel put it forward as an explanation of all kleptomania, an explanation which falls if we dismiss the entity of "kleptomania."

Another distinct combination of theft with sexual emotion has been described and clearly demonstrated by Healy. These cases occur in youths as well as girls who are led into sexual temptations which appear so abhorrent and wicked to them that they yield to what seems the less abhorrent temptation to steal. The mental process here is the reverse of that found in kleptolagnia, for the theft is not a real or symbolic gratification of sexual desire, but an escape from it.

BIBLIOGRAPHY

HAVELOCK ELLIS, *Studies in the Psychology of Sex,* Vol. VII, "Kleptolagnia."

HEALY, *Mental Conflicts and Misconduct.*

STEKEL, *Peculiarities of Behaviour.*

Exhibitionism

Another symbolistic manifestation of the sexual impulse, serious in adult life, may occur innocently, and not abnormally, in childhood. This is exhibitionism. Several writers have pointed out that at puberty, and even in adolescence, an impulse of ostentation extending to the developing organs of sex (in girls more especially to the breasts) is not uncommon. It is a common infantile tendency which seems perfectly natural. Freud refers to the exhilaration even very young children experience in nakedness ; they love to dance about naked before going to bed, often raising their little garments, even before strangers, a reminiscence, as Freud views it, of a lost Paradisiacal state, to become later in exhibitionists a morbid obsession, and often even normally re-asserted after puberty in a definite though restrained form. Putnam thought that the frequency with which we dream of being in an insufficiently dressed state reveals a latent exhibitionism, though this view I cannot accept: it is overlooked that during sleep we actually are in such a state. Sometimes in childhood it is a mutual practice (even to the age of twelve) as a manifestation of simple interest in the sexual organs; it is often also due to an impulse of mischief or rebellion, though, when persistent, it may have an obscure sexual cause, and be the sign of an irritation seeking unknown relief, a kind of vicarious masturbation, to be dealt with in the same manner as ordinary masturbation. In adults exhibitionism is more definitely a symbol of coitus, and its forms fall into several groups.

First described and named by Lasègue in 1877, Exhibitionism is a form of erotic symbolism in which an adequate equivalent of coitus is found in the simple act of deliberately exhibiting the sexual organ to persons of the opposite sex, usually by preference to young and presumably innocent persons, often children. It would appear to be a not infrequent phenomenon, and most women, once or more in their lives, especially when young, have encountered a man who has thus deliberately exposed himself before them. It is indeed the commonest sexual offence, and Norwood East found that of 291 sexual offenders received for trial or on remand at Brixton Prison as many as 101 were cases of "indecent exposure," though it must be added that sexual offenders were, altogether, only about 4 per cent. of the total number of prisoners.

The exhibitionist, though often a young and apparently vigorous man, is satisfied with the mere act of self-exhibition and the emotional reaction which that act produces; he seldom makes demands on the woman to whom he exposes himself; he seldom speaks, he makes no effort to approach her; as a rule, he fails even to display the signs of sexual excitation. He seldom masturbates; his desires are completely gratified by the act of exhibition and by the emotional reaction he supposes that it arouses in the woman. He departs satisfied and relieved.

Various classifications of exhibitionism have been put forward; thus Maeder recognized three forms: (1) the *infantile*, to gaze and to be gazed at being normal in childhood; (2) the *senile*, which is a method of sexual excitement in the impotent; and (3) exhibitionism as a *method of sexual invitation*, which may occur in fairly normal persons of defective virility. This classification may not be complete, but it rightly insists on the element of sexual weakness, which is significant in exhibitionism, and on the fact that the aberration has a normal basis in the common actions of childhood. Krafft-Ebing divided exhibitionists into four clinical groups: (1) acquired states of mental weakness with cerebral or spinal disease clouding consciousness and at the same time causing impotence; (2) epileptics in whom the act is an abnormal organic impulse performed in a state of imperfect consciousness; (3) a somewhat allied group of neurasthenic cases; (4) periodical impulsive cases with deep hereditary taint. This classification is not altogether satisfactory. Norwood East for practical purposes divided exhibitionists into two main groups: the *psychopathic* (about two thirds of the whole with "visionaries" and mental defectives predominating), and the *depraved* (who have a vicious motive and include the remaining one-third). Most cases fall into one or other of two mixed groups (1) cases in which there is more or less congenital abnormality, but otherwise a fair or even complete degree of mental integrity; they are usually young adults, they are more or less conscious of the end they wish to attain, and it is often only with a severe struggle that they yield to their impulses; (2) cases in which the beginnings of mental or nervous disorder or alcoholic degeneration have diminished the sensibility of the higher centres; these subjects are sometimes old men (clergymen, etc.) whose lives have been absolutely correct; they are often only vaguely aware of the nature of the satisfaction they are seeking, and frequently no struggle precedes the manifestation; with rest and restorative treatment the health may be improved and the acts cease. It is in the first class of cases alone that there is a developed sexual anomaly. In the cases of the second class there is a more or less definite sexual intention, but it is only just conscious, and the emergence of the impulse is due not to its strength but to the weakness, temporary or permanent, of the higher inhibiting centres. Of this alcohol is a common cause, either by causing real mental confusion or by liberating latent tendencies; Norwood East remarks that the decreased consumption of alcohol in England has been accompanied by decrease in the number of convictions for indecent exposure (in England and Wales in 1913, 866 men were so convicted, in 1923 and among a larger population only 548).

Epileptic cases, with loss of consciousness during the act, can only be regarded as presenting a pseudo-exhibitionism. They are not so common as is sometimes supposed; Norwood East found none in a series of 150 cases (though epileptics were among them) and remarks that in his experience these cases are not as frequent as they are dramatic. It is undoubtedly true that cases of real or apparent exhibitionism may occur in epileptics, as was clearly shown by Pelanda in Verona many years ago. We must not, however, too hastily conclude that because these acts occur in epileptics they are necessarily unconscious acts. When the act of pseudo-exhibitionism is truly epileptic, it has no psychic sexual content, and it will certainly be liable to occur under all sorts of circumstances, when the patient is alone or in a miscellaneous concourse of people. It corresponds exactly to the cases in which epileptics sometimes carry out the act of urination, during a psychic attack, in an apparently purposive but really unconscious manner. Such an act is automatic, unconscious, and involuntary; the spectators are not even perceived; it cannot be an act of exhibitionism, for the act of exhibition implies deliberate and conscious intention. Whenever, on the other hand, the place and the time are evidently chosen deliberately—a quiet spot, the presence of only one or two young women or children—it is difficult to admit that we are in the presence of a fit of epileptic unconsciousness, even when the subject is known to be epileptic.

Excluding these epileptic pseudo-exhibitionists, who, from the legal point of view, are clearly irresponsible, it must still be remembered that in exhibitionism there is usually either a high degree of mental abnormality on a neuropathic basis, or else actual disease. This is true to a greater extent in exhibitionism than in almost any other form of sexual deviation. No subject of exhibitionism should be sent to prison without expert medical examination. Hirschfeld believes that the exhibitionist is never mentally normal. In some cases the impulse to exhibitionism may be overcome or may pass away. This result is more likely to come about in those cases in which exhibitionism has been largely conditioned by chronic alcoholism or other influences tending to destroy the inhibiting and restraining action of the higher centres, which may be overcome by hygiene and treatment. When it occurs in youth it tends to be spontaneously outgrown, as in the masochistic Rousseau who records that as a boy he once or twice displayed his nates to girls at a distance. When travelling through Moravia many years ago I noted a young woman who had been bathing in a stream near the railway line and as the train passed turned her back to it and raised her chemise. (Here we have to bear in mind the ancient method of exorcism by displaying the nates, later degenerating into a way of showing contempt especially practised by women.) True exhibitionism is rare in the female except in childhood. As Douglas Bryan puts it, women in exhibitionism treat the whole body as a penis to be exposed.

Exhibitionism is an act which, on the face of it, may seem nonsensical or meaningless, but it is wildly extravagant to regard it as necessarily an inexplicable act of madness, such as it was once, if not still, frequently treated both by writers on insanity and on sexual perversion, even though in its extreme form it may be associated with either.

We must regard exhibitionism as fundamentally a symbolic act based on a perversion of courtship. The exhibitionist, if a male, displays the organ of sex to a feminine witness, and in the shock of modest sexual shame by which she reacts to that spectacle he finds a gratifying similitude of the normal emotions of coitus. He feels that he has effected a psychic defloration.

Exhibitionism is thus analogous, and indeed related, to

the impulse felt by many persons to perform indecorous acts or tell indecent stories before young and innocent persons of the opposite sex. This also is a kind of exhibitionism, the gratification it causes lying exactly, as in physical exhibitionism, in the emotional confusion which it is felt to arouse, though we cannot accept the view of Näcke that exhibitionism is simply a form of sadism and the satisfaction felt only due to the horror aroused. The two kinds of exhibitionism may be combined in the same person.

It is of interest to point out that the sexual symbolism of active flagellation is very closely analogous to this symbolism of exhibitionism. The flagellant approaches a woman with the rod (itself a symbol of the penis and in some countries bearing names which are also applied to that organ), to inflict on an intimate part of her body the signs of blushing and the spasmodic movements which are associated with sexual excitement, while at the same time she feels, or the flagellant imagines that she feels, the corresponding emotions of delicious shame. It is an even closer mimicry of the sexual act than the exhibitionist attains, for the latter fails to secure the consent of the woman nor does he enjoy any intimate contact with her naked body. The difference is connected with the fact that the active flagellant is usually a more virile and normal person than the exhibitionist. There is, however, only analogy here and not identity; we must not regard the exhibitionist (as is sometimes done) as a sadist. In the majority of cases the exhibitionist's sexual impulse is feeble, and he may even be suffering from an early stage of general paralysis, senile dementia, or other enfeebling cause of mental disorganization, such as chronic alcoholism. Sexual feebleness is further indicated by the fact that the individuals selected as witnesses are frequently mere children.

Psychologically the exhibitionist's act is not so inexplicable as on the surface it may appear. He is usually a shy and timid person, sometimes of rather infantile constitution; and his act is a violent reaction against his disposition. Fetishists are also apt to be similarly shy and reserved, and Hirschfeld has insisted that there is frequently an element of fetishism in the exhibitionist. He would indeed recognize two factors as present in all these cases: (1) an endogenous and neurotic factor, and (2) an exogenous factor which is usually fetishistic. It is never the face that excites the exhibitionist but, much more usually, the legs, which is why, Hirschfeld believes, the spectacle of children and schoolgirls so often induces these acts, as they are most likely to display naked legs.

The reaction aroused by the act may fall into one of three groups: (1) the girl is frightened and runs away; (2) she is indignant and abuses the culprit; (3) she is pleased or amused, and laughs or smiles. It is the last reaction which affords the exhibitionist most satisfaction.

It seems probable that a form of erotic symbolism somewhat similar to exhibitionism is to be found in the rare cases in which sexual gratification is derived from throwing ink, acid, or other defiling liquids on women's white dresses. Moll, Thoinot, Hirschfeld, and others have recorded cases of this kind. Thoinot considers that in these cases the fleck is the fetish. That is an incorrect account of the matter. The white garments in most cases probably constitute the primary fetish, but that fetish becomes more acutely realized, and at the same time both parties are thrown into an emotional state which to the fetishist becomes a mimicry of coitus, by the act of defilement. We may perhaps connect with this phenomenon the attraction which muddy shoes often exert over the shoe fetishist. Restif de la Bretonne associated his love of neatness in women with his attraction to the feet, the part, he remarks, least easy to keep clean.

Garnier applied the term *sadi-fetishism* to active flagellation and many similar manifestations such as we are here concerned with, on the ground that they are hybrids which combine the morbid adoration for a definite object with the impulse to exercise a more or less degree of violence. From the standpoint of the conception of erotic symbolism I have adopted there is no need for this term. There is here no hybrid combination of two unlike mental states. We are simply concerned with states of erotic symbolism, more or less complete, more or less complex.

The conception of exhibitionism as a process of erotic symbolism involves a conscious or unconscious attitude of attention in the exhibitionist's mind to the psychic reaction of the woman toward whom his display is directed. He seeks to cause an emotion which, probably in most cases, he desires should be pleasurable. But from one cause or another his finer sensibilities are inhibited or in abeyance, and he is unable to estimate accurately either the impression he is likely to produce or the general results of his action, or else he is moved by a strong impulsive obsession which overpowers his judgment. In many cases he has good reason for believing that his act will be pleasurable rather than the reverse, and frequently finds complacent witnesses among low-class servant girls, etc.

But the exhibitionist usually wishes to produce more than a mere titillated amusement; he seeks a powerful effect which must be emotional whether or not it is pleasurable. There is sometimes an evident effort—on the part of a weak, vain, and effeminate man—to produce a maximum of emotional effect. The attempt to heighten the emotional shock is also seen in the fact that the exhibitionist may choose a church as the scene of his exploits, not during service, for he always avoids a concourse of people, but perhaps towards evening when there are only a few kneeling women scattered through the edifice. The church is chosen, from no impulse to commit a sacrilegious outrage—which, as a rule, the exhibitionist does not feel his act to be—but because it really presents the conditions most favourable to the act and the effects desired, " just what is necessary," as one such said, " for an exchange of impressions." " What are they thinking? What do they say to each other about me? Oh! how I should like to know!" A patient of Garnier's, who haunted churches for this purpose, made the significant statement: " Why do I like going to churches? I can scarcely say. *But I know that it is only there that my act has its full importance.* The woman is in a devout frame of mind, and she must see that such an act in such a place is not a joke in bad taste or a disgusting obscenity; *that if I go there it is not to amuse myself; it is more serious than that!* I watch the effect produced on the faces of the ladies to whom I show my organs. I wish to see them express a profound joy, I wish, in fact, that they may be forced to say to themselves: *How impressive Nature is when thus seen!*" It is clear that we have here a trace of the same feeling which inspired ancient phallic worship, a feeling which is, indeed, sometimes found to-day, as Stanley Hall and others have pointed out, in youths at adolescence, as well as in women, though it is normally under restraint and merely exists as a certain pride in the possession of the fully developed male or female attributes.

That is why exhibitionism is in its most nearly normal forms a youthful manifestation. Norwood East found that as many as 57 of his 150 cases, over one-third, were below twenty-five years of age, the number gradually diminishing at successive later ages, while the great majority of the whole number are unmarried. That also is why so important a group (forty in Norwood East's cases) can be termed "visionaries." That is to say they are cultivating youthful fantasies of abnormal courtship, though, as East remarks, "in not a few one is reminded of the courtships of the farmyard and the love-antics and 'showing off' indulged in by certain animals."

It is by a pseudo-atavism that this phallicism is openly manifested by the exhibitionist. There is no true emergence of an ancestrally inherited instinct, but, by the paralysis or inhibition of the finer and higher feelings current in civilization, the exhibitionist is placed on the same mental level as the man of a more primitive age, and he thus presents the basis on which the impulses belonging to a lower culture may naturally take root and develop. When the hereditary neuropathic disturbance is not too profound there is often, under favourable conditions, a gratifying and complete return to normal conduct.

It will be seen that the exhibitionist is but carrying one stage further—as so often happens with sexual deviations—a sexual manifestation which has a primitive foundation, and within duly controlled limits and under proper conditions might even be considered legitimate.[1] He is often simply a too reckless narcissist. But under our present-day social conditions his conduct, however natural at its roots, cannot be tolerated ; it may lead to nervous or hysterical symptoms in the innocent girl who is subjected to it ; and the interference of the police is rightly called for.

But what is to be done with the exhibitionist when he is brought before the magistrate ? As Norwood East states, in a large proportion of cases the courts now themselves call for a report on the mental state. The problem has become a difficult one with the more intelligent view of sexual deviations which is tending to prevail. A small punishment has no effect ; a severe would be unjust and equally ineffective ; unless the offender is well-to-do he cannot be sent to an institution for expert investigation and treatment. I may here quote a letter from a friend who is a magistrate and a man of distinguished ability. " At quarter sessions yesterday there was a case of a man, a labourer, who had been repeatedly convicted of indecent exposure. The sentence was six months' hard labour. The difficulty seems to be twofold. One, there is, so far as we know, no place where such a man can be sent for detention and treatment, and two, as the prison doctor would only say the man was subnormal and would not certify, we had no power over him. The result is that a healthy man of 38, who may well live to be 68, will in six months be let loose and as likely as not repeat his offence. He had a very good army record. Other justices were much concerned about the case and I was cheered to notice that the feeling of the Bench was much against sending such a man to prison. The only alternative

[1] It must be remembered that it is only in recent times in England that nakedness has been regarded as a punishable offence. Before then it might be "indecent" but that was not an offence before the law until the eighteenth century. (In Ireland in the seventeenth century, as Fynes Moryson bears witness, aristocratic ladies would throw off their garments indoors, even in the presence of strangers.) I find indeed that as early as 1476 a London priest appeared before the Ecclesiastical Court charged with showing his privates to several women in the parish. No doubt his sacred profession led to scandal. We are not told that anything was done about it.

was to release him. Happily we are past the stage of flogging which is of course provided for under the Statute and would certainly have been inflicted two or three years ago."

Another magistrate, who is a physician and psycho-therapist, writes to me in this connection : " I have seen a good many such cases on the Bench ; they are very sad indeed. Some I have managed to get off ; others had to take their punishment 'according to the law.' There is no doubt that the majority need psycho-therapeutic treatment, being mental cases rather than criminal offenders. Many are genuinely horrified at their own practice which they strenuously try to control. Much propaganda is necessary in this matter to effect a change in the conventional outlook."

With regard to the therapeutic treatment, I should like to point out that it might be likely to prove effective if carried out in connection with a sun-bathing camp on nudist lines of the kind now becoming widely recognized and accepted. If the exhibitionist is often simply a narcissist of unusually pronounced type, presenting impulses which are not necessarily anti-social, and, indeed, under some conditions socially recognizable, to give him an opportunity for their legitimate manifestation is to confer upon him a new power of self-control. An exhibitionist who is encouraged to practise nudity among men and women who, being themselves completely nude, accept him as a matter of course is at once to gratify his narcissistic desires so far as they are innocent and to deprive them of their morbid intensity. If his impulses cannot be restrained within innocent limits, he faces the certainty that he will be deprived of the privilege conferred upon him. A wholesome and socializing channel is provided for an impulse which otherwise becomes isolating, perverse, and degrading.

The first advice to give to an exhibitionist who has not yet attracted the attention of the police is that he should never go out alone. Hirschfeld, who recognizes the importance of this rule, remarks that the advice is always taken in good part, for the exhibitionist tends to be in terror of his own impulses. When he is actually arrested and brought before the magistrate, the sensible and humane course on a first offence is to dismiss him with a warning on condition that he seeks medical advice. In many large towns there are now special clinics which are at the disposal of magistrates, police surgeons, and social workers at a negligible cost, and these should be oftener used. On the second offence there should be compulsory detention for at least a month in a home for examination and treatment. This is in line with the opinion of Forel that exhibitionists are not dangerous, and (unless when weak-minded) should not be detained for more than a short period for treatment in a mental home.

BIBLIOGRAPHY

KRAFFT-EBING, *Psychopathia Sexualis.*

HAVELOCK ELLIS, *Studies in the Psychology of Sex*, Vol. V, "Erotic Symbolism."

W. NORWOOD EAST, "Observations on Exhibitionism," *Lancet*, August 23rd, 1924.

Algolagnia (Sadism and Masochism)

Algolagnia is a convenient term (devised by Schrenck-Notzing) to indicate the connection between sexual excitement and pain, without reference to its precise differentiation into active and passive forms. The active form is commonly called *sadism*, after the Marquis de Sade (1740–1814), who illustrated it slightly in his life and largely in his books. The passive form is called *masochism*, after the Austrian novelist Sacher-Masoch (1836–1895), who has repeatedly described this sexual deviation, which he himself manifested, in his novels. Sadism is generally defined as sexual emotion associated with the wish to inflict pain, physical or moral, on the object of the emotion. Masochism is sexual emotion associated with the desire to be physically subjugated and morally humiliated by the person arousing the emotion. When fully developed, the actions which constitute the algolagnia—whether active or passive, whether real, simulated, symbolic, or only imagined—constitute in themselves an adequate gratification of the sexual impulse, and, in the last degree, ensure detumescence without the need for coitus.

The desirability of using the term algolagnia is shown by the existence of manifestations in this group which do not conveniently fall within the sphere of either sadism or masochism. Thus Krafft-Ebing and Moll refused to accept passive flagellation as masochistic, regarding it as simply a physical stimulant ; so it may be ; but in many cases it is definitely masochistic, active flagellation definitely sadistic. In either case there is an association of sexual emotion with pain. Thus the term "algolagnia" conveniently covers phenomena which are not always easy to include either under sadism or masochism.

Definitionally this merging of sadism with masochism is inconvenient, but psychologically it is sound. Masochism, as Freud put it, is sadism turned round on to the self, or we may say that sadism is masochism turned on to others. That indeed is the chief ground on which it is desirable to group sadism and masochism together under one heading. Clinically, they often exist separately, but there is no clear line of demarcation between them, and though it may be rare to find an element of sadism in the pure masochist, it is common to find an element of masochism in the sadist. Even de Sade himself was not a pure sadist, but had in him distinct elements of masochism clearly revealed in his works. The active and passive elements may be closely united, if not really identical. Thus a subject of mainly active algolagnia, for whom the whip is a stimulating fetish, writes : "My reaction is to the *active* side of the act. I have developed a slight interest for the passive side, but am convinced that this depends upon a semi-sub-conscious inversion or transference of the act, so that, though applied to me, it is imagined sub-consciously as applied by me to someone else." It is interesting to note, also, that while the masochist may sometimes seem masculine and robust in general temperament, the sadist is frequently a timid, delicate, and feminine personality. Thus Riedel, a sadist youth studied by Lacassagne (and finally sent to an asylum), who killed another boy, had voluptuous ideas of blood from the age of four and liked to play at killing, was of infantile physical development, very timid and delicate, modest (so that he could not urinate in the presence of another person), very religious, hating obscenity and immorality, and with a pleasant childlike face and expression. But the love of blood and murder was an irresistible obsession, and its gratification produced immense emotional relief. Another sadistic French youth, studied by A. Marie (and also sent to an asylum), was of similar temperament, very timid, easily blushing, unable to look even children in the eye, or to make advances to women, or to urinate in the presence of others.

Hirschfeld has sought to overcome some of the difficulties surrounding the definition of sadism and masochism by introducing the term *metatropism*, meaning thereby a kind of reversed or exchanged sexual attitude, the man taking on and exaggerating the normal feminine attitude of the woman, and the woman taking on and exaggerating the normal masculine attitude of the man. So that sadism in a man would merely be a heightening of the normal male sexual attitude, and masochism in a woman a heightening of the normal female sexual attitude, both sadism and masochism becoming totally different conditions according as they occur in a man or in a woman. Masculine sadism and feminine masochism are thus for Hirschfeld simply hyperæsthetic or erotomanic excesses of the normal sexual impulse, while in the opposite sex they become complete metatropic deviations from normality. This conception has not, however, been generally accepted. It awkwardly complicates the matter; it is based on a conception of normal sexuality which not all will accept; Hirschfeld himself admits that the sadistic man is often the reverse of virile, and the masochistic man the reverse of feminine in temperament, so that the metatropic conception is but lamely applicable. It still seems most convenient to speak of algolagnia, with its two opposite but often related forms of sadism and masochism, whether we are concerned with men or women.

A difficulty has been created out of the experiencing of pain as pleasure. In algolagnia, however, it is not the pain itself which is pleasure but the sexual emotion which it arouses. Algolagnic subjects are usually to be regarded as under-sexed rather than over-sexed, they present the reverse of the hyperæsthetic or the sexually athletic state. They need therefore a stronger than normal stimulus to arouse sexual activity. Strong sensations and strong emotions, even those of the most unlikely kind, such as anxiety and grief, are able to act as sexual stimuli, and so to produce pleasure though in themselves painful. Cullerre has brought forward a number of cases, mostly in persons manifesting symptoms of nervous exhaustion, both men and women, often highly moral people, in whom fits of anxiety and dread, sometimes of a religious character, terminated in spontaneous orgasm or masturbation. The widely extended implications of this fundamental psychological fact are taken advantage of, consciously or unconsciously, by the algolagnic subject to reinforce his feeble sexual impulse.

It must further be remembered that in a mild degree pain (with the associated emotions of shock, anxiety, disgust, contempt, etc.), whether witnessed in others or experienced in themselves, can for many people, especially if neurotically disposed, evoke a pleasurable psychic state without being intense enough to stimulate actually sexual sensations. The natural reaction to pain is pathetic or sympathetic; one is sorry for it in oneself, one is, to a less extent that varies with the affective nearness, sorry for it in others. But a certain element of pleasure or satisfaction is also possible. The classic expression of this is the passage in Lucretius (Book II.) concerning the feelings of the man safe on shore who witnesses others drowning, and it is interesting to see how Lucretius explained it: "It is sweet to contemplate from the shore the peril of the unhappy sailor struggling with death, not that we take pleasure in the misfortunes of others, but that it is consoling to view evils we are not experiencing." On newspaper placards there is no more frequent, and therefore presumably alluring, adjective than "amazing," and the "amazing" usually involves an element of pain or shock. The Grand Guignol type of play always finds fascinated spectators for its horrors, and it is noteworthy that the novels in which painful situations are made amusing, and pathetic figures ridiculous, are frequently the popular works of writers of high ability. It is evident that in a mild degree an element of what may be termed non-sexual sadism and masochism (what the Germans term *Schadenfreude*) is fairly widespread among the general population.

When we bear these considerations in mind we may understand how it is that the sadist is by no means necessarily impelled by the desire to be cruel. It is emotion that he is concerned to arouse, as well as to feel, more than pain. This is, for instance, illustrated by the active algolagnic subject already quoted, a man of intellectual habits and not extremely sadistic: "The actual act of whipping is the source of the fascination. There is absolutely no desire to humiliate the subject. She must feel pain, but *only as an expression of the vigour of the whipping*. The infliction of pain itself gives me no pleasure; on the contrary it is a source of repugnance to me. Apart from this sexual anomaly, I have a great dislike of cruelty. I have only once killed an animal and remember it with regret."

Our attention is apt to be fixed on the presence of pain in algolagnia because we fail to realize all the psychic phenomena involved. It is as though a musical instrument were sensitive: the supposition would be reasonable that a musical performance is the infliction of pain, and we should certainly have would-be scientific and analytical people concluding that the pleasure of music is the pleasure of giving pain, and that the emotional effect of music is due to the pain thus inflicted.

Algolagnia covers some of the most extravagant manifestations of the abnormal sexual impulse. Sadism leads to the most violent outrages against human nature; masochism to the most fantastic humiliations of human nature. It is, therefore, important to remember that both sadism and masochism are based on normal human impulses; they are the extreme term of tendencies which in a slight degree are strictly within the biological sphere.

The normal basis of algolagnia is complex and manifold. There are especially two elements to be borne in mind in this connection: (1) pain, inflicted or suffered, is a by-product of the process of courtship, alike in the lower animals and in man; (2) pain, more especially in enfeebled nervous conditions, congenital or acquired, is a nervous stimulant, whether suffered or inflicted, and is capable of acting powerfully on the sexual centres. If we steadily bear in mind these two fundamental factors we have little difficulty in comprehending the mechanism of the algolagnic processes, various as they are in form, and we have the clue to their psychology. Every algolagnic form of the sexual impulse is either a hypertrophied manifestation (sometimes perhaps atavistic in character) of some primitive phase of courtship, or it is the attempt of an enfeebled organism to secure a powerful aphrodisiacal aid to the attainment of tumescence.

All love, as the old English writer, Robert Burton, long since said, is a kind of slavery. The lover is his mistress's servant; he must be ready to undertake all sorts of risks, to encounter many dangers, to fulfill many unpleasant duties, in order to serve her and to gain her favour. Romantic poetry is full of evidence of this attitude of the lover. The further back we go among savages, towards primitive conditions, the more marked, on the whole, becomes this subjection of the lover in courtship and the severity of the trials he must undergo to win his mistress's favour. Among animals, the same thing is witnessed in a still cruder form; the male must exert his energies in the highest to win the female, and he often returns maimed and bleeding from contests with a successful rival. Alike to suffer pain and to inflict pain is an incidental if not essential part of courtship. The female, on her part, is inextricably mixed up in the same process, either by sympathetic or reciprocal, influences. And if in the process of courtship the wooer is her slave and she is able to view with pleasure the sufferings she is the cause of, alike to successful and unsuccessful wooers, she in turn becomes subjugated to her mate and later to her offspring, receiving her full share of the pain which the sexual process involves. Sometimes even in the course of courtship the female suffers pain, as among many birds when the male at mating time falls into a state of sexual frenzy, and the more passive female suffers : thus the chaffinch is a rough wooer, though as the female becomes submissive he is said to become gentle and considerate. The love-bite, again, is an animal as well as human device, and horses, donkeys, etc., gently bite the female before coitus.

That the infliction of pain is a sign of love is a widespread idea both in ancient and modern times. Lucian makes a woman say : " He who has not rained blows on his mistress and torn her hair and her garments is not yet in love." The same idea, that for a man to beat his sweetheart is an appreciated sign of love, occurs in one of Cervantes's *Exemplary Novels*, " Rinconete and Cortadillo." And a patient of Janet's said of her husband : " He does not know how to make me suffer a little. One cannot love a man who does not make one suffer a little." Reversely, Millament says in Congreve's *Way of the World*, " One's cruelty is one's power."

But algolagnic manifestations are more than a mere atavistic exaggeration of normal manifestations of courtship. They are, especially in organically feeble organisms, the manifestation of an instinctive attempt to re-inforce the sexual impulse. The incidental emotions of courtship, viz., anger and fear, are themselves stimulants to sexual activity. It thus becomes possible to invoke anger or fear artificially in order to strengthen a failing sexual impulse. The most convenient method of doing this is by the action of pain : if the pain is inflicted we are in the presence of sadism, if suffered in the presence of masochism, if simply witnessed we are in an intermediate stage which may be tinged with either sadism or masochism according to the direction of the sympathies of the algolagnic spectator. From this point of view the sadist and the masochist alike merely use pain as a method of drawing on a great reservoir of primitive emotion, which imparts energy to a feeble sexual impulse.

When we understand the foundations on which algolagnic deviations rest, we see that they have only an accidental and not an essential association with cruelty. It is not the desire to be cruel which impels the sadist, however cruel he may be in actual fact. He wishes to arouse his own flagging emotions, and in order to do so he in many cases arouses the emotions of his victim; the most potent method of doing so he knows of is to give her pain. But he frequently desires that she shall feel this pain as pleasure. Even in the sphere of normal love a man will often inflict small pains or hardships on the woman he loves, and all the time be anxious that she should like them, or even experience pleasure in them. The sadist merely goes a step further, and (as in one recorded case) sticks pins into the girl while insisting that she shall all the time wear a smiling face; it is not his wish to be cruel, he would prefer to give pleasure, though he is content with the mere appearance of the victim's pleasure. Even when the sadist goes so far as to kill his victim he is moved not by the desire to cause death, but to shed blood, so securing the emotional stimulus which is imparted almost universally by the spectacle of shed blood, and Leppmann has acutely observed that in sadistic crimes it is usual to find the wound in those parts of the body, like the neck or the abdomen, which will lead to the maximum shedding of blood.

Similarly the masochist has no wish to suffer cruelty. In that slight degree of passive algolagnia which Krafft-Ebing, Moll, and others regard as simply a heightened degree of a normal attitude and entitle "sexual subjection" (*Hörigheit*), there need be no serious violence, either physical or psychic, but only a complacent acceptance of the caprices and domination of the beloved person. There is no clear line of demarcation between sexual subjection and masochism—apart from the important fact that in sexual subjection the normal impulse to coitus remains, while in masochism it tends to be replaced by an abnormal impulse—and the masochist retains the same pleasure, and even in many cases ecstasy, as he experiences the manifold ill-treatment he desires. This ill-treatment may involve the reality, or the simulacrum, of a great many actions: binding and fettering, trampling, semi-strangulation, the performance of menial duties and tasks commonly felt to be disgusting by the beloved person, verbal abuse, etc. For the masochist such acts have become the equivalent of coitus, and the idea of cruelty, and in most cases even pain, never enters. If we bear this in mind the elaborate hypotheses which some psychologists (even Freud) have ingeniously constructed to explain masochism are seen to be completely unnecessary.

The manifestations of masochism, from their nature, are of little social significance and involve comparatively little danger to the community. It has thus come about that, though algolagnic phenomena of this kind may be traced far back in the history of civilization, masochism was not regarded as a definite perversion until Krafft-Ebing presented his masterly exposition of its characteristics in his *Psychopathia Sexualis.* Sadism, closely related as it is to masochism on the biological and psychological sides, has a very different social and medico-legal significance. Though at one end its variations range from so innocent and normal a manifestation as the love-bite, they extend to the most serious and dangerous anti-social acts as illustrated by the notorious case of " Jack the Ripper," the extreme type of a group of cases, not so very uncommon, which involve wounding from erotic motives, though by no means always murder. (This class of cases was especially studied by Lacassagne.) In another important group of cases, schoolmasters, mistresses, and other persons in authority over children and servant girls torture their charges from sadistic motives.

Sadism is manifested both by men and women. Masochism is more especially found in men ; this may be in part because in women a certain degree of sexual subjection, the primary stage of masochism, may fairly be regarded as almost normal, and in part because (as Moll pointed out) masochism being largely due to an attempt to attain a substitute or a stimulus for an enfeebled potency, women, who are normally more passive in the sexual act, do not require it.

Sadism and masochism, as has already been said, do not exhaust the manifestations of algolagnia. In the large sense, algolagnia is a great sub-division of erotic symbolism, and it includes all the cases in which sexual pleasure is associated, actively or passively, in reality or in simulation or in imagination, with pain, anger, fear, anxiety, shock, constraint, subjection, humiliation, and allied psychic states; for all these states involve recourse to a great reservoir of primitive emotion which may be utilized to reinforce the sexual impulse. It is in this way that flagellation—whether inflicted, suffered, witnessed, or thought about—may in some predisposed persons act as a sexual stimulant from almost the earliest age. In most cases both physical and psychic elements enter into the influence, and an important and extensive group of algolagnic cases is thus formed. In other cases the mere spectacle of various events which produce an emotional shock—such as an earthquake, or a bull-fight, or even the death and funeral of relations—acts erotically apart from any definite sadistic or masochistic attitude in the subject of the emotions.

Looked at broadly, the sphere of algolagnia is thus very large. There are, moreover, certain groups of cases which lie on its frontier though they may perhaps more accurately be classed with erotic fetishism. Garnier attempted to set up a group of "sadi-fetishistic" cases; but a case which he brought forward scarcely seems to prove the contention, for it belongs to the class of foot-fetishism. Abraham, while admitting diminished sexual activity, thought this need not be primary, but sometimes due to suppression or paralysis of an originally strong libido. He referred to the suggestion of Freud that osphresiolagnia and coprolagnia may sometimes play a part in the genesis of foot-fetishism, these elements later receding as unæsthetic, the visual pleasure remaining.

An occasional combination of algolagnia and fetishism is termed corset-fetishism. Here the corset is a kind of fetish, but its attraction is associated with pressure sensations and the attraction of fetters. Karl Abraham elaborated the rather complex case of a male student of twenty-two who presented foot-fetishism and corset-fetishism and the attraction of a fettering pressure as well as osphresiolagnia or the love of agreeable body odours, this last being regarded as the original manifestation and shown in relation to the subject's mother. There was also anal and urethral erotism. As in a case of a girl already mentioned, the subject in early life would sit on his heel pressed to the anus. There were eonist tendencies and he desired to be a woman in order to lace himself tightly and wear uncomfortable and polished high-heel shoes. The subject began to fetter himself at puberty in an old corset of his mother's, and there was no accidental association found to account for the fetishisms.

Necrophily, or vampyrism, the sexual attraction of corpses, is again a phenomenon often included under sadism. In such cases there is, strictly, no pain inflicted or suffered, so that we are not here concerned with sadism or masochism, but, in so far as the sexual stimulation may be said to be due to the emotional shock of the contact with a dead body, these cases come under the broad definition of algolagnia. Occasionally they may be said to belong more accurately to the group of erotic fetishism. When, however, we investigate these cases in their clinical aspects they are generally found to be in a high degree psychopathic, or mental feebleness is present; they are usually dull-witted and insensitive persons, not infrequently anosmic (as in the typical " vampire du Muy " recorded by Epaulard); they are men whom women reject, and their resort to corpses is almost a kind of masturbation, or at all events comparable to bestiality. The cases in which the corpse is not only violated but mutilated, as in the famous old case of Sergeant Bertrand, have sometimes been termed *necro-sadism*. There is of course here no real sadism in the narrow sense; Bertrand began with phantasies of ill-treating women, later imagining that the women were corpses; the sadistic ideas were incidents in the emotional evolution, the object throughout being not to inflict cruelty but to procure strong emotion; any mutilation is carried out in order to increase the emotional excitement. Such cases are highly abnormal.

BIBLIOGRAPHY

KRAFFT-EBING, *Psychopathia Sexualis*.

HAVELOCK ELLIS, *Studies in the Psychology of Sex*, Vol. III, " Love and Pain."

STANLEY HALL, "A Study of Fears," *American Journal of Psychology*, 1897 and 1899.
W. A. F. BROWNE, "Necrophilism," *Journal of Mental Science*, January, 1875.
FREUD, "The Economic Problem in Masochism," *Collected Papers*, Vol. II, and "Instincts and their Vicissitudes," *ib.*, Vol. IV.

Sexual Senility

There is a frequent well marked tendency in women at the menopause to an eruption of sexual desire, the last flaring up of a dying fire, which may easily take on a morbid form. Similarly in men, when the approach of age begins to be felt, the sexual impulse may become suddenly urgent. In this instinctive reaction it may tend to roam, normally or abnormally, beyond legitimate bounds. This tendency is by no means confined to men who have been lovers of women in youth; it is sometimes most conspicuous in those men who in earlier life have been severely restrained by moral considerations and now act from a sort of subconscious impulse to make up for lost time before it is too late. It is the experience of most women that sexual attempts on them in early life—the most daring and, it must be added, often the most successful attempts—have been made not by young men, whose attitude towards the women who attract them tends to be more respectful and even reverential, but by elderly married men, often by those whose character and position render such attempts extremely unlikely.

Apart from senility, there seems (as Leppmann long since concluded) to be no congenital perversion directed towards children. There may exceptionally be a repressed subconscious impulse towards unripe girls, but the chief contingent before old age is furnished by the weak-minded.

It has to be recognized that with the advance of age there is not only the liability to this eruption of sexual activity, but also to the development of a certain egotism and callousness which facilitates its manifestations. This is in other respects beneficial because it protects enfeebled old age from the risks of strong emotion, but it is liable to abuses of which the most dangerous occur if there arises an efflorescence of activity in the sexual sphere.

This late exacerbation of sexuality becomes still more dangerous if it takes the form of an attraction to girls who are no more than children, and to acts of indecent familiarity with children. There is normally an attraction, of a more or less sexual character, on the part of the elderly towards the young ; it is a counterpart of the sexual attraction often felt by young girls towards elderly men and by boys towards adult women. But in old men the attractiveness of the young may take on an abnormal and mischievous form owing to the senile decline of potency which renders mere sexual contacts an adequate gratification. The older the man the more easily he is satisfied and the less compunction he appears to find in seeking such satisfaction, so that in sexual assaults, as Brouardel long ago showed, the average age of the victim regularly decreases as the average age of the perpetrator increases. So long as the physical state is fairly sound and the mental state fairly intact, such impulses, when they occur, are doubtless easily restrained, and we are not called upon to regard as morbid, even if it is sexually tinged, the pleasure which the aged take in the freshness of the young. But with physical irritation, such as may arise from an enlarged prostate, and with psychic loss of control from incipient mental decay, there is risk that the barriers may be removed, and the man become a danger to himself and to others. It is in this way sometimes that senile dementia begins to declare itself before intellectual failure is obvious.

It was formerly thought (as by Krafft-Ebing and Leppmann) that offences against children occur in old men mentally sound as a simple result of " satiety " in normal sexual relationships, but this is doubtful. Hirschfeld in his wide experience has never seen a child violator who was mentally sound. There should certainly always be a careful psychiatric investigation.

BIBLIOGRAPHY

KRAFFT-EBING, *Psychopathia Sexualis.*
THOINOT and WEYSSE, *Medico-Legal Aspects of Moral Offences.*

The Social Attitude Towards Sexual Deviations

"The pathology of love is a Hell of which the gate must never be opened," said Remy de Gourmont in his *Physique de l'Amour*. That melodramatic declaration could only have been made by a philosopher of love, however admirable on his own lines, who was without scientific training, and it is surprising to find it endorsed by a gynæcologist like Van de Velde. It is a great thing, as Aristotle said, to be a master of metaphor, and here a Gate of Hell is the wrong metaphor. We are not here on the stage of a divine comedy such as Dante presented, but in the realm of biology, where the physiological is for ever passing into the pathological, and blending with it almost imperceptibly, without the opening of any gate. The elements of pathology are already to be found in the physiological, and pathological processes are still following the laws of physiology. Every normal man in matters of sex, when we examine him carefully enough, is found to show some abnormal elements, and the abnormal man is merely manifesting in a disordered or extravagant shape some phase of the normal man. Normal and abnormal, taken in the mass, can all be plotted as variations of different degree on the same curve. The loving woman who exclaims: "I could eat you!" is connected by links, each in itself small, with Jack the Ripper. We all possess within us, in a more or less developed form, the germs of atrocities.

It is not, therefore, because it is "abnormal" that a sexual act becomes reprehensible. That view once prevailed. A narrow conception of what is "natural" was held; everything else was "unnatural" and to be vituperated, if not to be punished, even severely punished, for it was perhaps a crime, almost certainly a sin.

Now that our knowledge of what is "natural" has grown, and the existence of endless variations in nature has to be admitted, a different conception is tending to prevail. We find that we have to discriminate. The question is no longer: Is the act abnormal? It becomes: Is the act injurious? Society is not concerned with the varieties of sexual couples, but with the question of determining those variations which inflict injury. That question is of some importance since it is believed by experienced physicians that many "perversions," as such variations of sexual activity are still usually called, have become more common during recent years. Numerous causes may contribute to this result. In part, significance is attached to a diminution of prostitution, and to a greater repugnance to intercourse with prostitutes, with the substitution of sexual gratification with women who, through moral scruples or fears of pregnancy, are unwilling to permit actual intercourse.

In addition there is probably to be considered a greater degree of refinement in the advance of civilization, which leads lovers to find pleasure in ways which among primitive folk, or even between themselves in the absence of passionate love, might appear disgusting. There are, of course, also, those who by some deep-rooted deviation of sexual feeling, such as inversion or masochism or fetishism, can only find sexual satisfaction possible when the stimulus reaches them through some abnormal channel. Even here what we call a "perversion," when not carried to an extreme point, is, as Wolbarst states, "often found as a normal constituent in the lives of normal individuals." Freud, indeed, has said, and probably with truth, that there is no healthy person in whom some such element of "perversity" does not sometimes occur.

The conclusion we are to-day slowly reaching is that the abnormal gratification of the sexual impulse, however unusual or even repugnant it may seem, calls for no condemnation or interference, except in two classes of cases, the one affecting medicine, and the other the law. That is to say, in the first class, the subject of the abnormal activity may be injuring his health, in which case he needs medical or psycho-therapeutic treatment. Or, in the second case, he may be injuring the health or the rights of his partner or of a third party, in which case the law is entitled to interfere. There are a number of various ways in which this may happen, while there are also various ways in which in different countries the law reacts, or, in the opinion of some, should react, to the injury inflicted. Such injuries are the seduction of a minor, the injury to conjugal rights by adultery, the conveyance of a venereal disease by intercourse, the infliction of what on the objective side (even if not so intended) is cruelty to obtain sexual gratification, etc. On many of these questions there is general agreement. A matter on which there is still wide difference of opinion, and in different countries of practice, is with regard to homosexuality, with the manifestations of which we shall be concerned in the next chapter.

Homosexuality has always and everywhere existed. It is one of the intersexual conditions within the natural and inevitable range of variations. Apart from that, and apart also from being based on the relative sexual indifference of early life, it has in some lands and in some cultures been popular as a fashion or cherished as an ideal. It cannot be eradicated either by legal enactments, however severe, or by social reprehension. In the early Christian centuries, after the State had, with Constantine, been captured for the new religion, homosexuality was the object of ferocious decrees, and in France, even to the eve of the Revolution, pæderasts were occasionally burnt. After the Revolution, however, with the Code Napoléon, all acts of simple homosexuality carried out in private by consenting adults ceased to be punishable, though still severely punished if effected in public or with a minor. That rule is now followed in those lands which have been influenced by the Code Napoléon. In other countries, however, and notably in England and the United States, the ancient harsh attitude still persists and it seems difficult to modify the old laws ; all that has so far been done is, in some degree, to refrain from carrying them out.

There is much still to be effected by the growth, which we are bound to expect, of a more enlightened attitude in society. Apart from the consideration that sexual acts and attitudes, when not made a cause of public offence, are for the persons concerned, and no one else, to decide, we have to remember that such acts and attitudes are largely the outcome of innate constitution. When so-called or seeming congenital cases of sexual deviation come before the physician, a difficult problem is sometimes presented. Shall he endeavour to make the patient " normal " when for him " normality " may be what for a genuinely normal person would be unnatural and a " perversion " ? I agree with Wolbarst that " we may possibly find ourselves on the correct road if we act on the theory that any sexual deviation which has always given satisfaction without injury to a particular individual must be considered normal for that individual," though it must be added that our attitude will be modified if at the same time injury is inflicted on some other individual. We are not called upon to attempt the fruitless task of drastic suppression, although we should facilitate the medical, or even surgical, treatment, of those who wish to escape from what they may find a burden, congenital or acquired, too heavy to be borne. We must aim not only to be just, but also to be sympathetic.

The greater tolerance in sexual matters now seen to be desirable is not alone a matter of justice to those persons who vary from the norm. It has weight in the whole social constitution and adds a new stability to the moral system. Not only is it a hopeless task to deal with sexual varieties as immoralities or crimes, but the moral system is thereby discredited by its failures, and the prevalence of varieties is fostered, for in such matters, as we know (it is now well recognized as regards alcohol), prohibitions are incitements. Licht, the historian of sexual manifestations in Greece, has pointed out the rarity of sexual perversions (homosexuality not being so regarded but as a normal supplement to marriage) in Greece. The reason was, he remarks, that for the Greeks sexual matters were outside morals (except where children or violence were involved), which was concerned only with injustice, offences against the State, and crimes. Where normal relationships are free, variations are not artificially fostered, and, if they occur, tend to pass unperceived. " It may sound paradoxical, but it is true," Wolbarst states, " that the spread of sexual perversion in American communities in recent years has been very largely fostered and abetted, unwittingly of course, by moral agencies."

We cannot expect or desire to return to Greek morality, and its ideal of " the beautiful alike in body and soul " may be out of our reach. But there can be little doubt that we shall gradually break down the false notions and the rigid attempts at legal and social prohibitions which have caused so much trouble and confusion in the sexual history of our recent past. In so doing we shall purify our spiritual atmosphere and strengthen our moral code by removing from it prescriptions which were merely a source of weakness.

BIBLIOGRAPHY

HAVELOCK ELLIS, *Studies in the Psychology of Sex*, Vol. II, " Sexual Inversion."
W. McDOUGALL, *Outline of Abnormal Psychology.*
A. L. WOLBARST, " Sexual Perversions : their Medical and Social Implications," *Medical Journal and Record*, July, 1931.
HANS LICHT, *Sexual Life in Ancient Greece.*

CHAPTER V

HOMOSEXUALITY

Sexual Inversion

WHEN the sexual impulse is directed towards persons of the same sex we are in the presence of an aberration variously known as "sexual inversion," "contrary sexual feeling," "uranism," or, more generally, "homosexuality," as opposed to normal heterosexuality. "Homosexuality" is the best general term for all forms of the anomaly, in distinction from normal heterosexuality, while "sexual inversion" is best reserved for apparently congenital and fixed forms. It is the most clearly defined of all sexual deviations, for it presents an impulse which is completely and fundamentally transferred from the normal object to an object which is normally outside the sphere of sexual desire, and yet possesses all the attributes which in other respects appeal to human affection. It is a highly abnormal aberration, and yet it seems to supply a greater satisfaction than any other aberration can furnish. It is probably this characteristic of sexual inversion which renders it so important. This importance is manifested in three ways: (1) its wide diffusion and the large part it has played in various epochs of culture; (2) its frequency in civilization to-day, and (3) the large number of distinguished persons who have manifested the aberration.

The fundamental and what may be called "natural" basis of homosexuality is manifested by its prevalence among animals. It is common among various mammals, and, as we should expect, is especially found among the Primates most nearly below Man. G. V. Hamilton, studying monkeys and baboons, states that "the immature male monkey typically passes through a period during which he is overtly and almost exclusively homosexual, and that this period is terminated at sexual maturity by an abrupt turning to heterosexual ways." Zuckerman has closely observed the homosexual behaviour of baboons and chimpanzees, sometimes finding it more pronounced in the females than in the males, and he is even inclined to assimilate homosexual and heterosexual behaviour among the apes, finding no pronounced differences.

Among many savage and barbarous peoples homosexuality has been conspicuous and sometimes treated with reverence. This was so even among the ancient civilizations on which our own is founded. It was known to the Assyrians, and the Egyptians, nearly four thousand years ago, attributed pæderasty to their gods Horus and Set. It has been associated not only with religion but with military virtues, and was in this way cultivated among the ancient Carthaginians, Dorians, and Scythians, as it was later by the Normans. Among the ancient Greeks, finally, it was idealized not merely in association with military virtue, but with intellectual, æsthetic, and even ethical qualities, and was by many regarded as more noble than normal heterosexual love. After the coming of Christianity it still held its ground, but it fell into disrepute, while as a psychological anomaly, consisting in an idealization of persons of the same sex even apart from homosexual acts, it was forgotten or unknown. It was only recognized after Justinian's time as sodomy, that is to say as a vulgar vice, or rather as a crime, deserving of the most severe secular and ecclesiastical penalties, even burning at the stake.

In the Middle Ages it is probable that sexual inversion flourished not only in camps, but also in cloisters, and it is constantly referred to in the Penitentials. It is not, however, until the Renaissance that it plays a conspicuous part in the world; Latini, Dante's teacher, was inverted, and Dante refers to the frequency of this perversion among men of intellect and fame. The distinguished French humanist Muret was from this cause in danger of death throughout his life; Michaelangelo, the greatest sculptor of the Renaissance, cherished homosexual ideals and passions, although there is no reason to suppose that he had physical relations with the men he was attracted to; Marlowe, one of the chief poets of the Renaissance in England, was clearly of the same way of feeling, as also, there is ground for believing, was Bacon.

It is quite true that the invert seldom places himself under a physician's hands. He usually has no wish to be different from what he is, and as his intelligence is generally quite up to the average level, if not above it, he is careful to avoid discovery and seldom attracts the attention of the police. In this way the prevalence of inversion is unknown to those who do not know where to look for it or how to detect it. In Germany, Hirschfeld, whose knowledge of homosexuality is unrivalled, has shown that a large number of separate estimates among different classes of the population reveal a proportion of inverted and bisexual persons varying between 1 and 5 per cent. In England my own independent observations, though of a much less thorough and extensive character, indicate a similar prevalence among the educated middle class, while among the lower social classes homosexuality is certainly not rare, and even if not innate there often appears to be among them a remarkable absence of repulsion to homosexual relations; many inverts have referred to this point. Among women, though less easy to detect, homosexuality appears to be scarcely less common than among men, in this respect unlike nearly all other aberrations; the pronounced cases are, indeed, perhaps less frequently met with than among men, but less marked and less deeply rooted cases are probably more frequent than among men. Some professions show a higher proportion of inverts than others. Inversion is not specially prevalent among scientific and medical men; it is more frequent among literary and artistic people, and in the dramatic profession it is often found. It is also specially common among hairdressers, waiters, and waitresses. Artistic aptitude of one kind or another, and a love of music, are found among a large proportion of educated inverts, in my experience as much as 68 per cent.

In America among the educated and professional classes, M. W. Peck among sixty college men in Boston, representing all departments of the University and College life, found seven who were definitely homosexual, six of them admitting adult overt experiences. Two others were clearly though unconsciously homosexual; he considers that 10 per cent. college men are homosexual, whether or not there are overt practices. G. V. Hamilton found that only forty-four of his 100 married women could deny all memory of homosexual play in early life; while forty-six men and twenty-three women owned to friendship with their own sex involving stimulation of the sexual organs. Katharine Davis found that 31·7 per cent. women admitted "intense emotional relations with other women," and 27·5 per cent. unmarried women admitted homosexual play in childhood, 48·2 per cent. of them dropping it after adolescence.

The importance of homosexuality is, again, shown by the prevalence of homosexual prostitution. This has been specially studied in Berlin, where the police tolerate it, on the same basis as female prostitution, in order to be able to control and limit its manifestations. Hirschfeld considers the number of male prostitutes in Berlin to be about 20,000; more recently and more cautiously Werner Picton estimates it as 6,000. More than one-third are judged to be psychopathic, less than a quarter of them to be homosexual themselves. Unemployment is a commonly assigned cause, as of female prostitution, but probably various other elements enter into the causation.

Although sexual inversion is thus so important a phenomenon it is only in recent times that it has received scientific study, or even recognition. This first took place in Germany. At the end of the eighteenth century two cases were published in Germany of men showing a typical emotional sexual attraction towards their own sex. But although Hössli, Caspar, and especially Ulrichs (who invented for it the term "uranism") further prepared the way, it was not until 1870 that Westphal published a detailed history of an inverted young woman, and clearly showed that the case was congenital and not acquired, so that it could not be termed a vice, and was also, though neurotic elements were present, not a case of insanity. From that moment the scientific knowledge of sexual inversion rapidly increased. Krafft-Ebing, who was the first great clinician of sexual inversion, brought together a large number of cases in his *Psychopathia Sexualis*, which was the earliest scientific book dealing with abnormal sexuality to attract general attention. Moll, with a more critical mind than was Krafft-Ebing's, and a wider scientific culture, followed with an admirable treatise on sexual inversion. Then Magnus Hirschfeld, with an unrivalled and most sympathetic personal knowledge of inverts, greatly contributed to our knowledge, and his book, *Die Homosexualität* (1914), not yet translated into English, is an encyclopædia of the whole subject. In Italy, where the term "inversione sessuale" seems to have originated, cases were from an early period brought forward by Ritti, Tamassia, Lombroso, and others. In France, where Charcot and Magnan first took up this study in 1882, a series of distinguished investigators, including Féré, Sérieux, and Saint-Paul (writing under the pen-name of "Dr. Laupts"), have elucidated our knowledge of sexual inversion. In Russia, Tarnowsky first investigated the phenomena. In England, John Addington Symonds, son of a distinguished physician and himself a brilliant man of letters, privately published two notable pamphlets, one on sexual inversion in ancient Greece and another on the modern problem of homosexuality. Edward Carpenter (also at first privately) printed a pamphlet on the subject and later a book (first published in German) on *The Intermediate Sex*. Raffalovich published a notable book in French, and my own book on sexual inversion was published first in Germany (*Das Konträre Geschlechtsgefühl*, 1896), and then in England and America, where also, at an earlier date, Kiernan and Lydston had given attention to the facts and theory of sexual inversion. The most notable recent book in English (1932) is Marañón's, translated from the Spanish.

The amount of study lately devoted to the subject has not yet resulted in complete unanimity. The first and most fundamental difficulty lay in deciding whether sexual inversion is congenital or acquired. The prevailing opinion, before Krafft-Ebing's influence began to be felt, was that homosexuality is acquired, that it is, indeed, simply a "vice," generally the mere result of masturbation or sexual excesses having produced impotence in normal coitus, or else (with Binet and Schrenck-Notzing) that it is the result of suggestion in early life. Krafft-Ebing accepted both the congenital and the acquired varieties of homosexuality, and the subsequent tendency has been towards minimizing the importance of acquired homosexuality. This tendency was well marked in Moll's treatise, Hirschfeld and Marañón consider that there is always a congenital element in homosexuality, and Bloch, Aletrino, etc., separated off the non-congenital homosexual persons who, for some reason or another, indulge in homosexual practices, as belonging to a group of "pseudo-homosexuality"; this was also the view of Näcke who considered that we have to distinguish, not between congenital and acquired inversion, but between true and false, and who regarded homosexuality appearing late in life as not acquired, but "retarded" or delayed homosexuality on a congenital basis. Some authorities who started with the old view that sexual inversion is exclusively or chiefly an acquired condition (like Näcke and Bloch) later adopted the more modern view. Many psycho-analysts still cherish the belief that homosexuality is always acquired, but as at the same time they also recognize that it is frequently fixed, and therefore presumably constitutional, the difference of opinion becomes unimportant.

Another fundamental point in regard to which opinion has changed is the question as to whether sexual inversion, even if congenital, should be considered a morbid or "degenerate" state. On this matter Krafft-Ebing at first ranged himself with the ancient view and regarded inversion as the manifestation of a neuropathic or psychopathic state, but in his latest writings he judiciously modified this position and was content to look on inversion as an anomaly and not a disease or a "degeneration." This is the direction in which modern opinion has steadily moved. Inverts may be healthy, and normal in all respects outside their special aberration. This has always been my own standpoint, though I regard inversion as frequently in close relation to minor neurotic conditions. We may agree with Hirschfeld (who finds hereditary taint in not more than 25 per cent. inverts) that even if there is a neuropathic basis in inversion the morbid element is usually small.

We are thus brought to what may be regarded as the fundamental basis in biological constitution on which, when we go outside the psychological field, homosexuality can be said to rest. It may seem easy to say that there are two definitely separated distinct and immutable sexes, the male that bears the sperm-cell and the female that bears the ovum or egg. That statement has, however, long ceased to be, biologically, strictly correct. We may not know exactly what sex is; but we do know that it is mutable, with the possibility of one sex being changed into the other sex, that its frontiers are often uncertain, and that there are many stages between a complete male and a complete female. In some forms of animal life, indeed, it is not easy to distinguish which is male and which female. In all these cases sex may be regarded as one of the devices (for there are other devices in Nature) for securing reproduction, though we are justified in studying the phenomena of sex apart from the question of reproduction. However true it may be that reproduction is Nature's primary aim, it is equally true that sexual reproduction is only one of several devices for attaining that end.

We are bound to assume that in every sex-chromosome, whether XX or XY, resides the physical basis of an impulse which tends to impose the male type or the female type on the developing individual. When two individuals of different races, as of some moths (in which the phenomena have been specially studied) are bred together, the offspring often ceases to be normal, and the male offspring may show a tendency in the direction of femaleness, or, under other circumstances, the female offspring show a tendency to maleness, the strain thus able to give an impress being termed "strong" and the other "weak." Here we see already, in a low zoölogical form, the condition of *intersexuality* which when we proceed to Man and enter the psychological field has sometimes been considered (though incorrectly) to constitute an "intermediate" sex. It is, more strictly, the result of a quantitative disharmony between the male and female sex-determining factors. Being part of the hereditary constitution of the individual, it is inborn, likely to become more pronounced as development proceeds, and, in the higher mammals, to manifest itself in the psychic sphere.

When dealing with moths, it is found that this intersexuality, more simple than when occurring higher in the zoölogical scale, may be produced by mixing different races of the same species. When we approach nearer to Man, the forms of intersexuality differ, are less pronounced, or not at all, in the external physical aspect, and are due less to mixture of different races than to varied individual deviations from the normal, while sometimes at all stages external factors may be influential.

We begin to come closer to the actual mechanism by which intersexuality is produced when we turn again to the action of the hormones. We may view these as taking up the guidance of the sex process after the influence of the initial sex-chromosomes, XX or XY, has been exhausted. The somatic, or general, tissues of the body possess the potency of developing the characters of either sex under the stimulus of the special complex of sex-hormones which they receive. The ovary, indeed, it is believed, does not at any early stage exert any marked influence upon the soma, the female development being seemingly innate, though the developed female sex-equipment depends on the sex-hormones for its maintenance. Male differentiation, on the other hand, requires the male testicular hormone for its development. Thus the female, it is held, represents the neutral form which the soma assumes in the absence of the male sex hormone. When the male hormone appears later than usual some form of inter-sexuality thus results, and the later its appearance the more femaleness there is in the result. "The degree of abnormality," as Crew puts it, "will be determined by the time at which the male sex-hormone becomes operative." That helps to explain why an individual who appears female in early life assumes male characters at sexual maturity.

To the adrenal cortex is specially attributed the formation of a hormone which exerts a masculinizing influence in the same direction as that of the testes. This result, " virilism " as it is now sometimes termed (formerly " adreno-genital syndrome "), is associated with hypertrichosis and in males with precocious sexual and somatic development, while in females there is atrophy of the uterus, with changes in the ovaries, under-development of the labia and overgrowth of the clitoris, atrophy of the mammæ, narrowing of the hips, broadening of the shoulders, with either marked muscular development or adiposity. There are disturbances of sexual function and even complete sterility. Four types of virilism have been described, depending on the time of onset: (1) *Congenital type* (with feminine pseudo-hermaphroditism, the sexual glands remaining female while the secondary sex characters are male); (2) *Puberty type* (beginning near puberty, with hirsutism and menstrual disturbances predominating); (3) *Adult type* (rather similar but less marked); (4) *Obstetrical type* (after the menopause with obesity, excess or loss of hair, psychic disturbances and asthenia). The exact method by which the adrenal hormone acts is still a matter of dispute.

Looked at largely, the inter-sexual transition falls, as Hirschfeld puts it, into four classes: (1) *Genital hermaphroditism* (blending of male and female sex organs); (2) *somatic hermaphroditism* (blending of bodily sex differences); (3) *psychic hermaphroditism* (eonism or blending of psychic differences); (4) *psycho-sexual hermaphroditism* (homosexuality).

When we deal with homosexuality we are still in the inter-sexual sphere, and we are no doubt still largely concerned with the action of the hormones, but we are on a psychic plane where physical syndromes are usually difficult to trace. There is no doubt that in a slight degree, and occasionally in a marked degree, they still exist, but they are unimportant, though many years ago Weil and others sought to demonstrate the presence of slight but measurable physical differentia of congenital origin in the homosexual. Apart from such measurable differences, there can be little doubt that certain individuals, in organic constitution, and probably as a result of unusual hormonic balance, possess a special aptitude to experience sexual satisfaction with persons of their own sex. There are a larger number, as is well known, presumably normal, both in Man and among lower animals, who when deprived of the presence of individuals of the opposite sex can find temporary sexual satisfaction in their own sex.

It may seem hazardous to assert that every individual is made up of mixed masculine and feminine elements, variously combined, and that the male invert is a person with an unusual proportion of female elements, the female invert a person with an unusual proportion of male elements ; it is a schematic view which will scarcely account altogether for the phenomena. But when we put aside occasional homosexuality in presumably normal persons, we seem justified in looking upon inversion as a congenital anomaly—or, to speak more accurately, an anomaly based on congenital conditions—which if it is pathological is only so in Virchow's sense that pathology is the science not of diseases but of anomalies, so that an inverted person may be as healthy as a colour-blind person. Congenital sexual inversion is thus akin to a biological variation. It is a variation doubtless due to imperfect sexual differentiation, but often having no traceable connection with any morbid condition in the individual himself.

This view of sexual inversion now tends to prevail and has gained much force recently. But it may be traced some way back. Ulrichs, so long ago as 1862, declared that inversion is "a species of hermaphroditism." Kiernan in America in 1888 insisted on the significance of the fact that the ancestors of the human species were originally bisexual ; Chevalier in 1893 put forward a theory of inversion based on fœtal bisexuality. Letamendi of Madrid in 1894 set forth a theory of panhermaphroditism according to which there are always latent female germs in the male, and latent male germs in the female. Finally, about 1896, Krafft-Ebing, Hirschfeld, and I (all, it seems, more or less independently) adopted a somewhat similar explanation.

The prevalence of these general views of sexual inversion has influenced the clinical classification of its varieties. Krafft-Ebing accepted four different varieties of congenital inversion and four different varieties of the acquired form. Moll rejected this elaborate classification, recognizing only psycho-sexual hermaphroditism (or, as it is now usually termed, bisexuality) and complete inversion. This corresponds to the division now recognized by most authorities. That is to say that when we have put aside the people who are exclusively attracted to the opposite sex, we have those who are exclusively attracted to the same sex, and those who are attracted to both sexes. When we go beyond this simple and elementary classification we encounter an endless number of individual variations but they do not easily admit of being arranged in definite groups. Even the bisexual class is not rigidly uniform, for it certainly contains many individuals who are congenital inverts with an acquired heterosexuality.

When we consider well-marked cases of sexual inversion, we find certain characteristics which frequently tend to recur. While a considerable proportion (in my experience over 50 per cent.) belong to reasonably healthy families, in about 40 per cent. there is in the family some degree of morbidity or abnormality—eccentricity, alcoholism, "neurasthenia," etc.—of slight or greater degree. The heredity of inversion is well-marked, though it has sometimes been denied; sometimes a brother and sister, a mother and son, an uncle and nephew, are both inverted, even unknown to each other; I find this family or hereditary inversion in 35 per cent. cases, and von Römer has found exactly the same proportion. It is alone sufficient to show that inversion may be inborn. The general personal health is in about two-thirds of the cases good, and sometimes very good; among the remainder there is often a tendency to nervous trouble or to a more or less unbalanced temperament; only a small proportion (about 8 per cent. in my experience) are markedly morbid.

In the great majority the inverted tendency appears in early life, often at puberty, but frequently there are indications of it before puberty. Sexual precocity appears to be marked in a large proportion, and there is often a tendency to sexual hyperæsthesia. Many inverts describe themselves as "sensitive" or "nervous." The influence of suggestion can be not infrequently traced, but in these cases there is usually also evidence of predisposition. Masturbation has been practised in a large proportion of cases, but masturbation is also common among the heterosexual, and there is no reason to suppose that it is a factor in the causation of inversion. The erotic dreams of inverts are usually inverted, but this is by no means invariably the case, and even inverts who appear to be such congenitally sometimes have normal dreams, just as normal persons occasionally have homosexual dreams.

The satisfaction of the inverted sexual impulse is effected in a variety of ways. Among my cases nearly 20 per cent. had never had any kind of sexual relationship. In 30 to 35 per cent. the sexual relationship rarely goes beyond close contact, or at most mutual masturbation. In the others, inter-crural connection or occasionally *fellatio* is the method practiced. In woman, gratification is obtained by kissing, close contact, mutual masturbation, and in some cases *cunnilinctus*, which is usually active rather than passive. The proportion of male inverts who desire *pædicatio* (more often active than passive) is not large. Hirschfeld places it at 8 per cent. cases ; I have found it to be nearer 15 per cent.

In male inverts there is a frequent tendency to approximate to the feminine type, and in female inverts to the masculine type ; this occurs both in physical and in psychic respects, and though it may be traced in a considerable number of respects, it is by no means always obtrusive. Some male inverts, however, insist on their masculinity, while many others are quite unable to say whether they feel more like a man or like a woman. Among female inverts, there is usually some approximation to the masculine attitude and temperament though this is by no means always conspicuous. Various minor anomalies of structure or function may occur. The sexual organs in both sexes are sometimes over-developed, or perhaps more usually, underdeveloped, in a slight approximation to the infantile type; gynecomasty is at times observed; in women there may be a somewhat masculine development of the larynx, as well as some degree of hypertrichosis. (Marañón finds that male traits tend to appear on the right side of the body, female on the left.) Male inverts are sometimes unable to whistle. In both sexes a notable youthfulness of appearance is often preserved into adult age. The love of green (which is normally a preferred colour chiefly by children and especially girls) is frequently observed. A certain degree of dramatic aptitude is not uncommon, as well as some tendency to vanity and personal adornment, and occasionally a feminine love of ornament and jewellery. Many of these physical and psychic characteristics may be said to indicate some degree of infantilism, and this is in agreement with the view of inversion which traces it to a fundamental bisexual basis, for the further back we go in the life-history of the individual, the nearer we approach to the bisexual stage.

Morally, inverts usually apply to themselves the normal code, and seek to justify their position. Those who fight against their instincts, or permanently disapprove of their own attitude, or even feel doubtful about it, are a small minority, less than 20 per cent. This is why so few inverts seek medical advice. They are fortified in their self-justification by the fact that not only in France but in several other countries (Italy, Belgium, Holland, etc.), which have been influenced by the Code Napoléon homosexual practices *per se* are not touched by the law, provided there has been no violence, no outrage on a minor, and no offence against public decency. England and the United States are probably the chief countries in which the ancient ecclesiastical jurisdiction against homosexuality still retains an influence. In these countries, however, the law in this matter causes much difficulty and dispute; it is difficult to decide what homosexual actions amount to a criminal offence; it is only in a few cases that the culprits are detected, or even sought, for, as a rule, the police carefully avoid pursuing their traces; and there is not the slightest reason to suppose that the countries which legislate against inversion possess a smaller, or even less prominent, proportion of inverts. In France, for instance, under the ancient monarchy, when an invert was, according to the law, liable to be burned, inversion was sometimes fashionable and conspicuous ; at the present day the reverse is the case. In view of these facts there is to-day a movement, which finds support alike in medical and in legal quarters, in favour of abolishing the punishment of homosexual acts except when the circumstances under which the acts are committed give them an anti-social character. It is a powerful argument in favour of such abolition that it at once puts a stop to the movement of agitation, and the tendency to the glorification of homosexuality—which is undesirable and even in many respects harmful—prevailing in those countries which still regard homosexuality as a crime.

BIBLIOGRAPHY

HAVELOCK ELLIS, *Studies in the Psychology of Sex*, Vol. II, Sexual Inversion.

F. A. E. CREW, Art. " Sex " in *Outline of Modern Knowledge.*

G. MARAÑÓN, *The Evolution of Sex and Inter-sexual Conditions.*

M. W. PECK, " The Sex Life of College Men," *Journal of Nervous and Mental Diseases*, January, 1925.

G. V. HAMILTON, *A Research in Marriage.*

K. B. DAVIS, *Factors in the Sex Life of Twenty-two Hundred Women.*

L. R. BROSTER, " A Review of Sex Characters," *British Medical Journal*, May 2nd, 1931.

WERNER PICTON, " Male Prostitution in Berlin," *Howard Journal*, 1931.

The Diagnosis of Sexual Inversion

It has already been remarked that the sexual impulse tends to be more diffused in children than it subsequently becomes in adults. Probably as a result of this diffusion, it is not so precisely focussed on individuals of the opposite sex. Max Dessoir went so far as to say that up to the age of fourteen or fifteen in both boys and girls the sexual instinct is normally undifferentiated. More recently Freud (following William James and others) has repeatedly stated that in all young subjects there is normally a homosexual streak. Theoretically that view is entirely sound. Since every individual contains the physical germs of the opposite sex, it is reasonable to suppose that he should also contain the psychic germs, and since in childhood his own sexual characters, physically and psychic, are still undeveloped, we should expect the opposite traits to be relatively prominent.

The appearance of a homosexual tendency in early life harmonizes with the results independently reached by the physiologists. Thus Heape concludes that the evidence shows that "There is no such thing as a pure male or female animal; . . . all animals contain the elements of both sexes in some degree." Some of the reasons for this conclusion are fairly obvious and it has long been recognized as the most reasonable explanation of inversion. It is quite intelligible that the latent sexual element should more easily come to the surface in early life when the dominant sexual element is still too undeveloped to be able to suppress it. "I have never," wrote Freud in 1905, "yet come through a single psycho-analysis of a man or a woman without having to take into account a very considerable current of homosexuality." If we may accept this statement by so penetrating and experienced an investigator as true for the morbid subjects of psycho-analysis, it must be added that for more normal persons, between whom and those who become patients there is no clear line of demarcation, this current may also be present, however slight, and not to be detected after adolescence.

The acceptance of the homosexual current does not therefore involve the belief in a completely undifferentiated state of the sexual impulse in early life. In some large schools, it is true (notably in some of the large English Public Schools), homosexuality is known to flourish, aided, it would seem, by a kind of tradition. But these appear to be exceptions. Many of us are unable to recall from the memories of school life and early associations any clear evidence of the existence of homosexual attractions, such rare sexual attractions as existed being exclusively towards the opposite sex.

It remains true that a certain liability to more or less romantic homosexual affection is found among boys, while girls, much more frequently, cherish enthusiastic devotion for other girls somewhat older than themselves, and very often for their teachers. Even, however, when these emotions are reciprocated, and even when they lead to definite sexual manifestations and gratification, they must not too hastily be taken to indicate either a vice calling for severe punishment or a disease demanding treatment. In the great majority of these cases we are simply concerned with an inevitable youthful phase.

In dealing, therefore, with such manifestations, which are in most cases purely sentimental, and with only a vague sensual tinge, though they sometimes take crude and even cruel shapes, it is important to realize that we are probably in the presence of an early stage of what may be a more or less normal development. Much injury may be done to a boy's nervous and mental character, to say nothing of his future reputation, by the over-hasty assumption that such manifestations are diseased or vicious. They can adequately be dealt with, when they need to be dealt with at all, by a kindly teacher or guardian, who in the course of imparting general sexual information inculcates in the boy self-respect and regard for the welfare of others. In girls these manifestations usually escape serious treatment, partly because they are so common, and partly because women, more often than men, are disposed to view them indulgently, if not indeed sometimes to share them.

It remains, however, of considerable importance to distinguish between these temporary manifestations of homosexuality and the congenital sexual inversion which is likely to indicate a permanent life-long direction of the sexual impulse and ideals. In some children the sexual impulse, far from being either undifferentiated or directed towards the opposite sex, is definitely directed towards the same sex from the first. A diagnosis of congenital inversion cannot, however, always be made with certainty until the period of adolescence is entirely completed. A refined and intellectual youth with æsthetic tastes, at the University, for instance, surrounded by attractive and congenial persons of his own sex, may remain indifferent to women and continue to cherish ardent sentimental friendships and admirations, reaching the conclusion that he must be an invert by nature. Yet, when he leaves the University for the world, he discovers that, after all, he shares the common passions of ordinary humanity. It is not, indeed, until the age of twenty-five has been reached or even later, that we can be fairly sure that homosexual impulses are not a phase of normal development. Even after maturity has long been reached the homosexual impulse may veer towards the heterosexual, or else become genuinely bi-sexual.

But at a much earlier period it may be possible to see good reason to consider that we are dealing with a congenital invert. If we find unusual sexual precocity combined with complete sexual concentration on the same sex without any sexual attraction to the opposite sex, though with perhaps an attraction to feminine interests and avocations, and if the family history shows a considerable tendency to nervous abnormality or to eccentricity, we may suspect, although we cannot be certain, that we are dealing with a certain type of congenital invert.

In other cases, however, the homosexual tendency may not appear until late in life. It was formerly taken for granted that in these cases the condition is acquired and not congenital; this is, however, to-day disputed by many who regard these cases as due to the late development of a really inborn tendency, retarded congenital inversion.

In this way it comes about that we have to distinguish between true congenital sexual inversion (early or retarded), bisexual attraction in which the individual's sexual impulse goes out towards individuals of both sexes (most though not all of these cases being apparently inverts who have acquired normal habits), and the large and vague class of the pseudo-homosexuals, whose anomaly is due either to temporary circumstances (as among sailors), to senile impotency, or to a deliberate search for abnormal sensations. Even in pseudo-homosexuality we have to recognize, according to the prevailing view, that the homosexuality rests on a natural germinal basis, and cannot therefore be regarded as completely acquired, but as the development of a latent aptitude.

Sexual inversion has specially high significance because it tends to occur in individuals who are above the average in intellect and character, even when we put aside many notable monarchs, statesmen, poets, sculptors, painters, composers, scholars, etc., both past and present. That is perhaps a reason why they are not easily recognized. Many physicians believe that they have never seen an invert; even so experienced an alienist as Sir George Savage once stated that he scarcely ever met with inversion. The experience of another distinguished alienist is instructive. Näcke at one time, never having to his knowledge met an invert, wrote to Hirschfeld, whose experience in this field is wider than that of any other physician, asking for an invert to be sent to his house. Great was Näcke's surprise when the visitor proved to be a man he was already well acquainted with, a near connection of his own by marriage. It is not usually until some circumstance has opened our eyes that we begin to discover that in every social environment inverts are to be found. It is, however, usually only those of the lowest, most degenerate, and sometimes mercenary class who are willing to betray their peculiarity. The suicides and mysterious disappearances which occur from time to time among highly placed persons, often of great ability, are frequently connected with inversion, though even after their fate has overtaken them, the cause of it often remains a mystery to the general public. These persons have probably never confided in a physician. They realize that it would be futile, that the average physician is quite unprepared to deal with their case, if, indeed, he would not be shocked or disgusted.

A physician, a man of high character and intelligence, who is himself a congenital invert, though his moral traditions have not allowed him to seek the satisfaction of his impulses, writes as follows regarding his education at a world-renowned medical centre: "The first reference bearing definitely on the subject of sexual perversion was made in the class of medical jurisprudence where certain sexual crimes were alluded to—very summarily and inadequately—but nothing was said of the existence of sexual inversion as the normal condition of certain unhappy people, nor was any distinction drawn between the various non-normal acts, which were all classed together as manifestations of the criminal depravity of ordinary or insane people. To a student beginning to be acutely conscious that his sexual nature differed profoundly from that of his fellows nothing could be more perplexing and disturbing, and it shut me up more completely in my reserve than ever. It was still more unfortunate that neither in the class of systematic medicine nor in the course of the lectures on clinical medicine was there the slightest allusion to the subject. All sorts of rare diseases —some of which I have not met with in twenty-one years of busy practice—were fully discussed, but we were left entirely ignorant of a subject so vitally important to me personally, and, as it seems to me, to the profession to which I aspired." This absence of reference to sexual problems in medical teaching has probably been the experience of most of us, though such defective teaching has usually been less unfortunate for the student personally than for those whom he might have been enabled to help. Fortunately this is a state of things which will now rapidly cease to exist.

It is not, however, only among the people who are in other respects obviously exceptional, whether "degenerates" or men of genius—though among these indeed it seems to be peculiarly prevalent—that sexual inversion is found. It is also found among a fair proportion of the apparently average population, among people who are indistinguishable from the average. Inverts are sometimes referred to, even by physicians, as an "effeminate" class. That is scarcely the case. A certain group of them may indeed be so styled, they are physically and mentally flabby, self-conscious, vain, fond of jewellery and adornment; these men have the inclinations of the prostitute and in some cases actually become male prostitutes. But they are not more typical of inversion than the female prostitute, actual or temperamental, is typical of womanhood. A large number of inverts, indeed, are unusually refined, sensitive, or emotional, but the same may be said of many slightly neurotic people who are not homosexual. Others, both men and women, are not obviously distinguished by any special character which could reasonably suggest an abnormal direction of the sexual impulse. It is this fact which accounts for so many people believing that they have never come across an invert, while yet the proportion of inverts in the general population has by careful and well-informed investigation been found so considerable as to be at the least well over 1 per cent.

It seems probable, as already pointed out, that the prevalence of inversion varies but very slightly in different countries, though in certain special regions of Southern Europe it is said to be considerable, perhaps owing to the special habits or traditions of the people. It is sometimes said by people of various countries that sexual inversion is not so prevalent in their land as it is abroad. But they speak in ignorance of the real facts. The apparent variations are merely superficial and mostly due to the social and legal attitude towards inversion which prevails in a country. This does not mean that it flourishes where the laws are lenient, for the existence of harshly repressive laws may merely serve to arouse an enthusiastic propaganda for their abolition which calls attention to the prevalence of inversion. Homosexuality is the most prevalent of all the sexual deviations, for though the erotic symbolisms, in a slight and undeveloped degree, are probably more common, they are not nearly so often met with in a fully developed degree as is inversion. This prevalence is still further emphasized by the energy and character, in many cases, of the subjects of the anomaly.

It is the gradual recognition of the prevalence of inversion among people of ordinary normal intelligence and conduct which has modified the opinions of alienists concerning the nature of this and, indeed, other sexual anomalies. In mediæval and earlier days homosexuality, in its only recognizable shape as sodomy and tribadism, was a sin and a crime, often expiated at the stake; it continued to be regarded only as a manifestation of disgusting depravity until well on in the nineteenth century; then there was a tendency to look on it as a sign of insanity, or at all events of degeneracy. That view is now out of date, as is inevitable when we find that such deviations and the like occur in mentally capable and morally well-conducted and self-controlled people, many of whom are by no means over-mastered or obsessed by their impulses and some of whom have never yielded to them at all. Occasional homosexuality is a tendency to which Man is everywhere liable in common with that part of the animal world to which he is most nearly allied. Congenital sexual inversion is an anomaly, an inborn variation of which we are beginning to understand the causes; it is, even when extreme, only pathological in the same sense as colour-blindness or albinism or transposition of the viscera is pathological.

BIBLIOGRAPHY

MOLL, *The Sexual Life of the Child.*

HAVELOCK ELLIS, *Studies in the Psychology of Sex,* Vol. II, "Sexual Inversion."

FREUD, *Collected Papers*, Vol. III.

KATHARINE DAVIS, *Factors in the Sex Life of Twenty-two Hundred Women.*

EDWARD CARPENTER, *The Intermediate Sex.*

Eonism (Transvestism or Sexo-Æsthetic Inversion)

This is a condition, not to be identified with homosexuality though it sometimes tends to be associated with it, in which the subject more or less identifies himself or herself with the opposite sex, not merely in dress, but in general tastes, in ways of acting, and in emotional disposition. The identification usually falls short of the opposite sex's sexual attitude; the normal heterosexual attitude is frequently pronounced, yet it may be convenient to introduce the consideration of it here.

Eonism is rather a puzzling condition to define and to label. I met with it many years ago and put it aside for further consideration. Meanwhile, Hirschfeld in Germany, who was already a leading authority on homosexuality, became interested in this condition, which he recognized as distinct from inversion and called "transvestism." He made it the chief subject of several books. In my own first study of the condition (1913) I called it "sexo-æsthetic inversion," a sort of sexual inversion of tastes. Both these names are unsatisfactory; "transvestism" is altogether inadequate, since a longing to wear the garments of the other sex is only one of the traits exhibited, and in some cases it is scarcely or not at all found, while "sexo-æsthetic inversion" may wrongly suggest that we are here concerned with homosexuality, though that is usually not present.

"Eonism" is the name I finally devised (1920) for this condition. It has been accepted by many and still seems the most convenient term, and adequately descriptive. Like "sadism" and "masochism," it is derived from a well-known person who exhibited the anomaly in a typical form, the Chevalier d'Eon de Beaumont (1728–1810), a Burgundian of good family, employed as a French diplomatic agent under Louis XV. and finally dying in London where he was generally regarded as a woman, though the autopsy revealed him as a normal male. A less known personage, also French, the Abbé de Choisy (1644–1724), and also of aristocratic family, is in some aspects an even more typical example of Eonism, and he wrote his own memoirs, which reveal him, as from other sources he is also known, as a man of urbane and sociable temper, generally popular in spite of his anomaly, refined, amiable, and rather feminine, a devoted admirer of women, with rather less than the average degree of sexual passion, but the father of at least one child, a man of genuine intellectual ability, the esteemed friend of many of the best people of his day. He became a distinguished ecclesiastic, the historian of the Church, and the Doyen of the French Academy. Among notable women of analogous temperament have been Lady Hester Stanhope, and also James Barry, who spent a long and distinguished life in masculine garments and became Senior Inspector-General of the English Army Medical Department. There is no reason to suppose that either of these women was homosexual.

Eonism is a remarkably common anomaly; in my own

experience it comes next in frequency to homosexuality among sexual deviations. In ordinary life the subjects present no startlingly unusual traits and may seem quite ordinarily masculine, though sometimes sensitive and reserved, often devoted to their wives, but seldom of vigorous sexual temperament. Their secret ideals are usually unsuspected, even by those nearest to them. Not all of them desire to adopt cross-dressing (as Edward Carpenter termed it), but when they do, it is with complete success, very skilfully, and with a minute and almost instinctive adoption of little feminine ways, which, they feel, come to them naturally. Though they do not often desire inverted sexual relationships, male Eonists sometimes feel an almost passionate longing for a woman's experiences of pregnancy and motherhood. In mental ability they are above the average and may attain distinction as authors or otherwise.

Eonism is to be classed among the transitional or intermediate forms of sexuality. But it is not easy to explain its precise origin. We may agree with Kiernan that there is sometimes an arrest of development, similar, as I have suggested, on the physical side, to eunuchoidism, to which indeed it sometimes seems related. We may thus probably invoke some defective endocrine balance, and thereby see an opening, with better knowledge, for readjustment of the normal balance.

On the psychic side, as I view it, the Eonist is embodying, in an extreme degree, the æsthetic attitude of imitation of, and identification with, the admired object. It is normal for a man to identify himself with the woman he loves. The Eonist carries that identification too far, stimulated by a sensitive and feminine element in himself which is associated with a rather defective virile sexuality on what may be a neurotic basis. An abnormal childhood, with too close attachment to the mother, who may herself be rather abnormal, seems sometimes to encourage the appearance of Eonism. Fenichel considers that the specific factor of Eonism is a castration complex ; he would, however, say much the same of all sexual deviations, so that we are not thereby carried far ; while he admits that this view will not apply to female Eonists.

BIBLIOGRAPHY

HAVELOCK ELLIS, *Studies in the Psychology of Sex*, Vol. VII, " Eonism."

HOMBERG AND JOUSSELIN, *D'Eon de Beaumont : His Life and Times.*

O. FENICHEL, " The Psychology of Transvestism," *International Journal of Psycho-analysis*, April, 1930.

FLUGEL, *The Philosophy of Clothes.*

The Question of Treatment

A condition so unique as that of sexual inversion raises special problems. On the one hand there is the similitude of a complete variation combined in many cases with a state of general good health. Yet we are not in the presence of a specific human mutation. The variation affects a special function, even though it happens to be a function with a widely pervading influence on the whole organism. It is only a variation in the sense that colour-blindness is a variation. Oswald Schwartz in a recent searching study (though tending to be metaphysical) still insists that we must regard homosexuality as morbid, though he is careful to define " morbidity " as " the insubordination of an organ to the functional law of the organism," generally due, he holds, to a retained infantility, so that " morbidity " here has much the same definitional value as Virchow's " pathological." We are not here far from the position of Freud that predisposition and experience are indissolubly linked, or from those authorities who hold that all genuine homosexuality has an innate basis, while acquired forms, due to external pressure, are only pseudo-homosexuality.

We are not here primarily concerned with therapeutical considerations. They have been fully discussed by Marañón and others. But the question of treatment has constantly come to the front in connection with homosexual states, whether or not innate inversion is suspected. And as the proposed treatment is usually psycho-therapeutic, we are bound to discuss its psychological advisability.

I put aside the question of surgical treatment as that has not yet come into common practice. Lipschütz mentions the case of a homosexual man who after transplantation of the testicle of a normal man, became heterosexual, and within a year felt able to marry. We need a much larger number of observations than are at present available before coming to conclusions as to the possibility and desirability of such a proceeding. More considerations than are at first obvious need to be regarded. At one time the necessity of attempting some such treatment in all cases was taken for granted. That is not so now, though still some authorities are in favour of this course, even in cases of clearly congenital inversion, where the patient is anxious for the attempt to be made. If, however, we are clearly in the presence of a deeply-rooted and complete case of inversion, even the attempt at a radical unsettlement of the organized habits, conceptions, and ideals, involving a violation of the individual's fundamental nature, should not be made without careful consideration. It must be remembered that when we are dealing with a really fixed condition, all normal methods of treatment become difficult. Hypnotic suggestion, which was formerly found useful in many cases of the most various kinds of sexual anomalies, is of comparatively little service in well-developed congenital deviations. It cannot even easily be applied, for the subject resists the suggestion, just as the normal subject usually resists under hypnotism the suggestion to commit a crime. Schrenck-Notzing, many years ago, when sexual inversion was not commonly regarded as innate, expended great time and trouble in treating inverts by hypnotism, aided by visits to the brothel, and believed that he had been successful. But an appearance of success, when success is merely shown by the ability to effect intercourse with the opposite sex, is admitted to be possible, with much good will on the patient's part ; it by no means follows that the ideals and impulses have been really and permanently turned into a new or even desirable channel ; the result may merely be, as one such patient expressed it, that masturbation *per vaginam* has been achieved.

The psycho-analytic method of Freud has also been employed therapeutically in these cases, and for this method also some success has been claimed. There is now, however, a tendency among psycho-analysts to recognize that when the state of inversion is fixed (whether or not it is regarded as innate) it is useless to apply psycho-analysis in the expectation of a change of sexual direction. I have known many homosexual persons who have subjected themselves to psycho-analysis. Some stopped the treatment at the outset; some considered that there had been little or no effect of any kind; some found distinct benefit, mainly, however, through the increased self-knowledge and self-realization thus obtained rather than by any change in the direction of the sexual impulse; I do not know of any cases in which a complete and permanent transformation of homosexuality into heterosexuality was thus achieved. Moll's associational therapy may, perhaps, be said to constitute a third psycho-therapeutical method calling for notice in this connection, though it represents no new departure in manner of application. It is, however, sound in theory and practicable, and consists in finding a bridge by which the subject's abnormal desires may be brought into association with normal ends. Thus, if the subject is attracted to boys he may be led to cultivate an attraction for boyish women. It was already known that the invert is affected by such considerations as these. Thus one of my subjects who leads a healthy and active life, is masculine in habits, represses his homosexual desires, and would like to marry and have a son, made various fruitless attempts at coitus. Later at Malta, at a public dance, he met an Italian girl who invited him to her home: "She had a very slim boyish figure and a boyish face and hardly any breasts. I went to her flat by appointment and found her dressed in a man's pyjamas. I felt decidedly attracted, but even then was unable to play the man's part. I came away, however, without the usual feeling of repulsion, and on returning the next night, the result, to my great delight, was satisfactory. I went on several occasions before leaving Malta, but although attracted by this girl, I never really enjoyed the act, and as soon as it was over had a desire to turn my back. Since then I have had intercourse with about a dozen girls. But it is always an effort, and leaves a feeling of repulsion. I have come to the conclusion that for me normal sexual intercourse is only an expensive and dangerous form of masturbation." But that is the best that psycho-therapeutics can generally hope to achieve.

It must be added that all these methods, even in so far as they can be said to attain success at all, when applied to deeply-rooted cases of inversion, at best, for the most part, lead to a condition of bisexual attraction, by which the patient is enabled to find gratification with persons of either sex. This artificial shifting or loosening of the anchorage of the sexual impulse is not favourable to stability of character nor to any high morality. Neither is it altogether a matter of congratulation to render an invert capable of procreation. The offspring of an invert united to a sound partner have, indeed, a fair chance of turning out satisfactorily, but the risks are too serious to enable us to say that they may be lightly run. When an invert is profoundly dissatisfied with his condition and keenly anxious to become normal it is not easy to resist the attempt to render him normal. But it is not possible to take a sanguine view either of the prospects of success or the results of success when it is achieved.

There may still be ample room for treatment, even when no direct attempt is made to suppress the inverted tendency and the cheerful and easy-going view (which I have seen advocated) is adopted of regarding homosexuality as merely "a form of bad manners." The invert is, in a considerable proportion of cases, generally and sometimes sexually, what used to be termed neurasthenic; in some cases he is sexually hyperæsthetic with the irritable weakness which commonly accompanies hyperæsthesia; he is often sensitive and emotional, sometimes liable to panics of apprehension or anxiety in connection with his abnormality. In such cases the ordinary treatment of the condition is indicated, whether by sedatives, such as the bromides, or, in some cases, tonics.

Electricity, balneo-therapy, physical exercises, wholesome occupation, change of air, etc.—all these ordinary methods of combating nervous exhaustion have been advocated as likely to prove beneficial in dealing with forms of sexual deviation. Many inverts are little worried by the existence of their sexual anomaly so long as they are in good health, so that it is on this ground alone highly necessary to apply any special medical treatment that may be required and to insist on the cultivation of physical and mental hygiene. The inversion will not thus be removed, but with intelligent comprehension and sympathy the anxiety it causes may be allayed, its excesses may be restrained, and it may be brought under rational self-control. This is in most cases all that is necessary, and in many all that is desirable.

The question of marriage sometimes arises in the case of inverts, although it is most usually settled without reference to the physician. As a method of treatment, whether the patient is a man or a woman, marriage must certainly be rejected, absolutely and unconditionally. It may perhaps enable the invert to become bisexual if the sexual instinct has not already taken on this double aspect, but the chances that it will abolish the inverted impulse, unless it is already on the way to do so when the marriage takes place, are of the smallest. On the contrary, marriage, by the difficulties and the disgust which it may force the inverted partner to contend with, sometimes exacerbates the inversion. Cases have occurred where it was not until shortly after an apparently happy marriage that an invert has recklessly placed himself within the clutches of the law. In or out of marriage, normal sexual intercourse cannot be regarded as a remedy for inversion, least of all in the form of prostitution, which tends to present women in the aspect which is most repulsive to the invert. Platonic friendship with a refined and intelligent person of the opposite sex is more attractive and more helpful, and if the Platonic friend is of a type which in the same sex would appeal to the invert, there is more likelihood of the relationship serving as a method of associational therapeutics than when the question of sexual intercourse is directly approached. The invert whose anomaly is based on an innate predisposition tends to be an invert all through, and any influences that modify his psychic state must be gradual and manifold.

While sexual intercourse, in or out of marriage, must never be regarded as a therapeutic method, it is not necessary to conclude that here—and the same is true of other profound sexual deviations—marriage is always to be prohibited. It is not unusual to find inverts marrying. But it is desirable that such marriages should not be made in the dark or with illusory hopes. The conjugal partner should not be too young, and should be accurately informed beforehand as to the precise condition of affairs and the probable prospects. Unions so formed sometimes prove tolerable and even happy, should the couple be congenial to each other. But it must always be remembered that the chances of complete sexual satisfaction on either side are small. The invert, unless genuinely bisexual (most bisexual persons are predominantly homosexual), cannot experience with a person of the opposite sex that intimate unreserve and emotional extravagance which are of the essence of sexual love, and though potency is possible, it may only be secured by imagining that the partner is of the same sex, or even by concentrating the thoughts on some attractive individual of the same sex. This state of things fails to give great satisfaction to the inverted partner, while the other partner, even if not clearly conscious of the imperfect character of the relationship, instinctively feels some degree of dissatisfaction and depression, if not repulsion. A union of this kind is often more happy when the attempt to secure sexual satisfaction is excluded, and the relationship is based on the satisfaction of other interests common to both partners.

Whether offspring should be one of these interests is a serious question which it is not always easy to decide resolutely in the negative. Certainly it may be laid down as a general rule that it is not desirable a person constitutionally predisposed to homosexuality should procreate. When, however, the inverted partner is otherwise healthy, and belongs to a fairly sound family, and the other partner is entirely sound and normal, there is a reasonable hope that the children may turn out fairly well. Children are frequently desired by the invert; they also form a consolation for the other partner and may serve to consolidate the union. But a marriage of this kind is often unstable; there is a prospect of separation or of alienation of the partners, so that the risks of an unsatisfactory home life for the child are considerable.

Much the best result seems to be attained for the congenital invert, as modern society is constituted, when, while retaining his own ideals, or inner instincts, he resolves to forego alike the attempt to become normal and the attempt to secure the grosser gratification of his abnormal desires, even though finding occasional auto-erotic relief inevitable, however unsatisfactory. This is not rare in persons of fine character. One such, who had some homosexual experiences before the age of nineteen, but not since, writes: "Occasionally I go for several months without masturbating, and find that when I do this my mind seems more self-satisfied, though I develop a more uncontrolled desire for masculine love, and my best men friends would be surprised to know that I am a sentimentalist in regard to them. Only to myself do I appear what I am. To my friends I am sexually normal. I believe that there is nothing about me to suggest to the most discriminating observer that I have a passion so generally associated with degenerates. I do not feel a degenerate. I have never felt ashamed of my desires, though I would be ashamed for people to know, as then I would lose caste."

Another man, who has never had any homosexual relations, a naval officer living an active life, has found considerable satisfaction in non-sexual friendships. He writes: "I am not in any way effeminate and by my own choice I have led a hard and often dangerous life. My desire for the companionship of men who have a sexual attraction for me is very great and the happiest days of my life have been spent in the companionship of such. My desires are not only sexual, but composed of about 50 per cent. of the desire for complete mental harmony which accompanies such attraction. Fear of losing this has kept me from ever making advances, and I imagine that with a male prostitute such harmony would be impossible. I have got over my shame at being different from other men, and look upon my condition as natural for myself."

For some, no doubt, this is scarcely possible, and for many it involves painful struggle and impaired vital energy for the tasks of life. But in a large proportion of inverts the sexual impulse—although its abnormality may cause it to be unduly present to consciousness and the prohibition of gratification artificially emphasize the need for it—is not really strong. It may find a large measure of satisfaction in a Platonic friendship with a congenial person of the same sex. Such friendship may be fortified by a study of the ideals that are inculcated in the writings of Plato himself and the Greek poets who were touched by homosexual emotions; such modern writers as Walt Whitman and Edward Carpenter and André Gide may also be named.

It must, further, be remembered that the inverted sexual impulse is peculiarly apt for the ends of sublimation. Freud considers that sublimation in the direction of friendship and comradeship and *esprit de corps* and the love of mankind in general may be developed *after* heterosexual impulses are established. But to wait for that must usually be the postponement of sublimation until (according to the ancient phrase) the Greek Kalends. Fortunately, we may often witness what may fairly be called sublimation taking place at a much earlier stage and in persons in whom the homosexual impulse can be considered fixed. It has often happened that inverts have devoted themselves with ardour to valuable social and philanthropic work for the benefit of the young of their own sex, and found joy and satisfaction in the task.

A man of Quaker antecedents, belonging to a family including many members displaying both nervous tendencies and distinguished mental ability which he himself shares, has homosexual impulses to which he has never yielded except in a very slight degree, and is married, although his heterosexual impulses are not strong. He writes: "The bisexual seems to love all mankind instead of only one person ; perhaps it is a noble and more useful kind of devotion. To reproduce one's life through scientific papers of originality seems more useful to-day than to add to the spawning which one sees on every hand." Not infrequently the homosexual tendency passes into a religious rather than a scientific channel. A correspondent, who has much studied Dante and regards himself as bisexual in tendency, writes : " I think a close correlation exists between sex and religion. The inverts I know well (four males) are all devout believers. I am myself a server in the Church of England. On my personal theory the essence of love is unselfish devotion, and I believe that service is the only key to genuine happiness. Invert or no, one must refuse admission to some thoughts, however loudly they knock. I can see a wealth of beauty in both boys and girls, but I utilize the inspiration in my religion and daily work, and try not to be unduly sentimental. I have passed the stormiest point in my psychic development. Perhaps one day I shall meet the right girl and have the joy of being myself the father of boys."

It is true that these motives only appeal to the superior invert. But, it may be repeated, such form a considerable proportion of the whole group. They are apt to feel at first that they are homeless wanderers in a universe that was not made for them. It is worth while by increasing their knowledge to increase also their happiness and their usefulness, so enabling them to feel that for them also, even as they are, there is still a place in the world, and often even an enviable place.

BIBLIOGRAPHY

HAVELOCK ELLIS, *Studies in the Psychology of Sex*, Vol. II.

EDWARD CARPENTER, *The Intermediate Sex*, and also *My Days and Dreams* (Autobiography).

Edward Carpenter : In Appreciation, Edited by G. Beith.

GEORGE IVES, *The Græco-Roman View of Youth*.

ANOMALY, *The Invert and His Social Adjustment* (Introduction by Dr. Thouless).

MRS. HAVELOCK ELLIS, *The New Horizon in Love and Life* " Eugenics and Spiritual Parenthood."

CHAPTER VI

MARRIAGE

Introductory (The Problem of Sexual Abstinence)

MARRIAGE in the social sense, and even to some extent in the biological sense, is a sexual relationship entered into with the intention of making it permanent, even apart from whether or not it has received the sanction of the law or the Church. But before entering on its consideration it may be desirable to touch on the problem of sexual abstinence, and the troubles, real or alleged, that may be associated with it.

This problem has passed through several phases. A century ago it scarcely came before the physician, and if it did, all he could legitimately say was that for men sexual abstinence outside marriage was moral and sexual intercourse immoral (though left privately free), while for women, who had no recognized sexual needs, the question could not arise. Then, within the lifetime of many of us, with the emergence of new social conditions and a somewhat more open attitude towards them, the physician began to be approached and he was asked to proclaim general principles in this matter for the world at large. This demand led to the formulation of various vague propositions concerning the harmlessness of continence, which meant nothing and might be used in senses not intended by the formulators; they could, for instance, be quoted with much satisfaction by those persons who advocated no sexual intercourse except for the production of children, that is to say, perhaps two or three times in a lifetime. No doubt continence in the use of the muscular and glandular system generally is not injurious to health; continence likewise in the use of the specifically sexual muscles and glands is equally not injurious to health. Such frivolous exercises in verbal juggling were, however, felt to be rather beneath the dignity of the medical profession and more suitably left to the charlatans who take advantage of the sexual ignorance and prejudices of the multitude. The physician is called to deal with the manifold cases of living men and women, not with abstract formulas. This is now realized, and since less rigid notions of sexual morality now prevail it is possible to deal more variously with the resulting problems.

The difficulties and dangers of sexual abstinence have in the past been both under-estimated and over-estimated. On the one hand it was emphatically stated, always by those who were over-burdened by the moral interests which they conceived to be at stake, that such difficulties and dangers are negligible. On the other hand were those who, partly by reaction against this extreme view and partly by ancient tradition, went to the other extreme, and declared that various forms of insanity, as well as of nervous disorder, were due to sexual abstinence. There seems no ground to believe that any serious psychosis or neurosis is caused by sexual abstinence alone in congenitally sound persons. The belief that it may is due to the familiar confusion between the "post hoc" and the "propter hoc"; similarly when insanity occurs in a person who has led a life of unbridled sexual licence, we are not entitled to put down his insanity to the sexual impulse. "The majority of those who compose our society," said Freud in 1908, "are constitutionally unfit for the task of abstinence," but he adds the significant remark, which we should always bear in mind, that it is in the presence of a disposition to neurosis that abstinence proves most troublesome, especially as leading to anxiety neurosis, while in his later *Introductory Lectures* he states that "we must beware of over-estimating the importance of abstinence in affecting neurosis; only a minority of pathogenic situations due to privation and the subsequent accumulation of Libido thereby induced can be relieved by the kind of sexual intercourse that is procurable without any difficulty." Since Freud has never under-estimated the importance of the sexual impulse in life, his testimony on this point is of peculiar value. Reference may also be made to the fact that, as has been pointed out by Löwenfeld, who has studied the matter in a judicial spirit on a basis of wide experience, Catholic priests usually enjoy excellent health in nervous respects and seldom suffer from abstinence, this being probably due, Löwenfeld remarks, to being brought up to their profession from youth.

We have always to remember that the whole art of living lies in a fine balance of expression and repression. For repression—understood in the wide sense and not merely in the special sense sometimes given to it by psycho-analysts—is as central a fact of life as expression. We are constantly at the same time both repressing some impulses and expressing other impulses. There is no necessary penalty in the repression, for it is essential to expression. It is far from being peculiar to civilization; it is equally marked in primitive stages of human life. It is even easily to be observed among animals. So natural a process can be nothing but wholesome in the main, even although it must be frequently liable to maladjustments, especially in those individuals who are not constitutionally organized for the task of attaining harmonious balance.

But it is not therefore to be denied that the difficulties of sexual abstinence, even though they do not involve any great risk to life or to sanity, are still very real to many healthy and active persons.[1] It is apt to cause minor disturbances of physical well-being, and on the psychic side much mental worry and a constantly recurring struggle with erotic obsessions, an unwholesome sexual hyperæsthesia which, especially in women, often takes the form of prudery. A student, for instance, who lives chastely, who is ambitious, who wishes to put all his best energies into his studies, may endure great anxiety and mental depression from this struggle. Many young women, also, actively engaged in various kinds of work, suffer similarly, and are sometimes thereby stimulated to a feverish activity in work and physical

[1] This has long been held by all competent authorities. Thus Näcke, a cautious and critical writer, stated over twenty years ago that the opinion that sexual abstinence has no bad effects is not now held by a single authority on questions of sex. The fight is concerned with the quantity and quality of the bad effects, which Näcke believed never to be of a gravely serious character.

exercise which usually brings no relief. One is sometimes, indeed, inclined to think that women have suffered more from this cause than men, not that sublimation is (as Freud believes) specially difficult for women, or because their sexual impulses are stronger, but because men have been, and are even still, more easily able to form sexual relationships outside marriage, while the spontaneous orgasms which in chaste men normally give relief during sleep are in women who have had no sexual experiences comparatively rare, even when sexual desire is strong. It is often the superior women who suffer most from this cause and they are precisely the women who are most anxious to conceal the fact.[1]

It may be interesting in this connection to consider the answers given by over a thousand women to the question in Dr. Katharine Davis's *questionnaire:* Do you believe sex intercourse necessary for complete physical and mental health ? It must of course be borne in mind that the replies to this question cannot be always, even if generally, based strictly on physiological and psychological considerations. We have inevitably to recognize the influence of moral, social, and conventional ideas. Still it is interesting to know how educated American women, brought up in the early twentieth century, privately regard this matter. It was found that 38·7 per cent. (394 in number) answered in the affirmative, a few emphatically, a large number with specific qualification, and some of them only dubiously. There remained a majority of 61·2 (622 in number) who replied in the negative, some emphatically and a few dubiously. Some

[1] I hear from many women who suffer acutely in this way; they frequently write from a distance or conceal their real names. One lady from whom I heard several times (who happened, without knowing it, to be well known to a friend of my own) is fairly typical: middle-aged, robust, well-developed and handsome, highly intelligent, has independent means and often lives abroad; has never had any sexual relationships. Though enjoying good health on the whole, some slight disturbances (notably a mental shock at sixteen which diminished menstruation) have stimulated sexual activity to an abnormal degree. There is constant sexual desire, and all the physical and mental methods of dealing with it which she can adopt are fruitless to relax this perpetual tension. Her character and traditions render any irregular gratification impossible, and prevent her even referring to her condition, while the occasional masturbation which she has been compelled to resort to at the monthly periods brings no relief but only remorse.

of the women answering affirmatively qualified their reply by saying "especially for men," or "for *mental* health," or "for a complete life," or "for some types." Of those who answered negatively, many qualified by saying "not necessary but normal," or "but desirable," or "not for *complete* mental health," or "no, but difficult," or "no, but people who do not have it seem harsh and shrivelled up." It is a significant commentary that, of those who believed sex intercourse unnecessary for health, 59·5—more than half—practised masturbation. It may not be surprising that of those who replied affirmatively a larger proportion (76·0 per cent.) acknowledged the same practice. It is natural to find that of those answering affirmatively a larger proportion than in the negative group had knowledge of sexual intercourse.

Those who belittle the difficulties of sexual abstinence may do well to consider the experience of the early Christian ascetics in the desert, as described, for instance, in the *Paradise* of Palladius. These men were vigorous and resolute, they were wholeheartedly devoted to the ideals of asceticism, they were living under the best possible conditions for cultivating such ideals, and their *régime* was austere to a degree that is for us impossible and almost inconceivable. Yet there was nothing that troubled them so much as sexual temptation, and this trouble to some degree persisted throughout life.

It may be added that another fact should warn us against any facile acceptance of mere platitudes in dealing with this question. I refer to the fact that, putting aside altogether the experiences of ancient ascetics and coming down to the present day, all careful investigation shows that the proportion of persons, even among physicians, who really live continuously in true sexual abstinence, that is without any manifestation of sexual activity, is really very small.[1] It is only considerable when we leave out of account the imperfect forms of normal sexual gratification involved in flirting, etc.,

[1] Meirowsky of Cologne, by inquiries among eighty-six physicians, found that only one had never had sexual intercourse before marriage. In English-speaking lands the proportion may well be larger, but on the other hand the proportion adopting auto-erotic practices also larger.

the abnormal forms of the impulse, and its various auto-erotic manifestations. Rohleder, an experienced physician in this field, believed some years ago that, when we thus widely look at the matter, there is no such thing as sexual abstinence, the genuine cases in which sexual phenomena fail to appear being simply cases of sexual anæsthesia. The seeming variations which we find would thus mainly be due to national differences in tradition which in some countries favour, in effect, resort to prostitution, and, in others, resort to masturbation. There are, indeed, two schools of physicians in this matter, one of which sternly reprobates any indulgence in the unmanly habit of masturbation, but is comparatively lenient to prostitution; while the other severely condemns any resort to the dangerous and immoral practice of prostitution, but is comparatively lenient to masturbation. (Forel, however, put both practices on the same level, prostitution with an indifferent stranger being "merely a form of masturbation.") Such considerations as these may profitably be borne in mind when we attempt to treat, or to palliate, the manifestations of unsatisfied sexual activity, such as local congestion, insomnia, irritability, depression, headache, vague hysterical and nervous symptoms. When the resulting troubles definitely approach the borderland of the psychoses it is usually found that other co-operative causes must be taken into account, and here psycho-analysts have sought out many devious paths in the Unconscious. Below the age of twenty-four, as Löwenfeld finds, men seldom suffer from abstinence, and even later rarely to a degree requiring medical aid, though Hirschfeld reports unfavourably of men who have lived abstinently to the age of thirty and then married. It is a bad constitution which makes abstinence a cause of nervous trouble, and this, as Freud, Löwenfeld and others have found, usually in both sexes takes the form of anxiety neurosis.

For the most part, however, as so often in the sexual field, treatment here usually resolves itself largely into hygiene, which, to be effective, must begin earlier than the conditions it is meant to combat: a simple life, plain food, cold bathing, the absence of luxury, avoidance of all strong physical or mental excitations, no evil companionship, abundant occupation and ample exercise in the open air, etc. The child who, being well born, is thus bred from his earliest years—however willing we may be to accept, in the abstract, the doctrine of infantile sexuality—has a fair chance, in the absence of unavoidable accidents, of prolonging sexual unconsciousness, even though sexual instruction may have been imparted, for a long time. But when once the organic sexual impulses have become irresistibly present to consciousness, all these excellent rules of regimen are no longer so effectual as they are sometimes represented to be. They are good to follow, in any cases, and sometimes they are not without effect in subduing the activity of the sexual impulse, but we must not expect from them what they cannot give. Healthy physical exercise, so far from repressing sexual desire, much more often, both in men and women, acts as a stimulant to evoke it, and only has a subduing influence when carried to an unhealthy and immoderate excess, producing exhaustion. Avoidance of a meat diet is equally ineffective, and Hirschfeld remarks that the carnivorous animals show less sexual ardour than the graminivorous. Mental work, likewise, sometimes even when of a purely abstract nature, is liable to cause sexual excitement. It is, indeed, obvious that the rules of general hygiene, being conducive to vigour, cannot fail to impart vigour in the sexual sphere ; we cannot take measures to generate vigour in the system, and then impede its overflow into sexual channels.

We may, it is true, transmute sexual energy into other more spiritual forms ; but only a small proportion of sexual energy can thus be sublimated ; as Freud well says, it is with sexual energy in the human organism as it is with heat in our machines, only a certain proportion can be transformed into work. Certainly we may resort to drugs, of which the bromides are the most generally employed, and probably the most effective. Such resort is perhaps especially beneficial in nervous and over-excitable persons whose sexual erethism is not the outcome of sexual vigour. In robust and temperamentally sexual persons the bromides are often useless unless pushed to an extent productive of a general deadening of the finer activities. This is not a satisfactory method of dealing with a great natural impulse capable of fine uses. We have to recognize the limitations of our powers in this field, refrain from platitudes in the face of difficulties which the social environment often renders inevitable, and leave to the patient himself the responsibility of solving those difficulties.

There are indeed some physicians who boldly declare that in this matter we must ourselves assume an unlimited responsibility. A patient comes—say, a Catholic priest or a married woman with an impotent husband—clearly suffering from nervous troubles as a result of sexual abstinence. It is our duty, they say, to these patients, firmly to recommend sexual intercourse. I do not think so. Apart from the fact that the physician obviously cannot guarantee the purity of the drug he is prescribing, apart also from the immorality of recommending in private a course of action entirely opposed to that which, in all probability, he implicitly or explicitly recommends in public, the physician who gives advice outside his own strictly medical sphere is bound to consider the wider effects of that advice on the patient himself. If—as in the instances mentioned—such advice leads a man into conduct antagonistic to his professional character, or leads a woman to place herself in a painful social position, the results, even to health, may be worse than those involved by the struggle to repress sexual desire ; one struggle has merely given place to another and perhaps more serious struggle. The physician would do well, when he goes beyond the purely medical sphere in this matter, to confine himself to a clear, wide, and impartial presentment of the issues that are before the patient, leaving to the patient himself the responsibility, which must rightly belong to him, of selecting the solution. The physician's part here is that of a judge charging the jury ; he must clear up the issues but not pronounce the verdict. In so doing he may at the same time bring his patient to a calmer and more rational attitude, and will perhaps prevent a rash attempt to cut the knot which it seems impossible to untie.

The conventional remedy for the ills of sexual abstinence—certainly also the best when it can be carried out under good conditions—is a fitting marriage.

BIBLIOGRAPHY

WALLIS BUDGE, *The Paradise of the Fathers.*

HAVELOCK ELLIS, *Studies in the Psychology of Sex,* Vol. VI.

FREUD, "Civilized Sexual Morality and Modern Nervousness," *Collected Papers,* Vol. II.

K. B. DAVIS, *Factors in the Sex-Life of Twenty-two Hundred Women.*

The Advisability of Marriage

The physician is nowadays consulted much more frequently than used to be the case concerning the desirability of a marriage when there appears some ground for anxiety as to the results of the union on the couple or their offspring. Moreover, the opinion of the physician on such matters is now taken more seriously than it formerly was. It is necessary, therefore, in such cases to avoid platitudes, which under the circumstances may be inconsiderate, and to give, so far as possible, a deliberate and circumspect opinion. The scientific material on which such an opinion can properly be based is for a large number of cases still imperfect and only now beginning to be co-ordinated, so that this whole subject belongs largely to a future, perhaps not remote, when it may be possible to forecast the probable results of sexual unions with much more precision than can now be done. At present, as Karen Horney also concludes in studying this question, even psycho-analysis (in which nevertheless she has much faith) will not furnish the insight necessary to enable us to prophesy concerning the future of a marriage. Moreover, the subject is, for the most part, outside the scope of the present chapter. There are, however, a few points in regard to which some indications may here be given.

A simple case which not infrequently occurs is that of the youth or girl who suddenly overwhelms relations and friends by announcing an intention to enter on a marriage which is flagrantly unsuitable, although it may not obviously clash with any eugenic principle. The physician is appealed to in order to ward off the dreaded marriage, and is sometimes expected to declare that the imprudent lover is not mentally sound. That is a matter for investigation, but it may be said that in most cases of this kind, while there may be a slightly neurotic heredity, the aberration, if it is an aberration, so little overpasses physiological limits that it cannot safely be combated on these grounds. The Romeo and Juliet lovers who disregard the social barriers which oppose their union are overcome by a temporary exaltation, but they are not insane, except in the sense in which Burton in his *Anatomy of Melancholy* copiously argued that all lovers are insane. In most cases of this kind we are concerned with young people who have not yet emerged from the storm and stress period of adolescence, and in whom the sudden eruption of the new erotic life produces an almost physiological disturbance of mental balance which will speedily right itself and never occur again.

A typical case which sometimes occurs is that of a chaste and upright youth who, having accidentally been brought into close contact with a prostitute, forms the design of marrying her, in such a case the obscure promptings of the sexual impulse being more or less disguised by the idea of redeeming a woman who seems never to have had a fair chance. Now it not infrequently happens that marriage with a prostitute turns out well when it is the result of deliberate choice by a mature and experienced man who clearly realizes what he is doing. But that is not likely to happen in the case of an ignorant youth blinded by the exaltation of his feelings. In these cases the best method of preventing the union is to temporize. Severe opposition will merely serve to increase the exaltation and lead to rash steps which will precipitate the dreaded marriage. By contriving to obtain delay, and in the meantime securing for the youth ample opportunity to see and study his beloved, he may be brought to view her in somewhat the same light as his friends.

In the case of a girl who contemplates a rash marriage, it may often be possible to remove her into a different environment in which new interests and relationships will gradually be formed. Sometimes (as was apt to happen during the

Great War); a young woman will, for a time, contemplate marriage with an attractive man of lower social class. Such a union should be strongly discouraged, however little value we may attach to class feeling, for it is very unlikely to work out, and the woman who has had such an idea seldom repents abandoning it. Lady Chatterley can never be the happy wife of her peasant lover. The unions which are the speedy result of a sudden infatuation so often produce a chain of disastrous results that it is always legitimate in such cases to introduce obstacles tending to cause delay, even though it is true that Absence is " the mother of ideal beauty," and that many a lover thus frustrated cherishes the belief that he or she thus missed happiness in life. The experience of Dickens, who when rejected by the girl he admired in youth, came to regard her as the supreme embodiment of perfect womanhood and moulded his heroines in her image, only to be repelled and disgusted when he at last met her again in the flesh, is an experience which has often been repeated in the lives of less distinguished persons.

These are special difficulties which may not often come under our notice. But whenever the question of marriage arises at all, there is at some point or another a problem to be solved, and such problems are more and more frequently brought before the physician. They can only be slightly touched on here, and it is scarcely necessary to say that there is seldom any definite and positive formula to be applied. Each case has to be considered individually, and the most desirable solution of one may be the most undesirable of another. It is probable that in the future all great centres of city life will possess institutions (of which the Sexual Institute of Berlin may be regarded as the pioneer) at which advice may be obtained concerning all the various problems of marriage.

The question of age may arise, the question of health and heredity, the question of physical examination, the question of preparedness or of preparation for marriage, the question of delayed procreation, and the highly important question of compatibility, physical or psychic, on which so often the happiness of marriage rests.

As regards the desirable age of marriage for marital happiness, as well as for the production of the best children, there is considerable difference of opinion, and at present few adequately convincing data on a broad basis. Hart and Shields in Philadelphia, measuring satisfaction in marriage by appearances in the Domestic Relations Court, found results opposed to early marriage, while Patterson, also in Philadelphia, failed to find a significantly larger proportion of marital difficulties when marriage took place under twenty years of age than in later marriage. Dickinson and Lura Beam found that the average age of wives who could be regarded as "adjusted without complaint," was some years over the average age, and in considering the length of married life of those couples who eventually separated or divorced, it was not found to be shortest in those who married youngest. Those who marry later are in the best position to know their own deepest needs and to form sound judgments, but at the same time they have often acquired psychic habits and physical troubles which render mental adjustment difficult, while the young girl is not only more adjustable psychically, but usually much more apt physically for coitus, and even for maternity, than is commonly supposed. The question is indeed not entirely of age but also of character, intelligence, and experience; the average age of marriage is probably at present quite as high as is desirable, and often too high. Burgdörfer is emphatically on the side of early marriage, while Hagen and Max Christian conclude that from the eugenic standpoint a man should marry at twenty-five and a woman earlier, courageously facing whatever difficulties may arise later. In Germany, where the age for men is around twenty-nine and for women twenty-five, a few centuries ago it was under nineteen for men and under fifteen for girls.

At whatever age marriage takes place, it is highly desirable, and ought indeed to be considered necessary, that full medical examination of each party should be made from the point of view of marital relationships and parenthood. This should be made at an early stage, and before the proposed marriage is made known to any wide circle of friends. It must, of course, include gynæcological examination of the woman and genito-urinary examination of the man. It has been argued that such certificates should be compulsory and some attempts have been made in that direction. But such an examination is so highly desirable for the welfare of both parties, even apart from all eugenic considerations with which we are not here primarily concerned, that no couple proposing to marry should wait for compulsion.

There is another kind of preparation for marriage, of an even more essential nature, which can only be made by the couple themselves in private. That is an examination into their own knowledge and feelings with regard to the intimate relationship they are proposing to initiate. What does each know about the anatomy and physiology of the other's body, and his or her own, and what are their emotional reactions to these matters? It has too often happened that, as Dickinson and Lura Beam put it, " the young husband finds her ' too sacred ' to consider her inner mechanism, or the wife thinks of herself as a tree with a solid trunk. The knowledge of anatomy of some of them is comparable with that of the early Persians." What, above all, are their feelings about intimacy in married love? There are husbands as well as wives who dread any private touch; there are husbands and wives who have never been in the bath-room together, because of some terror either on his part or on hers. But there can never be any real confidence and trust, never any real marriage union, without the possibility of a complete intimacy welcome to both. As Katharine Davis found, the percentage of happy marriages among women who were, in one way or another adequately prepared, was very much larger than among those who were not thus prepared.

It is not, of course, only on the sexual side that this mutual knowledge is needed. Marriage is much more than a sexual relationship. There are many marriages nowadays, and not always the least happy provided there is full mutual understanding, in which no sexual relationship ever takes place. It is, as so many investigations show, compatibility which is the chief clue to satisfaction in marriage. There are many temperaments which, however estimable in themselves, will not suit each other. This must be tested before marriage, it cannot safely be left till after. It is necessary for the couple to live together for considerable periods under some of the ordinary as well as extraordinary stresses of life in order for each to observe the other's reactions, not merely to each other—for such reactions are too often liable to be modified after marriage—but to outsiders. Such a noviciate, which the Catholic Church wisely regards as necessary before taking the veil for the cloister, is equally necessary before taking the veil before the altar of marriage, whether or not it is carried so far as actual sex relationships.

Not only is compatibility of temperament,—which by no means involves identity of temperament, but may even involve the opposite, provided there is harmony,—called for in marriage. A harmony of tastes and of interests is also in the highest degree desirable. A difference of temperament—as of extrovert with introvert—may be harmonious and complementary, and much more satisfactory to both parties than a tendency to identity of reaction. But a harmony, not necessarily an identity, of tastes and interests, is essential to a complete marriage union. Thus a distaste for music is not easily associated with a devotion to music; a difference in political ideals may not always be overbalanced by sexual compatibility; and where there are pronounced differences of religious conviction (such as Roman Catholicism and Evangelical Protestantism) marriage should be definitely discouraged. The wife is to-day no longer a purely domestic creature, with no interests outside the home, and it is not easy to imagine a satisfactory marriage in which there is no general agreement concerning the larger movements of social life in the world, whatever differences there must inevitably be concerning matters of method and detail.

It must always be remembered that all counsel concerning the advisability of a particular marriage is simply an attempt to foretell something which cannot be known beforehand with certainty. The couple, especially if young, will not be to-morrow altogether the same as to-day. As Exner well puts it, "psychologic marriage, marriage as a creative personal relationship, is *an achievement* between mates, and is not necessarily entered into at the wedding." It is often a very slow achievement, years of gradual progress may be needed before a relationship which can be called marriage in the full and deep sense is reached. It may never be reached at all.

There are many persons who, for some personal reason, cannot be advised to marry. Others for hereditary and eugenic reasons may be permitted to marry but not to procreate; in such cases by far the best method of contraception is sterilization of the husband.

BIBLIOGRAPHY

MAYO FOUNDATION LECTURES, 1923–4, *Our Present Knowledge of Heredity.*

LEONARD DARWIN, *Eugenic Reform.*

K. B. DAVIS, *Factors in the Sex Life of Twenty-two Hundred Women.*

DICKINSON AND LURA BEAM, *A Thousand Marriages.*

MRS. HAVELOCK ELLIS, *The New Horizon in Love and Life,* "A Noviciate for Marriage."

EXNER, *The Sexual Side of Marriage.*

R. L. DICKINSON, *Pre-marital Examination.*

LOPEZ DEL VALLE, "Pre-marital Medical Examination," *World's Health,* September, 1927.

Satisfaction in Marriage

In old times marriage was regarded as a sacred duty, appointed divinely or by the State. We do not marry for ourselves, said Montaigne. The question of satisfaction hardly entered, though it was assumed that happiness attended the fulfilment of an ordained duty, except for persons who were exceptional and perverse. That was the view sanctified alike by religion and by art; reputable novels of love ended in the unquestioned bliss of life-long union, and the Church romantically refused to admit that the end could be otherwise. Such a view is now antiquated; it was bound not to be in accordance with the real facts, partly because the facts had previously been disguised, and partly because the conditions now have actually become more complex. To-day many have gone to the opposite extreme of opinion and declared that, far from yielding life-long bliss, marriage hardly ever leads to even moderate satisfaction and happiness.

"Spiritual disappointment and physical deprivation become the fate of most marriages," declared Freud in 1908, and again, "a girl must be very healthy to 'stand' marriage." Numberless statements by less eminent writers could be quoted to the same effect.

It is to be noted, however, that all such expressions convey personal impressions, which are notoriously liable to be unreliable in scientific matters and are never placed on a statistical basis. Moreover, they do not coincide with the personal impression of other experienced observers. The evils of marriage, as we have known it, alike for husband and wife and children, however for a large part easily preventable, are frequent and undoubted. Where family troubles occur, Popenoe, of the Institute of Family Relations, Los Angeles, found that of 500 consecutive cases coming in 1930, all but one showed sexual maladjustment as a complicating factor. Yet, as Exner points out, there is no need to be unduly pessimistic about marriage, and there would be still less if society did not so often disturb the vision of the young and misguide their first steps. As the same writer well says, a high rate of dissatisfaction is not an unmitigated evil. It means a high ideal and a desire to attain it, for marriage is really an *achievement.* That, indeed, is a point often overlooked. In our civilization, possibly in any civilization, marriage in any full sense of the term cannot be reached at a bound. Considering the frequent extraordinary ignorance alike of self and of the partner with which marriage is approached, it would be strange if true marriage were not difficult to achieve. There are (as Karen Horney puts it), even on the strictly personal side, at least three aspects of marriage: (1) the physical relationship; (2) the psychic relationship; and (3) what may be called the associational relationship of a life encountered in common. It is almost inevitable that, with so inadequate a preparation, the difficulties met are often but slowly conquered, until finally, though perhaps after many years, a real and true marriage is attained. Even when, as is undoubtedly often the case, the marriage remains imperfect, we find on deeper insight, in most cases, that many compensations have been achieved. In no field more than in marriage does the Emersonian doctrine of compensation hold good.

To obtain a fairly clear vision of the facts a methodical investigation over a wide field is necessary. Even then an only faintly approximate result is possible. Many people are unwilling to admit, even to themselves, still less to others, that marriage is for them a failure. Others, on the contrary, in the thick of the inevitable little worries and irritations of marriage, lose sight of the central facts which can only be seen when one stands some way off and looks at one's life as a whole ; they are tempted to admit a failure where at another moment they would claim a great success. There is a yet more fundamental source of difficulty. So few people are aware of the nature of the satisfaction that may reasonably be found in marriage. They fail to realize that marriage is but life in miniature, and that if married life were all easy and all pleasant it would be but a feeble image of the world and would fail to yield the deepest satisfaction that the world can give to those who have drunk deeply of life.

We must, therefore, at least make the attempt to put the question on a statistical basis, even though we cannot secure an absolutely precise answer. Katharine Davis, assuming (though the statement may need some qualification) that "the sex relationship indisputably plays the major part" in marriage, found that among 1,000 presumably normal married women 872 unequivocally affirmed that their married lives were happy ; 116 were either partially or totally unhappy, incompatibility being the chief cause ; only 12 failed to answer.

Dickinson, among his gynæcological patients, who cannot be assumed to be so normal as Katharine Davis's subjects, found a somewhat smaller proportion of satisfied women ;

he concludes that 3 in 5 among 1,000 patients were "adjusted," in the sense of being at least "without complaint" of their married life. In composition the two groups of "adjusted" and "maladjusted" were not markedly different; they were of similar social and economic status; at some period about two-thirds in both classes had had considerable experience of auto-erotic practices; the adjusted were slightly more fertile than the other group; but the chief general difference seems to be that the outlook on life of the adjusted was more objective than that of the maladjusted; they were less self-centred and less troubled by mental conflicts. Yet he found a maladjusted group of 100 wives "socially normal," with "better than the average educational and economic standard," and in typical cases they were fine, well-dressed, sometimes beautiful or brainy women; 13 of them had definitely undesirable characters, and 19 came near to "profound total disturbance." They do not, however, greatly vary from the adjusted group in social and educational standing or in health, while the general externals of personality and environment are the same. The prevalence of auto-erotic practices before marriage had been almost the same, and sex was by no means always the beginning of the maladjustment, which was often due to incompatibility. The chief difference in the groups was the presence or absence of "mental conflict." We see here instructively how complex is often this question of "adjustment."

G. V. Hamilton among his smaller number of subjects, but of both sexes and all presumably normal, 100 married men and 100 married women, made a most elaborate investigation into their degree of satisfaction in marriage, with fourteen grades of happiness, according to the number of points to be assigned to each person. He found that husbands are definitely more satisfied with marriage than are wives. In the highest grades (7 to 14) there were 51 men and only 45 women, leaving 49 men but 55 women in the lower grades of satisfaction. Hamilton states that the result corresponds with his definite impression from personal contact that "the women, taken as a whole, had been more seriously disappointed with their marriages than had the men."

It cannot be said that this conclusion should cause surprise, and it seems to agree with my own experience. To some extent it lies in the relationship of the two sexes to marriage. To a woman marriage means more than to a man, because in the care of husband and child and household it necessarily absorbs a larger part of her being, so that if there is a sense of disappointment that disappointment is more serious. A man is more detached from home and family because his life is usually so much outside. Home occupies a smaller section of his field of activity; it constitutes a haven of rest. A woman, on the other hand, must often feel that marriage is her whole life, and deeper problems are thus stirred within her. This brings us to Dickinson's significant observation that the main difference between the adjusted wives and the maladjusted wives is that the former are more objective, and less troubled by mental conflicts. They are, in other words, more like the average husbands.

But the discontent with marriage which we so often find among wives, even though more or less below the surface, has a real foundation. It is associated with the new and larger claims on life which the women of recent generations have more and more taken, not content like their mothers to accept as natural and inevitable the predominance of men and their own place of subjection. The religious and social aspects of the world have changed for women without in any corresponding degree changing for men, because the change has for women been in large measure socially recognized and legally registered. The traditions of men have changed but little. So that when a woman enters marriage she is apt to become aware of a discrepancy which tends to become a mental conflict within herself. There are many women—old-fashioned romantically minded women brought up away from men as well as more modern girls—who realize even during the honeymoon the nature of man and of marriage for the first time and acquire a dissatisfaction which may never be entirely outgrown.

There is, as I have indicated, a still deeper ground for this discontent with marriage. The changes in the external order of marriage during recent times have too often left out of sight the fundamental facts of the relationship of marriage. They have concentrated attention on its more external features and they have made it appear that happiness in marriage depends on an easy readjustment of the external order. Above all, they have tended to put out of sight the fact, much better realized in old days, that such a relationship, penetrating so deeply into the spirit, can never be—save for the most shallow-spirited persons—without difficulty and trouble. The old conception of the inevitable pains of marriage is out of date. But they remain in new shapes and are of the nature of the relationship. Divorce may be no cure at all, even when we admit that there should be the greatest possible freedom for divorce. We constantly see people who divorce but are no happier in a second marriage. It is not marriage that was wrong; it was themselves that were wrong. Count Keyserling, in a subtle and penetrating analysis of the marriage problem, describes marriage as "an inter-polar tension"; there is a unity constituted by two foci: the two are held together by a tension—"a tragic tension" he elsewhere calls it—which cannot be abolished if the relationship is to remain intact. Such a relationship is a symbol of life itself, and, as in life generally, it is essential to its joy. So that no ascetic emphasis on pain or trouble for their own sake is here implied. As the poet-prophet Kahlil Gibran again and again asserts, joy and sorrow are inseparable. "Is not the cup that holds your wine the very pot that was burned in the potter's oven?" Long before that was said, the wise Montaigne, in the essay "On some lines of Virgil," which contains so many memorable sayings, had recalled the fact that the same muscles with which we weep are those with which we laugh.

BIBLIOGRAPHY

R. L. DICKINSON AND LURA BEAM, *A Thousand Marriages.*
G. V. HAMILTON, *A Research in Marriage.*

K. B. DAVIS, *Factors in the Sex Life of Twenty-two Hundred Women.*
EXNER, *The Sexual Side of Marriage.*
HAVELOCK ELLIS, "The History of Marriage," Vol. VII. *of Studies in the Psychology of Sex*, and *Little Essays of Love and Virtue.*
COUNT KEYSERLING, "Correct Statement of Marriage Problem," in *The Book of Marriage.*

The Monogamic Standard

Until modern times monogamy has been regarded as the only legitimate form of marriage for our Western civilization. Indeed, that has for the most part been assumed and taken for granted without discussion ; any exceptional person who disputed this dogma, or even discussed it, was regarded as, and usually in fact was, a crank, a negligible eccentric, if not something much worse. To-day the question of the form of marriage cannot thus be taken for granted and dismissed, as a matter that has for ever been fixed by religious, ethical, legal, and social regulations. Those who discuss it are no longer always negligible persons. So that any one who now concerns himself with the psychology of sex must be prepared to hold an opinion on sex relationships in regard to monogamy.

As a pioneer in the movement to bring our monogamic marriage system into the field of discussion, we may well regard James Hinton. It was half a century and more ago, though his arguments on the matter were not clearly published to the world until some forty years later. Hinton delayed any full public presentation of his criticism of Western monogamy until he had mastered the subject, and before then he died. He was not a man who could be put aside as abnormal or eccentric. He was a distinguished London surgeon and a philosophic thinker as well, in close touch with the scientific activities of his day, widely interested in general social questions, and in daily contact with life. The masses of manuscript he left behind are shapeless and unsystematic, but have made it possible to gather the general drift of his criticisms of monogamy and the conventional social system associated with it. He considered that no real monogamy existed, and that in Western Society, as he knew it, there are fewer men who are genuinely monogamic than are to be found in Eastern polygamic societies. Monogamy, as established, is, he held, an essentially selfish and unsocial institution, and is responsible for prostitution. We arrived at it too soon, for it is a mistake to convert an ideal, however good, prematurely into a universal legal form. The result has been that, though ostensibly existing to avert licentiousness, it has called out more licence than a polygyny would have led to. So it seemed to him that our marriage system is rotten, and rapidly breaking up. What we need, he believed, is a fluid order in our sex system, not rigid and unmodifiable, but permitting, when it seemed desirable, the union of one man with two women, though always leaving the order adjustable to the claims of human service.[1]

In more recent days, a rather similar thesis, though often on different grounds and seldom or ever with the same concentrated intensity as by Hinton, has been put forward from time to time. Simultaneously, it must be added, our marriage system actually has undergone modifications. If we compare its state to-day with the conditions in Hinton's time, many changes may be observed, and often in the direction he desired. Divorce is easier ; women have gained greater legal and social independence ; illegitimacy is viewed with somewhat less severity; the methods of birth control have become widely known; and greater freedom between the sexes is in all civilized countries admitted.

At the same time, in one sense or another, monogamy is to-day as firmly established as it has ever been, and even more so. By imparting to it a greater flexibility we to a considerable extent relieve it of the abuses to which in the former more rigid form it was subject.

[1] George Pitt-Rivers, in the Supplement to his suggestive work, *The Clash of Culture* (1927), argues that Man, like many animals, is a polygynous species (though Christian " monogamy " is " a disorderly mixture of polygyny and polyandry "), and that " a surplusage of adult females over males is a necessary condition of the stabilization and continued vigour of the human race." It must, however, be remembered that the normal sex-ratio inevitably limits any polygynous tendency, even if beneficial

Confusion has been introduced, it must be made clear, by using the word " monogamy " in the wrong sense. It is, for instance, common to say that one sex is more " monogamic " than the other sex, especially that men are " polygamic " while women are " monogamic." Strictly speaking, such statements are meaningless. At the outset it is obvious that since the sexes are born nearly equal in number (with, at the start, a preponderance of males), the natural order in a civilized society cannot work out as two wives for every male, and in the societies which recognize polygamy it is only practised by a small wealthy class. But it is incorrect to assert that in our civilization men (rare exceptions aside) ever desire two wives, whether in the same home or in separate homes ; there are various considerations of different orders which make such an arrangement undesirable for the majority of men ; while, for a woman, to carry on two families, with separate fathers, is still more impracticable ; she is necessarily " monogamic."

In fact, that is the wrong word to use. The people who discuss whether men are more " polygamic " than women, really mean more *poly-erotic*. That is to say, not whether they desire more marriages but more sexual freedom. To say that a man is monogamic still leaves open the question of whether he is *mono-erotic* or *poly-erotic*, and if it is decided that he is poly-erotic, that by no means implies either that he is polygamic, or that he is promiscuous, which involves indiscriminate sexual attraction without selection, a state of things not found, save occasionally in insanity. Much confused and futile discussion has been caused by this ignorant misuse of terms.

It would seem that most persons, women as well as men, are monogamic and poly-erotic. That is to say they only desire one permanent marriage, but they do not find that that relationship stands in the way of sexual attraction to one or more other persons, though the attraction thus aroused may be felt to be of a different nature to that experienced for the permanent partner, and it may prove quite possible to hold such attractions more or less in control. There appears to be no sexual difference in this matter. Women are fully as well able as men to experience affection for more than one person of the opposite sex, though on account of the deeper significance of sex for women they may be instinctively more fastidious than men in sexual choice, and on account of social and other considerations more reticent and cautious than men in manifesting or in yielding to their affections.

While, however, this seems the most frequent type of sexual attraction, there are other types and endless individual variations. We must not assume that one special type of sexual pattern is invariably of higher moral character and social value than the other types. Blonsky, in Soviet Russia, has discussed the two chief types of women (mainly among teachers), which he terms the monandric and the polyandric types, the first only drawn into serious relationship with one man, and the other who tends to form numerous relationships with men, either successively or simultaneously, though, of course, there are intermediate groups between the two marked types. Blonsky finds that the monandric woman, not only individually but socially, tends to be superior to the polyandric woman, who is more egoistic and assertive and more liable to undue nervosity, while the monandric women, who are twice as numerous, are more devoted to duty, better balanced, more capable organizers, and more successful in social contacts. These conclusions of Blonsky's doubtless have truth for the average, outside as well as inside Russia, but we must beware of generalizing too positively, and there are women of polyandric type for whom far more is to be said than Blonsky seems willing to admit. Exactly the same conclusions may be applied to men.

This is not a matter in which we are called upon to give advice. In matters of social morality, individuals are bound to take the responsibility for their own actions. But it is desirable for the psychologist to be able to view intelligently the psychic reactions occurring in the communities of to-day in which he lives. In this matter we undoubtedly witness a process of change, though it is much less extreme than many alarmists would make it out to be.

The "polygamy" which some people view to-day with consternation is mostly, as some one has improperly termed it, merely a "consecutive polygamy," due to an increased tendency to divorce. That is to say, it is simply an enlargement of the familiar monogamy. For the rest it is a recognition of the claim of variety in erotic affection. Every man and every woman, however monogamic where the central affections are concerned, is capable of a more or less erotically coloured affection for other persons, as we recognize to-day more frankly than it has been recognized in the past. The adjustments thus rendered necessary call for a generous and large-hearted understanding on the part of all the persons concerned, with mutual consideration, an equable sense of justice, and the conquest of those vestiges of primitive jealousy without which no wholesome civilized life can harmoniously be carried on.

But marriage in its main lines remains to-day, and is likely to remain, in the same form as we have always known it. To give it greater flexibility, to bring to it a finer intelligence, and to accord a greater sympathy to its varying needs, far from destroying it, is to impart to it a firmer stability.

Marriage, we must never forget—as too often happens—is more than an erotic union. To the truly "ideal" marriage there go not only an erotic harmony, but a union of many-sided and ever-deepening non-erotic affection, a community of tastes and feelings and interests, a life in common, a probability of shared parenthood, and often an economic unity. The erotic element tends to become less prominent as the marriage in other respects becomes a closer bond. It may even disappear altogether and the marriage remain unshakeably firm in mutual devotion.

BIBLIOGRAPHY

Westermarck, *The History of Human Marriage.*

Havelock Ellis, *Studies in the Psychology of Sex*, Vols. VI. and VII.

Havelock Ellis, *Little Essays of Love and Virtue* and *More Essays of Love and Virtue.*

V. F. Calverton, *The Bankruptcy of Marriage.*
Mrs. Havelock Ellis, *James Hinton : A Sketch.*

The Control of Procreation

Keyserling has remarked that those who are not able to accept the relationship of marriage in its fundamental sense would be well advised to avoid marriage and adopt some other form of sexual relationship.

Apart from that solution, however, there is one point which must nowadays always be held in mind when we are considering marriage from the eugenic standpoint in relation to the probable quality of the offspring. Formerly marriage and procreation were one and in aim indivisible. To recommend marriage meant to permit procreation ; to advise against procreation meant to prohibit marriage, and permanently to impair the happiness of the lives thus condemned to solitude, as well as indirectly to encourage prostitution or other undesirable methods of sexual relief. This necessity no longer exists among the educated classes in any civilized country. Contraception, the use of a variety of methods to permit intercourse while avoiding conception—whether or not it receives formal public approval—has become so general that the discussion of its desirability no longer subserves any useful purpose. It exists on a large scale even in countries where the law forbids its dissemination, and even among the adherents of creeds which disapprove of it.

Thus we have nowadays to distinguish between the desirability of marriage and the desirability of procreation, the latter question involving not only regard to the probable interests of the couple themselves, especially the wife, but also to the probable interests of the offspring. It is an undoubted advantage to be able to deal separately with the issues involved. Nor can it even be said that any revolutionary change has hereby taken place. It has long been customary in certain serious eventualities to enjoin abstinence from procreation for the future. It is only one step further to utter this injunction at the outset of marriage. It is well known that neuropathic persons tend to be attracted to each other. This is part of a general tendency of people to be attracted to their like, now known to prevail over the attraction to opposites, which was once imagined to be the rule; homogamy, that is to say, is more prevalent than heterogamy. The craving for opposite qualities is confined to the sphere of the secondary sexual characters, a very masculine man being attracted to a very feminine woman and *vice versâ*, but it fails, as a general rule, to extend beyond that sphere.

This fact has a bearing on the advice we may be called upon to give to neuropathic persons who contemplate marriage. Sensitive, intelligent, refined, as such a person often is, the neuropath finds an answering sympathy in a fellow neuropath, while the healthy normal person may seem irritatingly dull and insipid. In the same way the normal person finds the morbid and capricious temperament of the neuropath uncomfortable and unattractive. It is, therefore, somewhat futile to adopt the common advice that the neuropath should marry, if at all, a robustly normal person, with sound heredity. The advice is not even theoretically correct when we bear Mendelian conditions in mind. But it is unpractical because it overlooks the fact that the affinity between the normal and the morbid is not strong and that the chances of such a union proving satisfactory are not large. These chances are not considerable even in the case of two pronounced neuropathic people who marry each other, and such people may well be advised not to marry at all, alike for the sake of themselves and of their partners, however difficult the problem of sexual gratification may be to them in the unmarried state; the reasons against marriage in the case of such persons become all the more emphatic if there is a highly developed sexual deviation which the partner may not be able to gratify. But for the milder neuropathic cases these objections have less force, while the attraction is often so strong that opposing advice has but a small chance of being accepted. In such cases the necessity of distinguishing between procreation and marriage becomes stringent.

The necessity of birth control is now generally recognized,

not only by those who do not desire to have children but by those who do. The reason is that, both for the sake of the mother and for the health and well-being of the offspring, it is desirable that births should be properly spaced, allowing at the least an interval of two years between births, while there are various legitimate reasons, economic or other, why those who marry early do not see their way to become parents immediately. The child, therefore, however much desired, should come at a time when the parents are best able to receive it and to care for it. Moreover, the day of large families is over. Alike for the sake of the family, and in the interests of the nation and the race, an average of between two and three for each married couple suffices, and under the hygienic conditions of civilization is ample to keep up the population. When, for any good reason, such as the health of the mother or the existence in either parent of a bad heredity which should not be carried on, conception cannot be allowed, then strict birth control is compulsory.

We are not here concerned with methods of birth control. The literature of this subject is now extensive, though there is still dispute regarding the best methods, and even the best (sterilization apart), whichever they may be, are not always reliable. Fortunately birth control clinics are rising up rapidly in various countries, and here may be obtained practical help and advice, to the absence of which failure is often due among those who possess imperfect knowledge, though even with the best knowledge it is frequently difficult to maintain invariably the care necessary for success. It is true that the most ancient and common of all methods of contraception, *coitus interruptus*, requires no appliances and is practised without advice; and it is fairly certain. But though not so generally harmful as is sometimes supposed, it is frequently unsatisfactory, for in most men it involves undue haste, which is unpleasant for the husband and apt to be inadequate for the wife who may need satisfaction afterwards.

A common problem is indeed presented by interrupted coitus. This practice is held by the best authorities to be the commonest of all methods of preventive intercourse. It is also no doubt the most ancient and is referred to in the book of Genesis as being adopted by Onan in order to avoid conception. Its popularity is due to its simplicity ; it requires no forethought or preparation and it costs nothing. But there can be no doubt that, in relation to the well-being of the nervous system, the practice is sometimes open to question. It is quite true that in dealing with a practice so extremely prevalent, it is not enough to say that it is often found injurious. But it is clear that, in a certain proportion of cases—whether a large or a small proportion—various minor nervous conditions, indicating nervous irritability, in the woman, the man, or both, seem to be traceable to interrupted intercourse. It is easily intelligible that this should be specially so as regards women. Husbands do not always display the consideration necessary to ensure orgasm in their wives, and since orgasm is normally slower in women than in men it is obvious that, in the absence of such consideration, withdrawal must frequently take place before the orgasm has occurred in the wife, who is thus left in a state of acute nervous dissatisfaction and irritability. But the anxious apprehension and attention to his own state involved on the husband's part by premature withdrawal, and the jar caused by the sudden breaking off of the act at its culminating moment, cannot fail sometimes to be injurious to him. It is necessary to be alive to the possible existence of this practice, and to suspend it if the symptoms seem to depend on it. For a large number of people, there can be no doubt, interrupted coitus is unsuited and should give place to some better method of preventive intercourse. Interrupted intercourse should not be persisted in unless it can be so carried out, by mutual sympathy and co-operation, that no shock or apprehension is caused to the husband, and that the wife receives due satisfaction ; the latter point may be achieved by delaying intercourse until tumescence is well advanced and he is approaching the orgasm.

The opposite practice of prolonged or reserved coitus, with or without ultimate orgasm, has nowadays numerous advocates and a considerable body of practical adherents, not so many as interrupted coitus because it is less easy to carry out. It was the ordinary practice of the Oneida community, and was later advocated in Dr. Alice Stockham's well-known book, *Karezza*. There can be no doubt that prolonged intercourse is highly agreeable to the woman partner, and without the slightest evil results; for she is left entirely free and is not precluded from experiencing the orgasm at its own good time. All women who have had experience of this method seem to approve of it. Some doubts, however, have been expressed as to its effects on the men who practise it. There is reason to think that in some cases greatly prolonged coitus may produce some of the same nervous results, though usually in a milder degree, as interrupted coitus. But in a large proportion of cases this is certainly not the case. The practice is not usually easy except for men with sound and well-balanced nervous systems, and such persons do not usually seem to be conscious of any evil results from the practice, provided of course that it is not carried to excess.

When contraception fails—either owing to carelessness or the use of an unsuitable method—a serious situation may sometimes arise. But there is nothing to be done. It is still a criminal offence to aid a woman to procure abortion for personal, social, or even eugenic considerations. Women seldom understand this illegality, and cannot understand why, if poor, they are compelled to take injurious drugs in vain, or, if better off, be obliged (if English) to go abroad for the operation. When women have more influence than at present in effecting legislative changes there can be no doubt that the legal prohibition of abortion, which is based on grounds that are now antiquated, will be modified. And it will become clearly established that this is a personal question with which the law is not entitled to interfere. If inadvisable, it is for the doctor, not the policeman, to offer an opinion. There is already a movement in this direction in various countries, and in Soviet Russia, although abortion is not encouraged it is carried out with due medical precautions in the hospitals, pending a more widespread popular enlightenment with extended facilities for contraception.

The prevention of conception involves so much care and precaution that of recent years an alternative and more reliable method of attaining that end has received an increased degree of favour: the method of sterilization. By this method all risks are eliminated. It can now be effected, simply and harmlessly, without removal of the sexual glands, by vasectomy in men and ligature and section of the Fallopian tubes in women. As a method of treating any psychic condition its value is dubious, and if performed compulsorily it may be pernicious in its mental effects; but, adopted voluntarily, as a method of preventing conception, its advantages seem to be great, while it abolishes the need for those preventive precautions which most people, quite legitimately, regard with disfavour.[1] It is scarcely necessary to add that sterilization, being a permanent contraceptive measure, should not be adopted without due consideration.

It is sometimes imagined, even by medical men, that sterilization is at present illegal. There is no sound ground for this belief. The Eugenics Society has in England attempted to put forward a Parliamentary Bill to further sterilization, not, however (as some have supposed), to make it legal (for it is already carried out), but to bring its benefits within the reach of defectives and among the poorer class. The benefits have sometimes been questioned, even, it must be said with regret, in the medical profession. But there can be no reasonable doubt that, whatever the exact proportion of defective children born of defective parents, sterilization would here be personally, socially, and eugenically helpful, although it could not be possible in this

[1] In one of the earliest cases known to me, an American physician, in good health and with a family of several children which he had no wish to increase, submitted to vasectomy in order to avoid the routine of preventive precautions which was repugnant to himself and his wife. The pain and discomfort of the operation were not sufficient to interfere with his ordinary office work, and the result proved entirely satisfactory to both partners. It remained so several years later, when last heard of. There was no loss of potency or of desire. This case may now be regarded as fairly typical.

way to eliminate the mentally unfit element in the population. It would only be a beginning. In regard to this subject there is still much need for the spread of enlightenment.

An equally common problem is presented with regard to the frequency of coitus. Very widely divergent views are dogmatically set forth on this point. Some persons consider it normal and necessary to have intercourse every night, and they continue this practice for many years with no obvious bad results. Others assert that intercourse should never be practised except for the end of procreation—which might mean only two or three times in a life-time—and they argue that such a practice is alone natural and normal. It is undoubtedly true that this is the only end in the intercourse of animals, but in determining what is natural for man we are not entitled to consider the practice of the animals belonging to remote genera. We have to consider the general practice of the human species which by no means shows so narrowly exclusive an aim in procreation, although unspoiled and uncivilized peoples are on the whole (contrary to a common assumption) much more sexually abstinent than civilized peoples. But even if it were not so we are quite justified in departing, if we think fit, from the habits of the lower races. Certainly the sexual organs were developed for procreation, not for the sexual gratification of the individual; certainly also the hands were developed to serve nutrition, not to play on the piano or the violin. But if the individual can find joy and inspiration in using his organs for ends they were not made for, he is following a course of action which, whether or not we choose to call it "natural," is perfectly justifiable and moral. Those who advocate imitation of the lower animals by confining sexual intercourse to the "natural" end of procreation, are also bound to imitate the lower animals by, for instance, discarding the "unnatural use" of clothing. Human art legitimately comes into human activities, but it introduces no real conflict with Nature.

> "This is an art
> Which does mend Nature, change it rather, but
> The art itself is Nature."

Putting aside all dubious theories, it must be recognized, from a practical standpoint, that the natural range of variation as regards frequency of intercourse is very wide, and it is necessary to find out in each individual case what frequency best suits each of the partners, and how any discrepancy, if it exists, can be harmonized. Rules have, indeed, been laid down from antiquity : Solon advised three cohabitations a month, which agreed with the general opinion of Greek physicians. Luther's dictum of twice a week commends itself to most. Harvey, putting together various American tables, finds that the median frequency of coitus is about eight times per month, the middle 50 per cent. ranging between three and fifteen times. There are sometimes advantages in a certain irregularity, an unusually speedy repetition being followed by a long intermission ; this repetition may easily occur at the woman's desire, just after menstruation. As desire is usually more irregular and more capricious in the woman than in the man it is the wife who may properly be regarded as the initiator in this matter and the husband may find his advantage in according her this privilege. But, it may be repeated, it is in any case better to space out the acts of intercourse rather than to multiply their frequency. Its benefits, both physical and spiritual, tend to be lost by frequent repetition. Sexual union can only become the fine ecstasy it is capable of becoming when it is rare.

The cultivation of coitus as a frequent habit is also undesirable because it renders difficult the long intermission which may be necessary during absence, illness of one of the partners, or the period (a month or six weeks) following childbirth. The question of intercourse during pregnancy is difficult. The physician is usually reluctant to give advice in this matter on account of the domestic difficulties that may arise. It is largely, no doubt, a question of the predisposition to abortion, which varies greatly ; some women, it has been said, will abort if you sneeze in their presence, while others will not abort if you throw them out of the fifth floor window. Where the tendency exists, it is certain that sexual abstinence should be enjoined. It is also desirable that it should be cultivated, in any case, during the latter months of pregnancy. But it seems necessary to exercise a certain amount of circumspection in recommending abstinence during the whole of pregnancy. A sympathetic and intelligent couple can often find their own solution of the difficulty, and there is not much risk of a habit of masturbation under such circumstances. But the physician who enjoins sexual abstinence during pregnancy may sometimes find that he has evoked difficulties it may be beyond his power to remove.

We are not here primarily concerned with the regulation of the conditions of procreation, nor with the optimum number of children for a normally healthy couple. It is widely held that, unless when marriage occurs at an unusually late age, conception should not be allowed to occur at too early a period after marriage. Under present social conditions, that danger, however, is small. Nor is it by any means so injurious as is frequently supposed for a young woman to bear a child. Thus at the Edinburgh Obstetrical Society recently (June 8th, 1932) Miller gave the results of 174 cases of pregnancy and labour in girls of seventeen years of age and below at the Royal Maternity Hospital. The spontaneous deliveries were 85 per cent. and only in eight cases was any intervention necessary for disproportion, while the still-birth and neo-natal death rate was 6·5 per cent. as against 11·8 for all children born in the Hospital. Difficulty and danger are much greater for elderly women. Whatever the age at which childbirth begins, it is most certainly desirable, in the interests of mother and children alike, as well as of the husband and father, that an interval of at least two years should elapse between pregnancies. The optimum average number of children, under modern conditions, alike for the family and for the maintenance of the population, is between two and three. Formerly, under bad social conditions and with a high mortality, the number was higher. Eugenic considerations will here, as social enlightenment advances, become more and more influential, some families will be smaller, and others may legitimately be larger.

BIBLIOGRAPHY

G. V. HAMILTON, *A Research in Marriage.*
R. L. DICKINSON, *A Thousand Marriages.*
MARGARET SANGER, *The New Motherhood.*
MICHAEL FIELDING, *Parenthood: Design or Accident? A Manual of Birth Control.*
J. F. COOPER, *Technique of Contraception.*
M. C. STOPES, *Contraception: Its Theory, History and Practice.*
A. KONIKOW, *Contraception.*
Some More Medical Views on Birth Control, edited by NORMAN HAIRE.
CARR-SAUNDERS, *The Population Problem.*
LANCELOT HOGBEN, *Genetic Principles in Medicine.*
O. L. HARVEY, American *Journal of Sociology,* July, 1932.
LEONARD DARWIN, *Eugenic Reform.*
GOSNEY and POPENOE, *Sterilization for Human Betterment.*
J. H. LANDMAN, *Human Sterilization: The History of the Sexual Sterilization Movement.*
HAVELOCK ELLIS, *Studies in the Psychology of Sex,* Vol. VI., and *More Essays of Love and Virtue.*
The Eugenics Review.
The Journal of Social Hygiene.

The Problem of Childless Marriage

When we have put aside those married couples who have decided on mature consideration that it is best for them, whether temporarily or permanently, not to have children, and also those who, being childless but desiring children, have good reason to hope that by medical or surgical treatment they may be able to carry out that wish, a minority still remain who have become convinced that they will never be able to have a child but who still desire one. What are they to do?

This situation ought indeed seldom to arise. If there is a strong wish for children it is highly desirable that both parties should submit themselves to medical investigation before marriage, if only to ascertain that there is a fair probability of successful conception and parturition. This cannot, however, be more than a probability, as is sufficiently evidenced by the cases in which a couple cannot produce the child they are eager for, though, after divorce and subsequent re-marriage, they both become parents. Conditions, also, which could not be known or foreseen before marriage, may afterwards arise and prevent conception. There remain four possible solutions all of which have their psychic aspects.

(1) *To Accept the Situation.*—For many this solution may prove the best. While most people, and certainly most women, at some time desire children, the desire is by no means always permanent. It is realized that there are also other things in life. It is at the same time recognized that at the present time the world is not perishing for lack of children. It may also be found that the path chosen in life has proved so exacting and absorbing that it is not justifiable, especially for a woman, to undertake also the duties of motherhood, which is itself, if adequately performed, for some years of life equivalent to a profession, and even an exacting and absorbing one. Perhaps, also, there are no special aptitudes for such a vocation, or there is present the consciousness of an unsatisfactory hereditary constitution which it may not be desirable to pass on. But the instincts of parenthood may be in large measure sublimated; the maternal instinct may be directed to social ends. Instead of being the physical parents of children who may perhaps bring no benefit to the world or to themselves, it is possible to expend the energies thus liberated in far-reaching activities of unquestioned benefit. Many women have attained eminence, as well as satisfaction, in such ways and performed social services of immense value.

(2) *To Seek Divorce.*—This may be a legitimate solution of the difficulty for those couples who regard children as of the first importance. But, even apart from the difficulty under most legal systems of obtaining divorce honestly on such grounds, it is not a solution to be welcomed. It is possible to approve of facility for divorce as an abstract principle and yet to deprecate resort to it. Moreover, a second marriage may prove even more unfortunate than the first and equally unfruitful. Divorce is, further, at the best a confession of failure in the most vital of personal matters, and even at the worst there are probably bonds of union between the partners which cannot easily be treated as of

no account because there do not happen to be children. Married people who wish for divorce because they have no children usually, if the full truth were known, wish to be divorced because they feel incompatible. So that for them the problem of childlessness is really part of a larger problem.

(3) *To Adopt a Child.*—This is the solution which most readily presents itself, and with sound judgment it works admirably, all the more since now, at all events in England, it can be put on a firm legal basis. The marriage is not broken but probably strengthened, and a real child is provided for whom the wife can be a mother in all but the physical sense. There is even an element of social service involved, for the reasonable prospect of a happy future is bestowed upon a child who might otherwise have proved a burden not only to its parents but to itself and to the community. To many women, even with a full and intellectual life, the adopted child has proved an unspeakable blessing and a constant source of happiness.

There are obvious precautions to be taken if child-adoption is to prove successful. Not only must the child be taken when quite young, but the transfer must be absolute and complete. The chief question is of health and heredity. To neglect consideration of the child's parentage and ancestry may lead to bitter results. A child should never be adopted until all the ascertainable facts of its history have been carefully considered with the physician's aid.

(4) *To have a Child by a Union outside Marriage.*—This is the most difficult of all the solutions. It is sometimes contemplated but can only be carried out under exceptional circumstances. The difficulty arises from the fact that consent is required of three persons, each of whom can scarcely fail to view the matter differently from the others, and all of whom must feel that they are acting in a way which a large portion of the social group they belong to would disapprove. The conditions for satisfactory achievement are so rare that it is unprofitable to discuss this solution, and it would be impossible to recommend it.

It is true that there are two modifications of this solution :

one, altogether to be disapproved, when the wife takes the matter into her own hands, without consulting her husband, and another, which is the most practicable form of this solution, by artificial insemination. It has often failed and it presents obvious disagreeable features. But it is practicable, and is from time to time carried out successfully. The technique has recently been discussed by Van de Velde.

BIBLIOGRAPHY

Van de Velde, *Fertility and Sterility in Marriage*.

Impotence and Frigidity (Sexual Hypoæsthesia and Sexual Hyperæsthesia)

The limits within which the sexual impulse may vary—both as regards its strength and the age at its first appearance and final disappearance—are wide. In this matter Man differs from nearly all lower animals (except some of the higher apes), in whom the impulse is closely connected with the procreative life and is mostly absent at those times when it would be useless.

Manifestations of sexual impulse, as we know, both on the physical and the psychic side, are even in ordinary healthy children by no means so rare that we can regard them as abnormal. At the other end of life there are likewise no definite frontiers to the psychic sexual life. In women, the menopause is not always, or even usually, accompanied by the disappearance of the sexual impulse, and in men sexual desire, and even sexual potency, are often found at an advanced age.

There is the same kind of variation in the strength of the sexual impulse. If we seek to measure it in continent young men by the frequency of involuntary seminal emissions during sleep, it is found that while, in some, such emissions occur two or three times a week, without producing any seriously exhausting effect, in others they only occur once or twice a month, and in some individuals never occur at all. If, again, we seek to measure it by the frequency of coitus in those living in sexual relationship, it is found that while in some cases coitus takes place habitually every night during a long period of years without any obvious injury, in other cases even once a month is felt as the limit beyond which excess lies. Individual variations, even within what may fairly be considered a state of tolerable general health, are wide, and no general rules can be laid down.

Complete sexual anæsthesia (or anhedonia, as Ziehen termed it) in men is, however, extremely rare. Hypoæsthesia, or hyphedonia, that is a relative frigidity and indifference to sexual excitation is, however, common in men, much commoner than is sometimes supposed. In some cases, indeed, it is apparent rather than real, and is due to the concealed, or even merely latent and unconscious, existence of an abnormal direction of the sexual impulse, more especially to an unrealized homosexual impulse. In many cases frigidity may be merely the result of the exhaustion of excessive masturbation. In yet other cases it is the accompaniment of a strenuous development of other activities, psychic or physical, which use up all the superfluous energy of the organism, though in some of these we must probably admit that the sexual impulse was feeble at the outset. In others, again, it is due to a kind of infantilism, and is then a form of retarded development.

In civilization the strenuous demands of life and the more or less unnatural conditions under which the sexual impulse develops combine to produce a frequent inability, relative or absolute, to secure potency in coitus. Hamilton found that only 55 per cent. of his husbands and 38 per cent. of his wives, all belonging to what we must regard as the most civilized stratum of the community, regarded their potency as normal; and while there were a certain number of inconclusive answers among both men and women, the proportion of both husbands and wives who considered their sexual potency below normal was decidedly higher than of those who thought it was above, a result in contradiction of the common belief that both men and women are disposed to exaggerate their own sex qualities. It is also noteworthy that the number of husbands who thought their wives undersexed was about the same as of wives who thought their husbands undersexed. Hamilton found, further, that 41 per cent. husbands admitted that there was, or had been, a difficulty in securing potency, while 24 per cent. wives (not, it must be remembered, necessarily wives of the husbands examined) regarded their husbands' potency as defective. It may be noted, however, that both the husbands and the wives who regarded themselves as below the average in sexual desire presented a higher percentage of fairly to highly satisfactory marriages compared to those who rate themselves as equal to or above the average in sex desire. This is indeed a common experience and may well be remembered by those who look upon marriage as a mainly sexual relationship and imagine that a high degree of sexual activity is essential to happiness in marriage. Dickinson's gynæcological explorations, only indirectly concerned with husbands, seem to show that about 6 per cent. of them were impotent.

We have to bear in mind that both excess and defect of sexual feeling may co-operate to produce sexual impotence. It is an important consideration, since one of the great nervous terrors surrounding marriage in some men's minds—a terror which may also occur apart altogether from marriage as well as in later stages of the state—is connected with the doubt as to potency. A comparative absence of sexual power and sexual impulse, from one cause or another, is more common in men than is sometimes recognized. The number of marriages, indeed, is by no means small in which from this cause conjugal relations are not effected, and such unions are by no means always below the average in happiness. But the suspicion that he is impotent—although such sexual quiescence is a goal which others are vainly longing to attain—causes the average man extreme anxiety, so that he is prepared to adopt any course of treatment and often to resort to any of the quacks who are prepared to trade on these terrors. A temporary loss of potency under a high emotional strain may easily occur and is not of any serious import. Nervous and inexperienced men are specially liable to it. Montaigne long ago pointed out in his essay on the force of imagination that it is merely due to fear, and he sagaciously described how, by ingenious methods of neutralizing the fear, potency is perfectly restored.

In some cases, however, the defect of potency rests on an acquired habit of the nervous system. Chastity, masturbation, sexual excess—such are the causes commonly arraigned for such a defect in potency.[1] Moreover, the conditions of civilization are very favourable to a general nervous excitability, an over-hasty reaction to stimuli, which on the sexual side tend to produce an abbreviation of tumescence and a premature detumescence unfavourable to the satisfactory accomplishment of the sexual act.

I agree with Freud and others that the frequency of premature ejaculation is very great, though I do not agree with Löwenfeld in attributing this in 75 per cent. cases to masturbation. In a certain proportion, no doubt, this plays an important part, but even an extreme degree of masturbation has sometimes no serious effects on potency, while in any case it is so frequent that considerable caution must be exercised in asserting that it is the cause of anything. Usually, it is probable, we must regard neurasthenic impotence as in part a special manifestation of the general tendency to quick and sensitive reactions which marks all urban life under modern conditions (manifested in women by the tendency for pregnancy to come to a termination before full term), and in part as the result of ungratified desire during the period of adolescence, and beyond, leading to prolonged tumescence not followed by its natural relief even in masturbation, and a consequent impairment of the vascular mechanism of detumescence.

In most cases there is only a relative defect of potency. Erection more or less completely occurs and is followed, though too rapidly, by ejaculation. The subject may not be conscious that anything is wrong. But we cannot doubt that this defect of masculine potency counts for much in the prevalence of sexual frigidity among women.

When the loss of power is more absolute—whether due

[1] A definite psychic cause of another kind may be influential, for Dr. G. V. Hamilton informs me that of late he had found reason to believe that early mother-fixation leads to impotence.

to temporary psychic impotence or to real enfeebling conditions—the subject is often alarmed, even very alarmed. Under the influence of his nervous terror we often find a man constantly brooding over his own sexual powers, constantly trying to arouse them, constantly, perhaps, if he is unmarried, making appointments with prostitutes, to meet with frequent disappointment.[1]

We thus have two classes of cases, those of psychic impotence and those of what may perhaps still be termed neurasthenic impotence. In the former, the mechanism of detumescence is intact but its action is inhibited by psychic tension; the treatment, therefore, simply consists in removing the psychic inhibition by allaying the subject's doubts and suspicions. In the cases of neurasthenic impotence, the mechanism of detumescence is not inhibited but, on the contrary, more or less enfeebled, and the treatment is less promising, though it is usually quite possible, if not to restore the impaired mechanism, at all events to minimize the results of the impairment. In all these cases the main point is to allay the patient's terror, turn his thoughts out of sexual channels, and ensure the practice of a sound hygiene. Drugs are not here considered, and they are of secondary value though much advertised. Some have been found useful in some cases, but it remains doubtful whether they have any considerable real somatic influence on the condition; while a drug like nux vomica, notwithstanding its exciting effect on the sexual system, and the spinal cord generally, and its value as a tonic, is worse than useless when over-excitability already exists. The patient should be forbidden to attempt coitus and should especially be discouraged from making such attempts with prostitutes. Prolonged suspense and expectation is the worst prelude to coitus, especially in these cases, and all acute mental activity and emotional worry are unfavour-

[1] It is scarcely necessary to say that in the case of a chaste and refined man impotence with a prostitute proves nothing. Moll mentions the case of a man who, never having had sexual intercourse, visited a prostitute before marriage, on the advice of a friend, to ascertain if he was potent. He was quite impotent. But he married and was entirely potent with his wife.

able. A sensible and tactful wife is the physician's best assistant. The famous case of Rousseau is in this matter instructive. He was a man of extremely sensitive and erethic temperament, psychic and physical; his emotions responded to a touch, and his sexual impulse reflected this high nervous irritability. With a prostitute, or with a woman for whom he felt ardent passion, he was an ineffective lover. But with Thérèse, with whom he lived in calm and constant companionship, he was seemingly potent, and, if his own honest belief is correct, he was the father of numerous children. In these erethic cases everything that allays genital excitability is favourable; thus it is that after prolonged sexual abstinence the first ejaculation may be premature, but the second attain the normal result; the interval, of course, varies with the individual sexual constitution, and while it may be less than half an hour in one person, it may be several days in another. It may also be recommended not to attempt intercourse on retiring to bed, but only after a period of rest and sleep, or in the early morning, a time which some authorities advise as generally the best. With mental peace and rational hygiene fairly satisfactory results may be reached in these cases.

This indicates that sexual incapacity is largely a matter of personal and social adaptation. In most cases if the subject had been from youth in a natural and wholesome relationship with individuals of the opposite sex the difficulty or incapacity for harmonious union with a congenial member of that sex would not arise, and there would be little tendency to nervous terror, immature timidity, or aggressive frigidity in approaching a sexually desirable person. We are justified in believing that sexual incompetence is, to a large extent, a special manifestation of incomplete social adaptation. We must not ignore the constitutional factors, which may, for instance, involve a homosexual tendency, nor physical defect or weakness which calls for the surgeon's aid. But the wise surgeon himself admits that when he has done his best there often remains much for the psychologist and psycho-therapist.

We seem justified in believing that the sexual impulse

is never so feeble that it cannot, at times, under favourable conditions, become in some degree manifest. Krafft-Ebing accepted the existence of complete sexual incapacity in rare instances, but he brought forward no observations of his own in evidence, only a case of Legrand du Saulle's in which seminal emissions had still taken place and one of Hammond's in which there had even been transitory erections. These cases were undoubtedly marked by a considerable degree of hypoæsthesia, but the definite sexual manifestations they yet exhibited prevent us from accepting them as examples of complete sexual anæsthesia.

It seems equally doubtful whether complete sexual anæsthesia can exist in women. There can indeed be no doubt as to the extreme frequency of hypoæsthesia, or, as it is usually termed, frigidity, which has indeed been estimated—I do not know by what method—as occurring in nearly 70 per cent. of women. Such wild statements must be put aside. Among his 100 normal married women of the educated class Hamilton could only find one case of actual frigidity in the sense of persistent absence of sexual desire and sexual feeling; although a few women were only able to respond to auto-erotic or homosexual stimuli. In a long chapter on this subject in *One Thousand Marriages* Dickinson points out that "frigidity" is not to be regarded as a fixed state or a definite congenital condition. Its causes are multiple: in physique, temperament, education, habit (including ignorance and auto-erotic practices), the husband's inadequacy, etc. The most consistently "frigid," he remarks, are the auto-erotic; yet, strictly speaking, the auto-erotic are not frigid at all, and may be highly sensitive to those sexual stimuli which appeal to them.

The chief reason why women are considered "frigid" lies less in themselves than in men. It is evident throughout that while in men the sexual impulse tends to develop spontaneously and actively, in women, however powerful it may be latently and more or less subconsciously, its active manifestations need in the first place to be called out. That, in our society, is normally the husband's function to effect. It is his part to educate his wife in the life of sex; it is he who will make sex demands a conscious desire to her. If he, by his ignorance, prejudice, impatience, or lack of insight, fails to play his natural part, his wife may, by no defect of her own, be counted as "frigid." It so happens that, during a long period from which we are only now beginning to emerge, when all sex knowledge was suppressed or treated as unworthy of consideration, a large proportion of men were unable to become good lovers and a large proportion of women consequently remained "frigid."

There are thus many reasons why women should tend to be apparently frigid under the conditions of our civilization, since these conditions involve profound ignorance of sexual matters in both sexes, bad education, prudery, and an abnormally late age for the commencement of sexual relationships. But when it is asserted that an absolute sexual anæsthesia is common in women it is necessary to remember that the question is much more difficult and complicated in women than in men. Moreover, in women we have to distinguish between the presence of libido and the presence of pleasure in coitus. The first of these may be present in the absence of the second, and even when both are absent it cannot be affirmed that sexual anæsthesia exists. It is perhaps significant that Hamilton found that a high proportion (55 per cent.) of women with inferior capacity for orgasm yet rate themselves as above the average in sex desire. Cases occur in which a woman is frigid with a succession of men, but at last, perhaps in late middle age, the sexual impulse arises. Even if it never occurs at all in coitus it may be manifested in other forms, not merely in deviated activities, but also through the medium of outlying erogenous zones which in women are far more numerous than in men, and far more apt to be stimulated.

Thus it is much more difficult in a woman than in a man to affirm the presence of sexual anæsthesia. All we can say in a particular case is that we have not yet discovered the form in which the woman's sexual impulse is manifested, or may in the future be manifested. Even Otto Adler, who was confident concerning the frequency of sexual anæsthesia in women, when he wished to bring forward a final proof of the existence of the "femme de glace," the woman of "pure psychic sexual anæsthesia," went back to the case of a woman who died more than a century before he was born and of whom no medical history exists, Madame de Warens. Moreover, he relied on the narrative of Rousseau, who was by no means an accomplished lover, and he overlooks the recorded statement of M. de Warens that his wife was hysterical, a state, as we now know, leading to many subtle transformations of the sexual impulse which cannot be traced in the absence of a detailed medical history. We must be cautious in accepting any of the alleged cases of complete sexual anæsthesia in women. It is doubtful whether such a case has ever existed.

The existence of sexual hyperæsthesia in both sexes is, under the conditions of civilization, even commoner than hypoæsthesia, and is likewise largely due to those conditions. They tend to increase the excitations of sex while at the same time they impede the channels of its expression. A certain degree of hyperæsthesia is normal in courtship; in animals this manifests itself in the extreme excitement they show at this period and in man by a constant brooding on the charms of the beloved. Under the influence of sexual abstinence, also, hyperæsthesia usually occurs, and erotic excitation is found in objects and actions which have no normal relationship to the sexual sphere. When sexual hyperæsthesia goes beyond these limits it is abnormal and is usually associated with neurotic conditions.

Abnormal sexual hyperæsthesia by no means indicates any excess of genital force. The man of abnormal genital force, the sexual athlete, as Benedikt termed him, is not marked by hyperæsthesia; strength requires repose, and the sensations of the hyperæsthetic enjoy little repose. The appearance of genital force in hyperæsthesia is mainly a semblance, though it often suffices to delude the subject of it; the affinities of hyperæsthesia are with weakness.

Abnormal sexual hyperæsthesia may occur before puberty as well as in old age. It probably plays an important part in the constitution of various deviations, for it is only when an abnormal sexual excitation coincides with an abnormal state of hyperæsthesia that there is any likelihood of an unusual sexual association being formed. When sexual hyperæsthesia exists, anything connected with persons of the opposite sex, or even any non-sexual object or action which seems to show analogies to sexual objects and acts, arouses sexual associations and produces sexual feelings. Any part of the body, the garments even apart from the wearer, any unusual attitude or posture, however apart from sexual ends, the coitus of animals and even of insects, anything in Nature or in art which recalls the penis or the vulva or the act of coitus, all become not merely sexual symbols, as they normally may, but are apt actively to arouse sexual emotions. In such general sexual hyperæsthesia there is no choice and all suggestions are liable to be aroused indiscriminately. But the soil is thus furnished on which particular fetishisms may take root and flourish, though this is not usually the way in which fetishisms arise. It may be added that sexual hyperæsthesia may exist in a disguised form, and even without the active participation of the subject. Prudery is a form of sexual hyperæsthesia. The exaggerated horror of sexual things, as well as the exaggerated love of them, alike rest on a basis of sexual hyperæsthesia.

Sexual hyperæsthesia, while it is abnormal, and apt to be associated with neuropathic conditions, is by no means necessarily a manifestation of insanity ; it can be restrained and concealed, and it is more or less under the control of the will. In its more extreme degrees, however, when the motor and impulsive elements become pronounced, the power of control tends to be lost. In the extreme degree we may thus have what is termed satyriasis in men and nymphomania in women.

BIBLIOGRAPHY

HAVELOCK ELLIS, *Studies in the Psychology of Sex*, Vol. III., "The Sexual Impulse in Women."
HAMILTON, *A Research in Marriage.*
DICKINSON, *A Thousand Marriages.*
STEKEL, *Frigidity in Woman.*

Chastity

When we speak of abstinence we have in mind a negative state, that is to say the mere repression of a natural impulse. Such a repression has its motive in causes—frequently causes of a low order—outside the impulse itself, and in opposition to it. That is why it is liable to be harmful. It can never be in itself a virtue, though it may be the outcome of other motives which in themselves may be termed virtues or may be associated with virtues. As Flaubert wrote to George Sand, in an interesting discussion of this question in their correspondence, it is the effort that is good, not the abstinence in itself. Chastity, however, stands on a different level.

Chastity does not necessarily involve abstinence. It has sometimes been used as synonymous with absolute sexual abstinence, but it is not desirable to encourage that debased use of the term. It may be better defined as self-control within the sexual sphere. That is to say that, though it may sometimes involve abstinence, it may also involve indulgence, its essence lying in the acceptance of a deliberate and harmonized exercise of the psychic impulses. Thus understood it is not a negative state, but an active virtue. I once overheard a girl of about fourteen reproaching a companion of about the same age for greediness: " You have never learnt self-restraint!" " It's not necessary," replied the other. " It's not necessary," retorted the first, " it's nice." That girl would in later life have no difficulty in understanding chastity. It is the manifestation of temperance, of the Greek *sophrosyne*, in the sphere of sex.

Chastity is a virtue independent of all creeds and religions. It is true that in many parts of the world there have been religious sanctions to hold lust in check. That is to say that the exercise of sexual activity outside certain prescribed limits has been held to be a " sin." It was inevitable that religious communities, Christian or other, should take this attitude But, on a purely human basis, chastity has been and still remains a virtue.

Among savages, in many parts of the world, young children are freely allowed to play at sex and even to practice it.

That indicates that there is no abstract prohibition of sexual activity. But, as soon as the child approaches puberty, even in what we consider the primitive mind, a new attitude towards sex seems necessary: an attitude of control. Among peoples of low culture it is common to find sexual activity hedged in by a great number of limitations, quite apart from the formal Christian prohibitions of "fornication" and "adultery." And these limitations are for a large part conducive to the high estimation of sex, not only through the avoidance of it when its exercise is regarded as dangerous but by prescription when that influence is regarded as beneficial, and by associating its manifestations with sacred festivals. This kind of control, this regulated exercise accepted as good, we may properly call chastity, and it may be regarded as already built into the structure of savage life. A tissue of uses, often fanciful—though even then still helping to ennoble its exercise—have been popularly or traditionally assigned to chastity among lower as well as higher races. "Yet, to a remarkable degree," as Crawley well pointed out, "at least in primitive sociology, these uses, whatever their popular explanations, harmonize with biological facts, and the value of the explanations consists in having assisted the plastic nervous organism of man towards self-control, intelligent living, and general individual and social efficiency." If carried too far, as Crawley also pointed out, disintegration tends to follow; but the main process continues, having as its goal, "after many experiments, slowly but surely, a scientific development of that primal natural chastity with which man's sexual history began."

That fundamental fact tends to be obscured precisely because of the extremes, referred to by Crawley, to which the conception of chastity has sometimes been carried by religious creeds and social conventions. This has been well illustrated during recent centuries in our own civilization. When chastity is transformed into a mere compulsory abstinence it ceases to be either natural, or a virtue, or beneficial. Its essential character is lost sight of. It is then denounced as "unnatural," and regarded as the concomitant of an outworn religious creed or an effete political hierarchy. Thus it is that among ourselves the decay of ancient artificial restrictions in the sphere of sex has sometimes led to the other extreme—equally unnatural and undesirable—of licence and promiscuity as an ideal, if not even a practice.

Such violent oscillations of the just balance of chastity may take a considerable time to reach equilibrium, since any sudden rebound leads to another bound. We may observe this difficulty in Soviet Russia. In old Russia there was much conventional restraint and beneath it much concealed licence, each tending to produce its consequent reaction. The immediate effect of the liberation effected by the Revolution was largely in the direction of licence. To some extent that seems still to be felt, especially by those who regard restraint and regulation as *bourgeois* traits. But the main tendency is now a reaction against licence. Members of the Communist Party are expelled for their private sexual behaviour, as much as for political bad behaviour. The situation resembles that in eighteenth century Calvinist Geneva, for Russian Marxism is as rigid and as austere as Calvinism. " Frivolity, promiscuity, libertinism, rape (which may include several marriages in quick succession)," we are told, " are frowned on and their perpetrators expelled from the Party because such behaviour betrays the social purposes of the Party."

These oscillations are the more or less unfortunate exaggeration of a virtue which is still to be cherished. It is not only demanded for the sake of maintaining the vigorous activity of the sexual function but also for maintaining its human dignity. Beyond that, it is essential to any gracious art of love, which is, as it has been put, " the art of touching the things of sex with hands that remember their aptness for all the fine ends of life."

BIBLIOGRAPHY

A. E. Crawley, art. " Chastity," Hastings' *Encyclopædia of Religion and Ethics.*

Havelock Ellis, *Studies in the Psychology of Sex*, Vol. VI., Chapter V., " The Function of Chastity."

MARGARET MEAD, *Growing Up in New Guinea.*
MALINOWSKI, *Sex and Repression in Savage Society.*

The Menopause

The menopause cannot fail to constitute a psychological epoch in marriage, even though its importance was formerly exaggerated. Nowadays the pendulum has swung towards the opposite extreme. Various medical women now declare that the attribution of ailments to the climacteric is merely an "obsession," and that they rarely find any symptoms directly due to this cause.

Yet we have here a phenomenon which cannot be without direct psychological significance for the woman herself and an indirect bearing on her family and social life. It marks the end of her reproductive phase just as puberty marked its beginning.

The menopause, climacteric,[1] or "change of life," as it is variously termed, is the involutional period of the reproductive sexual system, and occurs between wide limits of age—thirty-five to fifty-five, but most commonly between forty-five to fifty, and is completed within two or three years. It is associated with changes in the functional activity of the endocrine glands, and also in the autonomic nervous system, with consequent emotional, vasomotor, and nervous symptoms, of which palpitations and flushing are found specially unpleasant and are due not so much to heightened blood pressure as to oscillations in that pressure. We are not here called upon to consider the possible initial causes of these changes. Marañón long since advocated a pluri-glandular theory of the menopause, fundamentally in the ovaries, thyroid, and suprarenals, and secondarily in the hypophysis. FitzGibbon regards it as an apparently spontaneous atrophy of the genital organs liable to produce toxins, whence a train of symptoms such as flushing, etc., which may be eliminated in severe cases by removal of the womb; but as flushing

[1] The menopause is sometimes distinguished from the climacteric, the former as the time when menstruation ceases, and the latter as the period of the cessation of ovulation.

and allied symptoms may occur to a pronounced degree after the womb is removed, on account of disease, at an earlier age, this view seems dubious at the best.

Although slight emotional and physical disturbances are almost invariable at this period, many women, even those of unstable nervous disposition, pass through this stage of transition with no serious trouble, though a few are liable to some degree of breakdown, physical or mental.

On the psychic side it is inevitable that the "change of life," the realization of the fact—which she has perhaps tried to postpone—that she is no longer young, should make a deep impression on a woman. The end of the reproductive life, moreover, appears as the end of the whole sexual life, though that is by no means actually the case. The woman awakes with a start to the fact that what seems the chief period of life is rapidly slipping away from her. There is thus sometimes a sudden increased sexual activity, with occasionally an unwonted tendency to be attracted to some new man and to make advances to him. In unmarried women who have lived respectable and conventional lives the same tendencies occasionally appear and are more apt to be accompanied by indications of mental unbalance. All such manifestations are familiarly known and their frequency often exaggerated.

Yet we have to recognize that the period of the menopause may sometimes be marked by such disturbances in the sexual psychic life, especially exacerbation of desire—a final flare of the generative flame—perhaps accompanied by various caprices and suspicions and occasionally by actual deviations of the sexual impulse. In married women the results are often aggravated by the fact that the husband is at this time beginning to lose sexual power, and his affection for his wife has entered into a stage of peaceful affection rendering it difficult for him to respond to her renewed ardour, which thus tends to go into other directions and perhaps to assume the form of jealousy. So that on the psychic side a number of unamiable traits may develop as well as painful troubles on the physical side. But on both sides, when these become at all grave, they are due not directly to the menopause but to the liberation at this period of tendencies already latent in the organism.

It is important to make clear that not only are such symptoms not essentially inherent in the menopause itself but that this time of life naturally brings with it many compensating advantages. "Among countless numbers of women," as W. J. Fielding remarks, "the climacteric has been the beginning of a golden period of achievement. Nor is there any reason why women, normally constituted, should lose their sexual charms at this time. As a matter of fact, many women are more attractive at fifty than they were at twenty-five; and if their personality has been developed and enriched by the passing years, they may be more charming at sixty than they were at thirty."

Hofstätter remarks that there become visible not only some physical male characteristics but what he terms "a surprising approximation to masculine habits and ways of thought: clarity, objectivity, a sense for conceptions of abstract justice, toleration, business aptitude, general social as well as political aptitudes." While recognizing these as possible psychic accompaniments of the post-menstrual life it is not necessary to call them masculine. They are non-sexual aptitudes, by no means so common in the male sex as some might desire. For many married couples, however, it may be said that it is only after the wife's menopause that marriage is finally achieved in its full sense as a happy and harmonious fellowship, even though it may sometimes seem to recall that of brother and sister. There is no doubt about the increased intellectual activity of women at this age and the active careers of many women of distinction have only begun after the sexual reproductive period was over. There are, indeed, some women who at this time use their increased activities in striving to interfere with the activities of their growing-up children, especially to dominate their daughters, if unmarried and still within the home-circle; many lives have thus been blighted, and kindly but firm rebellion is here necessary; for if some suffering is—though it should not be—inevitable it is better that the old should suffer than the young. But the wholesomely cultivated woman, while often devoted to her grandchildren, exercises her liberated maternal energies in the larger social world, which offers endless scope for wide activities.

It is a debated question how far there can be said to be any period in men corresponding to the menopause. If so it is certainly vague, as indeed is sufficiently indicated by the fact that the sperm-secreting function has no necessary final term and may be continued to advanced old age, even in one reported case to the age of 103. There are, however, times in a man's life when in some cases a recognition of a sudden turn in the road enters consciousness with disturbing effect. Since Kurt Mendel called attention to the point, such a phenomenon, corresponding to the menopause in women, has been widely recognized, though Krafft-Ebing and others have denied it. But even in ancient days a "grand climacteric" was recognized and placed at the age of sixty-three. We cannot, however, speak strictly of a "male menopause." On this ground Marañón prefers the term "critical age," meaning thereby a stage of organic evolution, having prominently at its centre the extinction or diminution of active genital life, although this is not the axis on which it turns. The biological foundation is genital decadence with changed neuro-endocrine reactions. Kenneth Walker would place the age of this change at about 55 to 60, Max Thorek 7 to 10 years later than in women, Rankin between 57 and 63, Max Marcuse between 45 and 55, and even at 40. In many cases, I would say, such a period occurs even near the age of 38. The man suddenly realizes that the period of expanding power has reached its limits, even that there is a comparative failure of power, this also manifesting itself in the sexual sphere, and by a sudden revulsion of feeling he may begin to feel that he is no longer a young man but an old man. Such a recognition with advance of age may involve not only the liability to an eruption of sexual activity but also the development of a certain egotism and callousness which facilitates its manifestations; this is on the whole beneficial, because it protects enfeebled old age from the risks of strong emotion, but it is liable to abuses of which the most dangerous occur should there be an efflorescence of activity in the sexual sphere. In abnormal cases there may be exhibitionism, the sexual attraction to young girls, or, sometimes, taking a homosexual turn ("retarded homosexuality"), to boys. The distinguished German novelist Thomas Mann has dealt in *Der Tod in Venedig* with this theme, which he has himself stated to be an illustration of the pathological male climacteric. Hirschfeld believes that this phenomenon is specially marked in unmarried men and widows, and Max Marcuse in sexually inadequate men.

The wider psychic aspects of this male climacteric are frequently said to include that loss of youthful aggressiveness and audacity, and the tendency to social and political conservatism, which is everywhere regarded as characteristic of old age, though there are notable exceptions to this tendency.

On the whole, since the reproductive life in men is of so much less intensity than in women, the male climacteric is a somewhat vague and comparatively unimportant period. Still it may induce a number of minor psychic traits of disagreeable character—irritability, meanness, miserliness, etc. —corresponding to traits found in women at the same period. It may also lead to a wider and calmer outlook on life, the psychic changes involved, however, being more endogenous, more within, on account of the normally greater activity of men in the world, than with women. There may be, as Rankin put it, "a new lease of life," even though on a plane of lessened activities, modified ambitions, and a chastened philosophy.

BIBLIOGRAPHY

F. H. A. Marshall, *The Physiology of Reproduction.*

G. Marañón, *The Climacteric.*

Kenneth Walker, "The Accidents of the Male Climacteric," *British Medical Journal*, January 9th, 1932.

Max Thorek, *The Human Testis.*

W. J. Fielding, *Sex and the Love-Life.*

W. Gallichan, *The Critical Age of Women.*

CHAPTER VII

THE ART OF LOVE

The Sexual Impulse in Relation to Love

THERE are many ways of regarding "marriage." In a bald and abstract elementary form it may be defined as "legalized cohabitation." Under civilized conditions it becomes a complex part of the *mores* or moral customs (morality being essentially custom) of a country, and is then a contract, and, as Max Christian puts it, "not only a contract to exercise and maintain a sexual relationship but also a true life community with economic and psychic foundations and moral (that is to say social) obligations." Yet more intimately, however, it is the association by free choice of two persons who suit each other, with the object of finding an unhampered field of exercise for all the varied manifestations of love.

By a common euphemism the word "love" is used to cover any manifestation of the sexual impulse. That is, needless to say, incorrect. We must distinguish between *lust*, or the physiological sexual impulse, and *love*, or that impulse in association with other impulses.

There is no verbal agreement as to the best definition of the distinction between love and lust. It can, indeed, be said that many of the definitions offered may be accepted as expressing some part of the distinction. Love may be regarded, roughly speaking, as a synthesis of lust and friendship. Or, looking at the matter physiologically, we may say, with Forel, that love is the sexual instinct as manifested through the cerebral centres. Or, with Kant, we may say that love is the sexual impulse released from its bondage to periodicity and made permanent through the help of the imagination. Pfister, after devoting a long chapter to various definitions of love, concludes that it may best be defined as "a feeling of attraction and a sense of self-surrender, arising out of a need, and directed towards an object that offers hope of gratification." It is an inadequate definition, and so are most of such definitions.

While love apparently becomes in its most developed forms a completely altruistic impulse, it springs out of an egoistic impulse and even when it involves self-sacrifice there is still an egoistic gratification. Freud, among others, has insisted in his *Introductory Lectures* on this egoistic source (even stating elsewhere, about the same time, that "love is primarily Narcissistic"), although recognizing that love later becomes detached from its source. Putting aside the specifically sexual element, the mother, as Freud and others hold, is the child's first real *love*-object, although later, in subjects who are not neurotic, this primary love-object falls into the background, with the naturally growing prominence of other love-objects.

In developing into love, the sexual impulse, which at the outset is predominantly egoistic, becomes also consciously altruistic. There are, under normal and natural conditions, altruistic elements from the outset of its sexual development. Without consideration for the other partner, even among animals, courtship fails, and coitus cannot take place. But with the development of love this altruistic element becomes conscious and highly developed; it may even lead to the complete subordination of the egoistic element.

This process by which love is developed may be said to be double. In part it is due to the irradiation of the sexual instinct through the whole organism, taking longer nervous circuits and suffusing regions which are outside the sexual sphere so long as the sexual impulse attains its ends speedily and without impediments. In part, it is due to fusion with other psychic elements of a more or less allied character.

At a stage after full sexual development love is reinforced by allied emotions derived from the relationship of parents to offspring. The woman's sexual love is thereafter mingled with the tenderness and patience which have been evoked by her children, and a man's with the guarding and protecting elements involved in the paternal relationship.

Sexual love thus becomes, in marriage, part of the structure of society, while in some of its highest manifestations it may be allied with the impulses of religion and the impulses of art. In this women seem often to have been pioneers. Letourneau pointed out that in various parts of the world women have taken a leading part in creating erotic poetry, and sometimes seem even to have monopolized the emotion of love. In this connection it may be mentioned that among primitive peoples suicide from erotic motives seems to occur chiefly among women.

It must, however, be remembered that the evolution of love from lust has proceeded but a little way among many lower human races, and is indeed rudimentary among a large number of persons in civilization. While " lust " is known all over the world, and there are everywhere words to designate it, " love " is not universally known, and in many languages there are no words for " love." The failures to find love are often remarkable and unexpected. We may also find it where we least expect it. Sexual desire became " idealized " even by some animals, especially birds, for when a bird pines to death for the loss of its mate this cannot be due to the uncomplicated instinct of sex, but must involve the interweaving of that instinct with the other elements of life to a degree which is rare even among the most civilized men. Some savage races seem to have no fundamental notion of love, and (like the American Nahuas) no primary word for it, while, on the other hand, in Quichua, the language of the ancient Peruvians, there are nearly six hundred combinations of the verb *munay*, to love.

Brinton, in making this statement, remarked that the words for love in some American Indian languages reveal four main ways of expressing the conception : (1) inarticulate cries of emotion ; (2) assertions of sameness or similarity ; (3) assertions of conjunction or union ; (4) assertions of a wish, desire, longing. Brinton adds that " these same notions are those which underlie the majority of the words of love in the great Aryan family of languages." The remarkable fact emerges, however, that the peoples of Aryan tongue were slow in developing their conception of sexual love, while the American Mayas, going beyond the peoples of early Aryan culture, possessed a radical word for the joy of love which was in significance purely psychic.

Even the Greeks were late in developing any ideal of sexual love. True love for the Greeks was nearly always homosexual. The Ionian lyric poets of early Greece regarded woman as only an instrument of pleasure and the founder of the family. Theognis compares marriage to cattle-breeding; Alcman, when he wishes to be complimentary to the Spartan girls, speaks of them as his "female boy-friends." Æschylus makes even a father assume that his daughters will misbehave if left to themselves. There is no sexual love in Sophocles, and in Euripides it is only the women who fall in love. In Greece sexual love, down to a comparatively late period, was looked down on, and held to be unworthy of public discussion and representation. It was in Magna Graecia, rather than in Greece itself, that men took interest in women, and it was not until the Alexandrian period, and notably in Asclepiades, as Benecke maintained, that the love of women was regarded as a matter of life and death. Thereafter the conception of sexual love in its romantic aspects appears in European life. With the Celtic story of Tristram, as Gaston Paris remarks, it finally appears in the Christian European world of poetry as a main point in human life, a great motive force of conduct. But such romantic conceptions still failed to penetrate the European masses who continued to regard "love" as a crude act of sexual intercourse.

When, however, love is fully developed it becomes an enormously extended, highly complex emotion, and lust even in the best sense of that word, becomes merely a co-ordinated element among many other elements. Herbert Spencer, in an interesting passage of his *Principles of Psychology*, analysed love into as many as nine distinct and important elements: (1) the physical impulse of sex; (2) the feeling for beauty; (3) affection; (4) admiration and respect; (5) love of approbation; (6) self-esteem; (7) proprietary feeling; (8) extended liberty of action from the absence of personal barriers; (9) exaltation of the sympathies. "This passion," he concludes, "fuses into one immense aggregate most of the elementary excitations of which we are capable." Even this comprehensive analysis omits the element of love, already mentioned, based on the parental impulse, yet that is a highly important element; when the specifically sexual element in the conjugal relationship has fallen into the background the emotional tone of the husband's love for his wife, and still more that of the wife for her husband, becomes easily that of love for a child. Every analysis of love serves to show that, as Crawley remarked, "love is as difficult to define as life itself, and probably for the same reasons. In all its forms love plays a part in society only less important than that of the instinct to live. It brings together the primal elements of the family, it keeps the family together, and it unites in a certain fellow-feeling all members of a race or nation."

Even so brief a discussion of love may serve to indicate that it is foolish for even the most superficial thinker to imagine that we are here concerned with a romantic illusion that may be dismissed, or, as some would-be analysts like to imagine, a mere transformation of hate. It is true, that, as Ibsen said, "no word is so full of falsehood and fraud as the little word 'love' has become to-day." Yet the thing the word stands for remains, and the extent of the abuse of "love" is the measure of its inestimable values, for it is only gold and diamonds and the most precious things that lend themselves to the abuse of imitation in paint and paste and cheap alloys and substitutes of every sort. There can be no self without others and the craving for others, and we cannot put aside others and the emotions which others excite without first putting aside the self. So that, properly speaking, love is involved in life, and if love is an illusion then life itself is an illusion.

When, indeed, we consider further, how love is bound up with the race as well as the individual, and with ends not only natural but such as we term spiritual, it seems, as Boyce Gibson puts it, "the great transforming and inclusive agency, the ultimate virtue of all life." So that, as it has been said, "Love is the supreme virtue," and "Virtue is love," or, as the early Christian epistolist sought to express it, "God is love."

BIBLIOGRAPHY

WESTERMARCK, *History of Human Marriage; ib. The Origin and Development of the Moral Ideas.*

HAVELOCK ELLIS, *Studies in the Psychology of Sex*, Vol. VI., "Sex in Relation to Society," and *Little Essays of Love and Virtue.*

EDWARD CARPENTER, *Love's Coming of Age.*

ELLEN KEY, *Love and Marriage.*

BOYCE GIBSON and A. E. CRAWLEY, articles, "Love" and "Primitive Love" in Hastings' *Encyclopædia of Religion and Ethics.*

FREUD, *Introductory Lectures on Psycho-Analysis.*

OSKAR PFISTER, *Love in Children and Its Aberrations.*

Why Love is an Art

Love has been defined (as by Boyce Gibson) as a "sentiment" and a "passion," this varying with the point of view. In either case it is a stable and complex organization of the emotional life, but when regarded as a sentiment it is a more intellectual, refined, and subtle emotional feeling, and when regarded as a passion it is an emotional complex of predominantly forceful kind, a "passion" being defined by A. F. Shand as "an organized system of emotions and desires," that is, more than a system only of emotions. In every passion, however, a system of self-control tends to arise—by whatever mechanism we may consider that it works—whereby its intensity is more or less effectively regulated. By reason of its systematic character and its unifying principle, it is possible to regard the passion of love as "stable, regulative, inclusive, and instinct with a profound rationality." But for its normal development—and at this point we discern the path with which we are here mainly concerned—the essential condition is (as Boyce Gibson again states) *joy in its object*, even though that condition of joy inevitably involves pain and the possibility of sorrow, these emotions being indeed co-operative and interpenetrating; sorrow thus enters with joy to strengthen the passion of love. It is by this complexity and inclusiveness that love may become in a supreme and unique sense the master passion.

We have not indeed, even at that point, reached the full significance of love in the large sense. The "master passion" may still be merely an enlarged egoism, an "*égoisme à deux*,' and, therefore, however justifiable, still not greatly more enlarging and ennobling than simple egoism. Love thus understood may be a source for the generation of energy, but if the two generating partners expend it merely on each other the energy is largely wasted. Love is one of the supreme things that make life worth while, but, as Bertrand Russell well points out, the love of two people for each other is too circumscribed to be by itself the main purpose of a good life. There must be purposes which stretch out beyond the individual couple into the great world outside and into the future, purposes, maybe, which can never be achieved but are always growing. "It is only when love is linked to some infinite purpose of this kind that it can have the seriousness and depth of which it is capable."

There remains a primary condition of love which, we see, the moralists admit, even if somewhat slurring over the details : *joy in its object*. There it is that we are brought to love as an art.

There was a time, and not so long ago, when the consideration of love as an art found no place either in manuals of psychology or of morals. It was left to the poets, who were quite content that it should be regarded as a rather illegitimate subject. That was so when Ovid wrote those poetic treatises on the Art of Love which remained famous, and sometimes infamous, for more than fifteen centuries, and so it still was in Christendom. It was not proper or respectable or moral to treat sexual love, either socially or in literature, as anything but a duty. It is sometimes said that, for modern times, the first beginnings of the art of love were discovered in France in the twelfth century, but it remained a rather illegitimate art.

To-day the situation is different. To regard love as an art is commonly justified, and moralists themselves are not behindhand in maintaining that justification. They recognize that duty alone is no longer an adequate motive for fidelity in marriage, and that to enlarge the basis of love, to multiply the motives that make mutual affection attractive, by converting love into an art, is to deepen the foundations of a marital union and to fortify its morality. We are not here directly concerned with morality, but we are entitled to allow for its claims.

Attempts to recognize this art date some time back in modern civilization. Ambroise Paré, a great pioneer in surgery, advised a considerable degree of love-play as a desirable preliminary to coitus. More recently Fürbringer, in his treatise on sexual hygiene in marriage, considered that the physician should be competent to expound to his patient the technique of conjugal intercourse. To return to France, the land with which the art of love seems in the first place especially associated, it was in 1859 that Dr. Jules Guyot produced his *Bréviaire de l'Amour Expérimental*, which most admirably presented the main points in the art of love, and was much later (1931) in part translated into English under the title of *A Ritual for Married Lovers*.

At this point we are brought back to the characteristics of the sexual impulse in women, and to that sexual coldness which has been commonly regarded as so frequent in women. For it is by the recognition of these characteristics that the art of love has been stimulated, and that the elementary fact becomes clear that throughout the animal world courtship tends to be an art.

Sexual frigidity, it has become recognized, produces domestic infelicity, suffering to the wife, and disappointment to the husband who is tempted to seek more congenial relationships elsewhere. In such cases there is either defective desire for sexual union or defective pleasure in union, commonly both, and either may call for the exercise of art in love.

In the biological game of sex the female normally plays the more passive part, and in civilized women this relative passivity is reinforced not only by Nature but by our conventions. It is true that the doctrine alike of the sexual activity of the male and the sexual passivity of the female needs to be qualified. It is fundamental, and constitutes, as is too often forgotten, the deep foundation for far-reaching psychological differences between men and women. As Douglas Bryan points out, sexual tension in the two sexes, being opposite and complemental, cannot fail to lead to different feelings and reactions in each sex: the excitable penis producing impulses of propulsivity, activity, mastery, etc., and the excitable vagina impulses of receptivity, passive submission, etc. That is to say, we have here the essence of what we call "masculinity," and the essence of what we call "femininity." But, as Douglas Bryan also points out, before this stage is reached, in the earlier phase of courtship, the parts are in some degree reversed; the male must be to some extent submissive, and the female to some extent active. The sexual centres are more numerous and more diffused in women, so that the impulse is more easily dispersed and gratified in remote and unconscious channels, while at the same time old traditions taught women to repress as disgusting and sinful the manifestations of the sexual impulse. It thus happens that in women more than in men the sexual impulse tends to be driven below the surface, to seek an outlet in remote and often unconscious paths, this indeed being the great fact on which Freud seized. But notwithstanding the special characteristics of the sexual impulse in women there is no good reason to suspect frigidity among women living under fairly natural conditions. Even among the poor in civilization (putting aside a certain proportion of domestic servants who even still sometimes live, like domestic animals, under artificial conditions) there are, as it is said, no "old maids," and this suggests, without actually proving, that there is no defect of sexual impulse. But the civilized woman, under the combined influences of Nature, art, convention, morality, and religion, has often tended to come into her husband's hands, usually at a rather late adult age, in a condition inapt for the conjugal embrace, which, if the bridegroom is lacking in skill or consideration, may cause her suffering or disgust, or merely leave her indifferent.

Certainly there are various conditions in the woman herself which in this circumstance may need direct attention. Auto-erotic and homosexual practices have frequently rendered normal intercourse difficult or repulsive. The sexual organs may be in a disordered condition, perhaps increased by neglect. Sometimes there is a tendency to vaginismus. In such cases the gynæcologist's aid is required, and it may happen that with his aid the natural sexual feelings quickly and satisfactorily develop and the orgasm is enabled to take place. But the main part of the task in curing sexual anæsthesia in a woman must usually rest with her husband. He is by no means always equipped for this treatment. One fears that there is still too much truth in Balzac's saying that in this matter the husband is sometimes like an orang-outang with a violin. The violin remains "anæsthetic," but it is probably not the violin's fault. This is by no means to say that husbands are consciously or intentionally brutal. Certainly much brutality may be exercised by a husband in sheer ignorance, from a sense of conjugal duty. But often the inexpertness is combined with a real desire to be considerate. The sad thing is, indeed, that the awkward husband is, in a great proportion of cases, awkward simply because he is virtuous and high-minded, has tried to live a life of chastity before marriage, and has never learned to know the nature and needs of women. It is true that the happiest marriages, marriages of life-long devotion on each side, have sometimes been made by two young people who have never known anyone but each other. But this innocence is a two-edged sword, and in many cases it is the other way that it cuts. Then the man who has faithfully lived by the rules of the morality he was brought up in may find that he has thus wrecked his own domestic happiness and his wife's. It must be added that the man whose pre-marital experiences have been confined to prostitutes is often by no means any better equipped, and either thoughtless crudity, or an exaggerated consideration for his wife's "purity," may prove equally unfortunate.

It must be admitted that the husband's task is often

difficult. The difficulty is increased by the late age at which in civilization a woman enters the state of marriage after a long period of years in which she has presumably been leading a life of chastity. During those long years there has been, we know, a constant generation of sexual energy which must be consumed along some channel or other. The woman has acquired habits and fallen into routines; her whole nervous system has been moulded and hardened. Even on the physical side of sex, the organs are by no means always so ready to respond normally to the exercise of their natural functions. The difficulties of late primiparity are paralleled by those of the late initiation of coitus. It is a mistake to suppose that early adolescence is an unfavourable age for coitus and involves a kind of violation; on the contrary, all the evidence goes to show that the young adolescent girl is more apt for the initiation of coitus than the adult woman. The reasons for the delay in initiating coitus are not based on natural facts, but on our civilized traditions. It is quite true that Nature has aimed through the course of zoölogical evolution at the delay of maturity, but that end is effected by making puberty late, and in the human species puberty is very late. The demands of civilization make it desirable that we should postpone the relationships between the sexes to a still later period, but in so doing it is inevitable that we should lay up for ourselves many troubles which only art can redress.

It is thus certainly true that we cannot regulate the sexual life of man without considering that of woman. But it is yet more emphatically true that if we wish to understand the psychological life of the woman on the sex side we must keep one eye on the man.

There are several reasons why it is essential to understand that the sex life of woman is largely conditioned by the sex life of man. They have already been touched on, but we need to recall them when considering the significance in sex psychology of the art of love. In the first place while it has been argued—and even with a measure of truth—that in this matter the woman dominates and that the man is merely a plaything in her hands, that is not the fundamental fact. Ultimately, throughout the zoölogical series we belong to and most of the others, in sex the male is the more active, the female the more passive agent. Anatomically, if not physiologically, the male is the giver, the female the receiver. The psychological relationship cannot fail to be essentially a reflection of this fact, even though, under varying circumstances, it may be departed from without disturbing the general norm of nature.

In the second place, apart from the natural animal relationship, all our traditions in the recognizable historic past are based on the dominance of the man in the establishment of the sexual relationship, and the assumption that the chief if not the sole part pertaining to woman in the sexual life is that of the child-bearer, any erotic part exercised by her being a more or less illegitimate by-play. Our social institutions have grown up and been established on this male dominance and this commonly received assumption: marriage, the legal headship of the husband with the legal irresponsibility of the wife, and outside marriage the recognition of prostitution with a sole view to the assumed needs of the man alone and not of the woman. We know that in all these matters both social opinion and law are changing, but ancient institutions, and still more the feelings and opinions rooted in them, can only change slowly, and even in a state of transition we are still profoundly influenced by the past.

There is a further important consideration, proceeding from those that go before, though belonging more intimately to the feminine psychological sphere. Modesty—both what may be termed natural modesty, which is more or less shared with the lower animals, and artificial modesty, which depends on social fashion and is easily modifiable—is more especially a feminine trait. Here is not the place to show that this is so, or to deal with the numerous qualifications that must be made to the statement. In the main it is not doubtful, and it is closely connected with the more passive part in sex activity played generally by the female in nature, and fortified by our social traditions. (But how modifiable is modesty may clearly be seen by the increasing number of societies established for the practice of what is termed "Nudism" whereby men and women in a completely unclothed state are enabled to meet socially without any embarrassment.) The modifications taking place in our traditions have not here yet produced any pronounced effects. They have indeed tended to produce in women a disharmony between the manifest and latent elements of consciousness. The woman is free to know what she latently feels and desires, but she is not yet usually free to manifest these feelings and desires. The result is that we have to-day a far larger body of women who definitely know what they want, but definitely know also that to make that clear would cause misunderstanding, if not repulsion, in the very men who are in need of that knowledge. So we are always brought back to men.

Even these considerations may suffice to suggest that we are in the presence of two different and sometimes conflicting ideals of the sexual sphere of women. There is one, very ancient in our civilization, according to which maternity is the central fact in the sexual life of women, a fact we cannot dispute, while outside that fact, the sexual sphere is mainly regarded as man's concern; woman having no sexual impulses (if any at all) which do not tend to motherhood, is thus by nature monogamous, while man, not being anchored to home and child, but with a wider scope of psychic variation, is by nature polygamous; so that, while the sexual problem for women is simple and obvious, for men it is more complex. That, one may almost certainly say, is the theory which has been regarded as natural and wholesome from classic times almost to our own, whether or not the actual facts fitted into it. Less than a hundred years ago the English surgeon Acton wrote a book which until near the end of last century was the standard authority on sexual questions, and he stated in it that to attribute sexual feelings to women was "a vile aspersion," while at the same period, in another standard medical work, it was laid down that only "lascivious women" showed any physical signs of pleasure when in the embrace of their husbands. And these absurd statements were generally accepted.

To-day we see arising another ideal, which is, we probably have to recognize, not only in accordance with our growing tendency to place the two sexes on the same level, but also more in accordance with the natural facts. Even outside the field here under consideration, we do not draw the sharp line of sexual distinction which was formerly accepted. We recognize differences that are indeed fundamental, and endless in number, but they are subtle differences. They do not involve two different sorts of human nature. They represent the same human nature with the same varying tendencies. These tendencies may in the male lead more often to modifications in one direction and in the female more often in the other, but the human nature still retains essentially the same common characteristics.

We have already come in contact with the old dictum, endlessly repeated, that man is polygamous and woman monogamous, and seen how far that dictum is true and how far it is false. The fundamental fact that in nature the sex act has weightier consequences for a woman than for a man renders her instinctively slower and more careful than a man in selecting a mate. This difference has always been pronounced. Yet there is a large minority of women, indifferent to the question of maternity, who can form a relationship of sex as easily as the average man, while women generally are just as sensitive as men to the claim of variety, and just as able—if not better able—to love two persons at the same time. The custom of establishing hard and fast oppositions between "man" and "woman," in this field as in others, will not bear serious consideration, though it is not yet extinct. Women, like their brothers, had fathers, and, however numerous the minor distinctions between masculine nature and feminine nature, they inherit the same fundamental human nature. It is, as we see, the existence of two different ideals belonging to two different stages of culture which is mainly responsible for an artificial opposition. It is the clash between these ideals which we witness in our phase of transition to-day.

That is why we should attribute importance to all precise and statistical studies, on a large scale, of the sexual situation in women, whether normal women or women belonging to special groups, as compared with men. Mere picturesque general statements, the dogmatic generalizations of psycho-analysts and others—inevitably coloured by the prejudices and the necessarily limited experiences of the man or woman making them—are no longer of much interest, and, fortunately, are no longer required. Precise groups of data are now being accumulated. It is indeed only to-day that they have become available, and that we possess valuable objective investigations by competently trained hands, such as those by Katharine B. Davis, R. L. Dickinson, and G. V. Hamilton.

Does the seeming greater passivity of women mean any fundamental psychic difference of feelings or physical difference of needs? A convenient measurement for testing this point, thoroughly explored alike by Hamilton, Davis, and Dickinson, is the relative prevalence of auto-erotic manifestations of the sexual impulse. When an auto-erotic act occurs in either sex we are justified in accepting—even though we may refuse to believe that the impulse was absolutely irresistible—the presence of an active sexual desire. Our investigators differ, as we might expect, in the figures they present, and it has to be remembered that their subjects, not being bound to answer the questions, sometimes preferred to pass them over, and some may consider that the women were specially likely to do so. It is therefore significant to find how frequently, as has already been pointed out in Chapter III., they admitted active auto-erotism. Thus Dickinson found that 70 per cent. of average women belonging to all classes experience sexual impulses of sufficient strength, and usually, it is evident, with considerable frequency, to induce them to resort to solitary gratification. Katharine Davis, among 1,000 unmarried women college graduates, found that 65 per cent. of those answering the question acknowledge that they had practised masturbation, about half of these admitting that they still do so, the general health of those who still carry on auto-erotic practices being in a larger percentage of cases "excellent or good" than among either those who have given them up or those who have never practised them, since a vigorous sexual impulse is the efflorescence of vigorous health. Hamilton, dealing with persons of position and ability above the average and all married, found that only 26 per cent. women stated positively that they had never masturbated, and he observed the tendency (which I have myself long since noted) for women, after childhood is passed, to begin the practice later in life than men, for only 1 per cent. men began after the age of twenty-five, but 6 per cent. women. Various interesting points came out clearly. The practice had not generally been taught, as is so commonly supposed to be the rule. In by far the larger proportion of cases, of both sexes, it was discovered by the individual spontaneously. It is significant that while 17 per cent. men and 42 per cent. women state that they have not masturbated since marriage, the number of women who state that they have done so " frequently " since marriage is nearly as large as of men and includes nearly half the women who do it at all after marriage, the infrequent practice being much more common among the men. That would seem to indicate that while in married men it is mainly due to absence from home, or other extraneous cause, in married women it expresses the greater incidence on them of dissatisfaction in marriage. It is further to be noted that a far larger proportion of men than of women consider that the practice has been physically or mentally injurious.

Hamilton was the only investigator of the three who was able to approach directly the question of the relative satisfaction in marriage experienced by husbands and wives, since his husbands and wives were comparable, equal in number and investigated in precisely the same manner. He made fourteen grades of satisfaction in marriage, and when the results were tabulated it was found that 51 per cent. of the husbands had attained to the seventh highest degree of satisfaction, but only 45 per cent. of the wives. The women, taken as a group, had been more seriously disappointed in their marriages than had the men. Katharine Davis confirms this, though only able to make the comparison indirectly, by finding that wives report a larger proportion

of husbands who were satisfied by marriage than they themselves show. My observations though less precise, both as regards English and American marriages, are in harmony with these. The difference may not be great, but it is recognizable.

It is becoming increasingly evident that there is no special sexual psychology of woman. That was a notion originated by ascetics and monks, though it has taken a long time to fall into discredit. Differences there are, and always must be. So long as men and women are not alike in body they cannot be alike in spirit. But these differences, on the psychological side, are not of substance. We see now that, essentially, men and women are of the same sexual composition, and the old notion that such a belief was " derogatory " to woman is for us merely moonshine.

We see, also, that—mainly, no doubt, as a result of the traditional ignorance and prejudice of the past—women tend to suffer more than men from the sexual situation. Apart from general expressions of satisfaction or of dissatisfaction in marriage, which seem always to show a less amount of satisfaction in marriage on the part of wives—although in old days it used to be said that marriage was magnanimously devised by men for the benefit of women—the more precise gynæcological evidence points in the same direction. Thus, among 1,000 patients, Dickinson records 175 cases of dyspareunia, that is to say more or less pain and discomfort in the physical relationship of sex, and 120 cases in which there was in that relationship some degree of frigidity or sexual coldness, which in the act of union must practically amount to dyspareunia. In the case of husbands both these conditions have practically no existence (their counterpart being an impotency which is a purely negative condition), so that here again we have an important disadvantage on the side of women.

How far is this feminine disadvantage rooted in the nature of things, and how far in circumstances which we can control? There is something of both. That is to say that physiological and psychological adjustment to the sexual relationship is under normal conditions less easily achieved by women than by men. That is a natural disadvantage but one that may be naturally overcome. The problem before us concerns the fact that this partly natural disadvantage has been more acutely felt in recent times than, so far as we know, it has ever been felt in human history before. "Why should not husbands be taught more?" asked one of Dr. Davis's subjects as she reviewed her own painful experiences. And what these experiences may have been we gather from the nature of the answers given by the married women to the question concerning their first reaction to marriage: "amused," "astonished," "bewildered," "disappointed," "frightened," "indignant," "resigned," "shocked," "stunned," while 173 merely "took it as a matter of fact." Naturally such answers came in a much larger proportion from the women who entered marriage in ignorance of all that it meant, and we are brought at the end to the point at which we started.

Formerly there was a kind of sexual adjustment, at all events on the surface, because women were trained beforehand, by a closer relationship to the life of their age, to know and to expect what they actually found on marriage. In more recent times, if not still, they have been trained, rightly or wrongly—if trained at all—to expect what they did not find. That is to say, that there has been a revolution quietly going on in the status of woman and in every field of women's activity, not directly touching the sexual impulse, but from every side having an undesigned repercussion on that impulse. No corresponding revolution has taken place in the status and activities of men and hence an inevitable lack of sexual adjustment. Since we cannot expect, nor even desire, the effects of the feminine revolution to be undone, the present sexual situation is mainly one with which men have to deal. A new husband is required to meet the new wife.

All life, as I have often had occasion to point out, is art. The statement has been denied by those who have confused art with æsthetic sensibility, which is quite another matter. All making and doing is of the nature of art, which is not confined to man's activities alone, and may even be said to be unconsciously true of all Nature. To say that life is art ought, indeed, to be a mere truism, and would be so if it were not so often denied or indifferently ignored, even by those who profess to accept it. As it is, one is tempted to say that if life is art, life is mostly bad art.

There is perhaps no field of life in which one may be more tempted thus to qualify the statement than in that of love. It is often said that it is the male rather than the female who reveals in Nature the stronger impulse to art, and there is no doubt that this is so in various zoölogical groups (it is only necessary to think of birds), but such a generalization could hardly have been reached, as regards modern man in the field of love, by reading the results recorded in the pages of Hamilton and Davis and Dickinson. This is unfortunate, because love, considered as the psychic side of sexual relationship, is life itself, the gesture without which, so far as we are concerned, life would cease. We can see to-day and coldly enumerate all the causes which led to the art of love falling into reprobation, neglect, and contempt: religious, moral, spiritual, æsthetic causes. We can also see to-day on how shallow a foundation all those causes worked. That vision is a necessary condition for the improvement of our art. We know that it is already becoming influential, even though not always in accordance with right knowledge. Some, indeed, have sought—not as had once often been done by unreasoning instinct but on principle—to eliminate any problems here involved by reducing sexual activity to a mere routine, involving no deeper thought than is involved by eating and drinking, or to a mere amusement like dancing or tennis. But, as an acute exponent and critic of modern fashions in life and love, Aldous Huxley, has truly remarked, following Robert Burns: "Nothing is more dreadful than a cold unimpassioned indulgence. And love infallibly becomes cold and unimpassioned when it is lightly made." Moreover, it must be added, we do not really touch the problem of the adjustment of the sexes by thus reducing love. We were far from Nature when, in the days now passing away, we made the sexual act a duty—with, or without, throwing in sentiment and romance—but we are equally far away if we make it a routine or an amusement. Not only in civilized man, but in the physiological facts of Nature, even going beyond the mammals, we are here concerned with an act which normally evokes resistances, and demands for its completely satisfactory achievement both passion and art. If we seek to disregard that essential fact, one way or another we inevitably suffer.

We are thus led to emphasize the therapeutic importance of the art of love. In old days not only would such emphasis have been impossible but the whole idea would not have been intelligible. The art of love in this connection could be ignored or spurned, partly because the erotic needs of the wife were never considered, partly because the erotic needs of the husband, it was generally conceded, could be gratified in silence outside marriage. But along both these lines our attitude has now changed. We are tending to concede to women the same erotic privileges as to men; we are also tending to aspire after a monogamy which, unlike our present system, may eventually be real and not nominal only. Thus it comes about that to-day the cultivation of the art of love is inseparably associated with the cultivation of monogamy, because without it any satisfactory marriage, as we now understand marriage, is scarcely practicable, while even with it marriage may still prove full of difficulties.

In its finest and subtlest manifestations the art of love is the outcome of a man's or a woman's most intimate personality. But in its lower ranges it is an extension of sexual hygiene and comes properly within the sphere of the physician who is called upon to give advice in the various difficult situations which may arise in marital life. Our advocates of sexual hygiene still too often ignore this matter, but such an attitude cannot be maintained and is indeed rapidly breaking down. It is no longer possible to assert that a knowledge of the methods of sexual courtship and intercourse comes by Nature. As Paget remarked many years ago, it is certain that in civilization such knowledge has to be taught. It may be added that the same is even true, to a large extent, of uncivilized races, and training in these matters is part of the serious initiation of life among various peoples. Moreover, it is not sufficiently realized that among peoples living in natural conditions great attention is often paid to the preliminaries of intercourse, and a considerable variety of methods of intercourse prevails. Both these points are highly important. The prolongation of the preliminary courtship before the act is necessary on the physical side, in order to ensure tumescence ; it is necessary on the psychic side because without it the ideal element of love, which is essential to real marriage, cannot well be developed. The recognition that a number of methods of intercourse, far from being vicious "perversions," come within the normal human range of variation, is required because it is often found that when one method is unsuitable to secure gratification another method proves more successful. Sometimes years elapse before the conditions and the method are found which alone render coitus agreeable or even tolerable to a woman. Due attention to the preliminary courtship of the act of intercourse and to the method most suitable for adoption suffices to cure the majority of cases of sexual frigidity in women.

These things, as we are now beginning to learn, cannot wisely be neglected by the physician. The sexual gratification of the woman is even a part of the act of fecundation, for her share in that act is not purely passive. A distinguished gynæcologist of an earlier generation, Matthews Duncan, placed stress on this need of sexual pleasure in the woman in order to ensure fecundation, and Kisch and some other later authorities have confirmed that doctrine. It cannot be essential when we think of the vast number of children who have certainly been conceived without pleasure on the mother's part. But Kisch found that dyspareunia (by which he means absence of gratification in intercourse) was with remarkable frequency associated with sterility ; he found it in 38 per cent. cases of sterility, but neglects to state its average frequency.

The elementary fact, to which reference has here so often been made, is that courtship is a natural and even essential preliminary to every act of sexual intercourse. Usually it is for the male to take the initiative in this, when he divines that the right moment has come (for he must not expect the woman to tell him this) and to take the most active part, although there is nothing really abnormal in his partner's assumption of the more active part, and the art of love can scarcely be exercised when the female is merely passive. On the purely physical side, it is not until, by the preliminary play of courtship, the woman's genital region is bathed in the glandular secretion liberated by emotions of pleasure that intercourse is either pleasurable or often even easy, so that, sometimes, artificial substitutes, which should not be needed, are recommended to replace the natural lubricant.

All this, though often ignored in civilization, is well understood among peoples in a less "advanced" stage. Thus among the Melanesians of British New Guinea, we are told, there is much freedom in selecting partners (so long as the rules of totem and blood-relationship are observed), but no question of marriage arises until after several months of intimacy. In some districts a custom exists by which a boy may sleep with a girl for the night, holding her in his arms and caressing the upper part of her body. Sexual connection seldom occurs; if it does marriage usually follows. With such a system the elementary principles, at all events, of the art of love are involved.

In the course of any preliminary courtship before intercourse it is natural and desirable that more or less contact, pressure, or friction should be exerted on the clitoris, which is from the first the chief focus of sexual sensation in women. It is sometimes said by psycho-analysts that this is only true for an early age, and that with adolescence sexual sensation is normally, if not constantly, transferred from the clitoris to the vagina. It is difficult to account for the origin of this notion which seems to have been devised in the study, and might easily have been dispelled by a little actual knowledge of women. The clitoris is a normal focus of sexual sensation and tends so to continue, frequently as the chief if not the only focus. That with the initiation of adult intercourse the vagina should also become a focus of pleasurable sensation is natural, but it is incorrect to speak of any "transfer." As so authoritative a gynæcologist as Dickinson truly states, "a large proportion of women have orgasm only from pressure in the clitoris region, and this is perfectly normal."

With regard to posture in coitus, it is sometimes assumed that there is only one right, proper, and normal posture, with the feminine partner supine, and that any other posture is unnatural, if not indeed "vicious." That is a mistake. The custom most usual in one particular phase in human history, or among one particular race, is not to be taken as a rule for other times and other peoples. The oldest picture of coitus we possess—of the palæolithic Solutrian age and found in Dordogne—represents the man as supine while the woman squats. At the present time many different customs as regards posture prevail among different peoples, and many peoples admit various postures. Van de Velde remarks as regards Europeans, that husbands seldom realize that the monotony of the marriage-bed—if such it is found to be—may be relieved by variations that come within the normal range; and even if they do realize this possibility they often put it indignantly aside as "licentious."

There is, indeed, more than this to be said. In many cases it may merely be a question of selecting an agreeable variation, but in other cases the question is more urgent. For some women there are postures—sometimes those most usually adopted—which may prove difficult or intolerable, while another and perhaps more unusual posture proves easy and pleasurable.

Taking sexual relationships in the widest sense, but still on the physical side, it is important always to bear in mind that whatever gives satisfaction and relief to both parties is good and right, and even in the best sense normal, provided (as is not likely to happen in sound and healthy persons) no injury is effected. *Fellatio* and *cunnilinctus* (the impulse to either of which frequently arises spontaneously in men and women who never heard of such practices) are perhaps the chief of these contacts. It is extremely common, I find, for nervous or scrupulous persons to inquire whether this, that, or the other unusual method of sexual gratification is wrong or injurious. A shock is often thus caused, for we seem to be in the presence of something which is "unæsthetic." It seems to be forgotten that not even the most recognized methods of sexual intercourse can well be described as "æsthetic." It is not understood that here, amid the most intimate mysteries of love, we are in a region where the cold and abstract viewpoints either of science or of æsthetics are out of place unless qualified by more specially human emotions. To the rigid formalist in these matters, well intentioned but ignorant, we may gently recall the endlessly wise words of Shakespeare: "Love talks with better knowledge and knowledge with dearer love."

It may be added that of the 100 married women investigated by Hamilton—presumably normal and healthy women and of good social position—he found that thirteen had had experience of *fellatio*, *cunnilinctus*, or both, but in no case could any ill effects be discovered. "No sex play is psychologically taboo," Hamilton reasonably concludes, while making certain reservations, of which the most important are that no injury to physical structure is involved and that there are no serious guilt reactions. That is important. Hamilton states that he has elsewhere met with a series of cases of naïve persons who had innocently practised some such "perversion," without knowing how formidable and objectionable it appeared to many, whereupon "the shock of suddenly acquiring a belief that they had been engaged in a loathsome and perverted practice appeared to precipitate serious paranoid symptoms." Nothing could better show how urgent it is to spread abroad more sensible notions on these matters. A woman should be "assured," as Dickinson, a wise and experienced gynæcologist, declares, "that there is nothing in the fullest sweep of passion that is not compatible with her highest ideals of spiritual love, and that all mutual intimacy of behaviour is right between husband and wife."

In a simple introductory manual we are not called upon to consider the art of love in detail. But it may be well to say that that art is far from being confined to the physical aspects of love. There is here an art, and a difficult art, even when physical love is not directly concerned, or when it has fallen into the background, or when physical relationships do not take place at all. The recognition of individual freedom, the allowance for difference of tastes and of disposition even when there is a fundamental unity of ideals, the perpetual call for mutual consideration, the acceptance of the other's faults and weaknesses with the acknowledgement of one's own, and the problem of overcoming that jealousy which because it is rooted in Nature every one has in some form and at some time to meet—all these difficulties and the like exist even apart from sex in the narrow sense. Yet they are a large part, even the largest part, of the art of love. Every failure here, moreover, may become a source of misery or of weakness in the whole art of living.

We have, it becomes clear, to take a wide view of the conjugal relationship, before we can grasp all the factors that constitute it in any complete sense. The satisfaction of all these factors is essential to individual well-being, and, in addition to therapeutic importance, possesses social significance as a guarantee of the probable permanence of the union. "It is not the physician's business to come forward with proposals of reform," said Freud in 1908. That notion now belongs to the past, as Freud himself seems to have realized, for since then he has meditated over some of the largest questions of life. To-day we may say explicitly, even if we thereby reverse the primitive conception of medical art, that it is no longer the physician's business to preserve evils in order to tinker at them. In every department of medicine—and now at last in the most intimate of all—it is our business so to adjust the conditions of life that, if possible, the evils may not arise. There is no field in which it is more necessary than in that now before us for the physician to acquire a wider knowledge or to exercise a finer intelligence.

BIBLIOGRAPHY

JULES GUYOT, *A Ritual for Married Lovers* (Part translation of *Bréviaire de l'Amour Expérimental* by Gertrude M. Pinchot).

HAVELOCK ELLIS, "The Art of Love," *Studies in the Psychology of Sex*, Vol. VI.; also Vol. III.

HELENA WRIGHT, *The Sex Factor in Marriage.*
VAN DE VELDE, *Ideal Marriage.*
EXNER, *The Sexual Side of Marriage.*
ISABEL HUTTON, *The Hygiene of Marriage.*
W. F. ROBIE, *The Art of Love.*
O. L. HARVEY, "The Frequency of Human Coitus," *American Journal of Sociology*, July, 1932.
MARGARET SANGER AND HANNAH STONE, *The Practice of Contraception.*
R. L. DICKINSON, *Pre-Marital Examination as Routine Preventive Gynæcology.*
DOUGLAS BRYAN, "Bisexuality," *International Journal of Psycho-Analysis*, April, 1930.
KISCH, *Sexual Life of Woman.*
C. G. SELIGMAN, *The Melanesians of British New Guinea.*

CHAPTER VIII

CONCLUSION

The Dynamic Nature of the Sexual Impulse

THE great fundamental impulses in human life, as among animals generally, are those of nutrition and of sex, of hunger and of love. They are the two original sources of dynamic energy which bring into existence the machinery of living in lowlier organisms, and in ourselves tend to constitute the most elaborate social superstructures.

It is the impulse of sex the ramifications of which attract the greatest attention, although it is the less essential to the individual; the very fact of its intermittence, and of its varying degrees of violence, together with its dependence on the response of another person, fully account for this prominence.

Yet the impulse of nutrition, though its significance has often been overlooked, has a similar dynamic energy, not to be confined within merely economic limits. It is equally susceptible of transformation into psychic channels, and even of sublimation into spiritual shapes. Our highest aspiration, indeed, we are accustomed to regard as a hungering and a thirsting. Dr. Audrey Richards, dealing primarily with the Southern Bantus of Africa, has recently developed this line of investigation with fruitful results. We are not here concerned with them. But unless we recognize the equal psychological primacy of hunger and sex, our conception of life will be one-sided and distorted.

Under the ordinary conditions of social life, as we know it in civilization, there are three main channels along which we may direct the energy of the sexual impulse: (1) We may avoid all overt manifestations, leaving the impulse to expend its dynamic energy along whatever paths, normal or abnormal, the organism may lend itself to; (2) We may be content with temporary or merely casual sexual relationships, of which prostitution is the familiar type ; (3) We may enter on marriage, that is to say, a sexual relationship set up with the intention of, if possible, making it permanent, and involving a community of more than sexual interests. There can be no doubt whatever that—whatever one's religious or moral principles may be or even in the absence of any—this third condition, even when there are no children, leads to the richest and deepest life experience.

But while it is the best path, it is without doubt a difficult path. Indeed, as we have seen, the whole path of sexual activity, and not only for the neuropathic but even for the normal, is beset with perils. This is in part due to the comparatively late period at which the sexual impulse, as compared to the other impulses, undergoes full development, even though it may begin early, in part to the periodic and violent nature of the impulse, and in part, not the least part, to the rigid rules which religion, morals, law, and convention have combined to lay down in the sphere of sex. A wise and watchful hygiene is here for ever necessary, and is the more imperative because, when it is defective, we are often faced by situations which it is not always altogether within the sphere of medicine to treat. We have to regard the sexual impulse as a force, generated, we are now becoming accustomed to think, by powerful ferments, springing up from within and capable of taking on endless forms, healthy and morbid, normal and abnormal forms that are sometimes scarcely recognizable as sexual at all, and which, while we can to some extent control or guide, we can never altogether repress. This dynamic conception of the sexual impulse has long been vaguely perceived ; Anstie used it, half a century ago, to explain some forms of what was later called neurasthenia ; James Hinton developed it more especially in its moral aspects ; it underlies the conception of auto-erotism ; it has been worked out with endless subtlety by Freud.

I have referred to sexual energy as " a force generated by powerful ferments." That is vague ; if we now try to define it more precisely than was attempted at the outset, we may perhaps say that the erotic personality rests on a triangular association between the cerebrum, the endocrine system, and the autonomic nervous apparatus. This last component has not come conspicuously to the front, but its importance may here be indicated. It is constituted by the digestive, circulatory, respiratory, and urinary systems, the secretory glands and their ganglionic nervous systems. This apparatus thus regulates what may be considered the fundamental function of living. It is largely responsible for setting in action what Kempf, who has insisted on the significance of the autonomic factor for behaviour, calls the acquisitive and avertive compulsions to action in relation to the environment. The animals with primeval autonomic systems which felt tensions of distress sought to protect themselves, and by surviving through the relief of these tensions transmitted them to higher organisms. We are thus helped to bring into line somatic causation and psychic causation and to understand the individual working as a unit. We are further helped to greater precision in the conception of the conations and desires, the *libido* if we prefer so to term it, or the Schopenhauerian Will to which the philosophers of the sexual impulse are apt to appeal. As Carlyle long ago wrote: "Perhaps the notablest God we hear tell of is one of whom Grimm the German Etymologist finds trace: the God Wünsch or Wish."

With his usual powers of luminous expression, Freud long since (1912) set forth the varying conditions under which the difficulties of the sexual life may lead to nervous disorder, and his exposition is the more important since it may be held to stand independently of many psycho-analytic doctrines which are in dispute. Freud himself admitted that it is unsatisfactory as a clinical classification of cases since the same case may exhibit the various conditions at different times, or even to some extent at the same time; but it is useful in helping us to a knowledge of those conditions. Four types thus become recognizable. (1) The simplest and most obvious sexual occasion of neurotic disorder—an occasion to which most people are in some degree liable—is that of denial; the subject is here quite healthy so long as his need of love is satisfied in a real object in the outer world; and only becomes neurotic when deprived of this object without any adequate compensation; under these circumstances there are two possibilities of preserving health in spite of the denial of sexual needs; either the psychic tension is directed towards activity in the practical world and finally finds a real satisfaction of sexual desire, or, such satisfaction being renounced, the inhibited desires are sublimated into energy which is directed to non-erotic ends. In this process there is a possibility of what C. G. Jung termed introversion, that is to say, the inhibited sexual impulse instead of being sublimated may be turned from real channels into imaginative channels where it occupies itself with dream-wishes. (2) In the cases of the second type the individual becomes morbid, not through any change in the outer world replacing satisfaction by the need for renunciation, but by his own inner efforts to attain satisfaction in the outer world. The subject becomes disordered by the inner difficulties which he finds in adapting himself to the real world and by his efforts to attain a normal method of sexual satisfaction which he is still unfitted for. (3) The next class of cases, in which various disorders occur through inhibition of development, is really an extreme group of the second class, and there is no theoretical ground for considering them separately, the sexual satisfaction remaining fixed on infantile aims which no longer accord with the individual stage of development, and the conflict arises in the effort to subdue the outgrown infantile impulses which still seek gratification. (4) In the fourth class of cases we find individuals who were formerly healthy becoming morbid without any change in their relation to the external world. But, on more careful examination, it is found that there has been, in consequence of biological changes such as the attainment of a certain period of life (puberty or the menopause), a change in the amount of sexual desire, this alone serving to destroy the balance of health and to introduce the conditions for the occurrence of neurosis. The inhibition of the sexual impulse through the external inability for its satisfaction here becomes pathogenic; the amount of sexual desire is not indeed measurable, it is a relative change in amount that causes the trouble, and the subject finds himself overburdened in the struggle with this relatively changed amount.

Although it has no objective clinical validity, this abstract analytical classification may be said to sum up conveniently the various conditions with which we have been dealing. It indicates the lines on which the treatment of sexual disturbances in the nervous and psychic sphere, and still more the hygiene of the sexual life, most properly lie.

However sound the individual's constitution may be, the inevitable difficulties of the sexual life, and its constant readjustments to inner and outer changes in the conditions, involve difficulties of the kind we have dealt with. These difficulties are emphasized when there is an inherited morbid predisposition. The sexual impulse is a force, to some extent an incalculable force, and the struggle of the man to direct that force, when he and it are both constantly changing, and the conditions under which they move are also changing, is inevitably attended with peril, even when the impulse is normal or at all events seeking to be normal.

The conditions are still further complicated when the impulse is abnormal, that is to say when it is not merely undue in amount or passing into undue channels, but when it has definitely taken on an abnormal form, a form which may sometimes be congenital, in so far as the forms of the sexual impulse can ever be said to be congenital.

It will have become fairly clear that while we set out without defining too precisely what we mean by "sex," or what Freud calls "libido," the term grows wider as we examine it. Freud himself has been led to an ever wider conception of "libido," and some of those psycho-analysts who were at first his disciples even go to an extreme in minimizing what is ordinarily understood as the impulse of sex; similarly F. L. Wells would substitute "hedonic" for "erotic" and "auto-hedonic" for "auto-erotic." This enlargement of libido is (as Cyril Burt has pointed out) in accordance with the general tendency of psychology, which now seems to regard the innate tendencies we inherit from our animal ancestors as merely specific differentiations of a single life-impulse. And McDougall, enlarging his earlier more rigid delimitation of instincts, is now almost inclined to unify them as part of "the great purpose which animates all living beings, whose end we can only dimly conceive and vaguely describe as the perpetuation and increase of life."

It is, indeed, interesting to note that Jung in his much criticized enlargement of the connotation of "libido," beyond the earlier Freudian exclusively sexual sense, was really returning to the original classical sense of "passion or desire in general." It thus comes into line with Schopenhauer's "Will" and Bergson's "élan vital," and Burt is able to define it as general conative energy proceeding from all the instincts.

If we are to use the word "instinct," let it be added, it seems best to regard an instinct as more primitive and fundamental than emotion, and not, as has sometimes been done, to regard emotional qualities as a central part of instinct. Where "instincts" are concerned, we are perhaps justified (with Garnett) in considering ourselves in the presence of *conational* rather than emotional systems. The associated impulse is that of a fundamental conation.

Freud once suggested (in 1918) that the instinctive factor in life may form the nucleus of that subliminal portion of the psyche to which as the "Unconscious" he attaches so potent an influence. This would be a primitive kind of mental activity, overlaid by human reason, corresponding to the instinctive knowledge possessed by animals. Repression, says Freud, would be the return to this instinctive stage, and man would be paying for his own new acquisitions by a liability to neurosis.

We are again brought to that rhythmic balance of expression and repression which is so dominant a feature in our civilized life, but is also to be seen in all animal life. As I have already pointed out, psycho-pathologists, in accordance with their own special experiences, are too often tempted to see here mainly a possibility of neurotic disorder.

Within the normal range, and in the sound organism, the play of expression and repression, it is essential to understand, is harmless and wholesome, even essential to any developed form of life. To hold that the Unconscious is always, or even often, in disharmony with the Conscious is a distortion of the facts. He is indeed an unfortunate person whose Unconscious is always out of harmony with his Conscious. A very little consideration shows that, for most of us, it is not so. We have only to appeal to dreams which furnish the most familiar revelation of the Unconscious. It must be within the experience of most normal people that dreams perpetually bring back to us, with even a heightened beauty or tenderness, the facts and emotions of our conscious waking life. Dreams are sometimes a revelation of concealed disharmonies. They are also the proof of unsuspected harmonies between our conscious and unconscious lives. We are too apt to be content with the superficial aspect of dreams, and fail to see their latent and more significant content.

BIBLIOGRAPHY

A. J. RICHARDS, *Hunger and Work in a Savage Tribe.*
E. J. KEMPF, *The Autonomic Factors in Personality.*
MCDOUGALL, *Psychology: the Study of Behaviour.*
C. BURT, *Eugenics Review*, January, 1918.
FREUD, *Collected Papers*, Vol. III., "An Infantile Neurosis."
C. G. JUNG, *Psychology of the Unconscious.*

Sublimation

The balance of expression and repression, however fairly maintained on the whole in a healthy organism, can seldom be achieved without difficulties, and in an unsound organism such difficulties are apt to be disastrous. A remedy commonly put forth is sublimation. It is usually offered too easily and too cheaply. There has, indeed, often been a tendency to believe that the stresses of sex can readily be put aside. For some persons they may, but, as we know, for many, even with the best will in the world, it is not so. Neither muscular exertion nor mental distraction here proves effective. The games in which schoolmasters seem to have faith do not arrest sexual activity, unless carried to an extreme and harmful degree. At school, it has been said, the best athletes are usually the most prominent rakes. We have, however, to form as clear an idea as possible of what it is we are seeking to do. If, as Garnett believes, we must distinguish between sex as an instinct and sex as an appetite (he considers that Freud tends to confuse them) the instinct is only aroused when the opportunity of sexual satisfaction is presented, and it may be possible to avoid such opportunity. But sex as an appetite, receiving its impulses not from without but from within, still remains. We are here concerned, as Ernest Jones would put it, not so much with sex in the narrow sense but with " the individual biological components of the instinct, *i.e.*, with the various infantile tendencies that later on form the basis of erotic desire as well as of many other (non-sexual) interests . . . a specific transference of energy from one given field of interest to another." It is important, at the same time, to remember that it is not usually in early life that this problem arises. Matsumato pointed out that the fact that the interstitial cells of the testes pass into a resting stage soon after birth, not to become active until after puberty, does not indicate the presence of strong sexual interests in early life (though, it must be added, we do not positively know all the sources of the sexual impulse), while in women such interests are frequently either latent or widely diffused, not to become acute sometimes until towards the age of thirty. Yet, sooner or later, we may expect this problem of sublimation to arise, and more urgently in the best constituted natures.

Plato said that love was a plant of heavenly growth. If we understand this to mean that a plant, having its roots in the earth, may put forth " heavenly " flowers, the metaphor has a real and demonstrable scientific truth. It is a truth which the poets have always understood and tried to embody. Dante's Beatrice, the real Florentine girl who becomes in imagination the poet's guide in Paradise, typically represents the process by which the attraction of sex may be transformed into a stimulus to spiritual activities.

The precise formulation of this doctrine has been traced back not only to Plato but to the more scientific Aristotle.

Lessing understood that philosopher's doctrine of *katharsis* as "a conversion of passion or emotion in general into virtuous dispositions." But that seems scarcely correct, for it was simply the alleviation brought by emotional discharges of pity or fear which Aristotle seems to have had in mind, and, as Garnett rightly points out, the mere "draining off" of emotion is not sublimation.

It is not until the coming of Christianity that the idea of *sublimation*, even as a concrete image, begins to take definite shapes. It is traced back to an early Father of the Egyptian Desert, Abbâ Macarius the Great, sometimes regarded as "the first scientific mystic of Christendom"; and Evelyn Underhill in *The Mystic Way* expounds his psychological view of a gradual transformation in the substance of the soul (which he did not regard as absolutely immaterial) into an ever less dense and more pure spirituality under the influence of the Divine Fire. "Like metals," he said, "which, cast into the fire, lose their natural hardness, and the longer they remain in the furnace are more and more softened by the flame." The painful fire becomes heavenly light, and for Macarius light and life are identical. Here we have, as definitely as possible, our modern conception of sublimation. Macarius was the friend of St. Basil, who was in the main stream of Christian tradition, and this idea constantly recurs in the later Christian mystics and is the foundation of St. Catharine of Genoa's doctrine of Purgatory—the fire of purgatory burning away the rust of sin.

Later it appears, apart from any religious doctrine, under the definite name of "sublimation," in the poets and still later in the moralists. To *sublimate* is to bring a substance by heat from what we usually regard as its grosser, more "material" and sordid form, to a state of vapour which we usually regard as more exalted and refined. The poets seized on this process as symbolizing what takes place in the human spirit, and they frequently used the idea in the early seventeenth century. Thus Davies in his *Immortality of the Soul* sang of turning "Bodies to spirits by sublimation strange." Prose writers, religious and other, seized on the conception. Jeremy Taylor spoke of " sublimating marriage into a sacrament"; Shaftesbury, in 1711, of the original plain principles of humanity being " by a sort of spiritual chemistry sublimated" to higher forms; and still later, in 1816, Peacock, reaching nearer to our use of the idea, referred to " that enthusiastic sublimation which is the source of greatness and energy." Schopenhauer subsequently attached importance to the conception.

In the field of sexual psychology, " sublimation " is understood to imply that the physical sexual impulse, or *libido* in the narrow sense, can be so transformed into some impulse of higher psychic activity that it ceases to be urgent as a physical need. The conception is now widely current in popular psychology. Those who adopt it, however, do not always seem to realize that this process of " sublimation " is even in its original imagery a process involving much expenditure of force, and in its metaphorical and spiritual form far easier to talk about than to achieve. That it stands for a real psychic transformation of physical impulses, by which the grosser physical desires are lifted on to a plane where their keenness is lost in the gratification of desires which correspond to the physical but are more, as we say, " spiritual " in nature, may be accepted. But that transformation, though possible, is not easy nor of swift attainment, and perhaps only possible at all for those natures which are of finer than average nervous texture. Thus, Hirschfeld, who prefers to speak of " sexual equivalents," is cautious in admitting sublimation, and denies that the sexually abstinent yield intellectual products in art or science superior to those yielded by persons not sexually abstinent. It is only in men of religion, and in those engaged in strenuous motor activities, that Hirschfeld would clearly admit sublimation.

Freud, however, recognizes sublimation, and is even prepared to assert that civilization itself may be regarded as a kind of sublimation of instinctive forces which include the sexual. He points out that the sexual impulses are exceptionally, as he would say, " plastic "; that they can be moulded into different shapes and even directed towards different objects. He remarks that artists are often, it is probable, endowed with a specially powerful capacity for sublimation.

Psycho-analysts in recent years have been concerned to explain and define " sublimation " in very precise ways, as well as to distinguish it from other processes with which it might be confused. Edward Glover has, for example, discussed this matter in a lengthy and elaborate manner. His treatment of the question will chiefly appeal to those who are interested in " metapsychology " (which may roughly be described as the metaphysics of psychology), but his main conclusion is that, though the conception of sublimation is still surrounded by some confusion, and we cannot attempt any binding formulations, it is legitimate to make use of the term.

For ordinary practical purposes, no doubt, we may remain in ignorance of the nature of the exact change in energy which takes place when sublimation occurs. It has to be recognized that the process is largely below the level of consciousness, and that, however readily the will goes with it, the will cannot suffice to accomplish it. Also, it is obviously necessary not to confuse sublimation with a simple displacement of unchanged sexual activity into another channel, or with the substitution of a morbid symptom. It is involved in the whole conception of sublimation that the change is into a form more precious ; a higher cultural level is necessarily involved. The victim of kleptolagnia who displaces sexual activity into theft has not achieved sublimation. It would not be necessary to state this if the notion had not been foolishly put forward.

By some psycho-analysts, carrying on the suggestion of Freud that all civilization may be regarded as a sublimation of *libido*, the idea has been pushed to extreme lengths. Thus, the Swiss school of analysts (notably as once represented by Maeder) have emphasized sublimation as helping to constitute a kind of psycho-synthesis, and even a kind of religion, the soul being led, as Dante was in his great poem, through Hell and Purgatory to Paradise, the physician as guide playing the part of Virgil.

The Italian psycho-therapeutist Assagioli more temperately attaches high value to sublimation when there is a contrast and conflict between excessive sexual energy and the obstacles to its normal gratification. He does not desire to explain all the highest psychic faculties as simply the product of the more elementary impulses, and, putting aside the efforts of direct psycho-analytic treatment, he attaches importance to auto-sublimation. He does not regard it as less real because we cannot register it on a revolving cylinder, and show a graphic curve, and he rightly points out that to gain the benefits of sublimation it is necessary to put aside the notion that sex is bestial and shameful, and " repression " therefore required. The sexual excitation may be intense, but it may at the same time be linked on to higher emotional and spiritual activities, and especially, he holds, by a complete change of occupation, to some *creative* work, for artistic creation is deeply but obscurely related to the process of sexual sublimation. (Hirschfeld has referred to *genus* and *genius* as having the same root.) Assagioli invokes Wagner's *Tristan* as a marvellous example of sublimation since it was clearly filled with the fire and passion of its composer's ungratified love for Mathilde Wesendonck.

Assagioli's advice may help to bring home to us the limits of sublimation. According to the second law of thermodynamics, " no machine converts nor can convert into work all the heat received ; only a small part of this heat is transformed into work ; the rest is expelled in the form of degraded heat." When we deal with sublimation we are treating the organism dynamically, and we must be prepared to accept and allow for a certain amount of sexual energy " expelled in the form of degraded heat," whatever the form may be. Even Dante had a wife and family when he wrote the *Divine Comedy*.

As Freud truly says in his *Introductory Lectures :* " The measure of unsatisfied Libido that the average human being can take upon himself is limited. The plasticity and free mobility of the Libido is not by any means retained to the full in all of us ; and sublimation can never discharge more than a certain proportion of Libido, apart from the fact that many people possess the capacity for sublimation only in a slight degree." So that, on the one hand, the possibility of sublimation, its value, and its far-reaching significance must always be held in mind; on the other hand it must also always be remembered that, even in the process of sublimation, a portion of the sexual impulse will be left, either to be dispersed in wholesome but more primitive ways or else to seek a channel in neurotic transformations.

BIBLIOGRAPHY

FREUD, *Introductory Lectures.*

ERNEST JONES, *Papers on Psycho-Analysis.*

S. HERBERT, *The Unconscious in Life and Art.*

A. C. GARNETT, *The Mind in Action.*

EDMUND GLOVER, "Sublimation, Substitution and Social Anxiety," *International Journal of Psycho-Analysis*, July, 1931.

GLOSSARY

Algolagnia. The association of sexual pleasure with pain, whether given or received.

Anhedonia. A term devised by Ziehen for sexual frigidity.

Auto-erotism. The spontaneous manifestations of the sexual impulse not directed towards a sexual object (or, as frequently understood by psycho-analysts, directed towards the subject himself).

Auto-sexual. An alternative to *Auto-erotic* proposed by Lura Beam and Dickinson.

Chalone. A hormone with an inhibitory action.

Chromosomes. The rod-like filaments into which the chromatin of the nucleus of the reproductive cell breaks up in the course of development.

Coitus interruptus. Sexual intercourse brought to an end by withdrawal when emission is about to occur.

Coitus reservatus. Sexual intercourse prolonged by control over the act of seminal emission, which may take place after withdrawal or not at all.

Contrectation. The term devised by Moll for the preliminary approaches of courtship needed to produce tumescence.

Coprolagnia. Also *Coprophilia.* The association of sexual pleasure with defæcation or with the fæces.

Cunnilinctus. Also, but incorrectly, *Cunnilingus* (which can only be correctly used for the actor, not for the act, and corresponds to *fellator* and not to *fellatio*). The apposition of the mouth to the female genital organs.

Detumescence. The stage of sexual excitement, following tumescence, during which the orgasm occurs.

Endocrinology. The science of the endocrines or hormones, products of the various ductless glands which influence the whole organism.

Enuresis. Bed-wetting, now frequently regarded as having a sexual association.

Eonism. The impulse to assume the dress, habits, and ways of feeling of the opposite sex.

Erogenic or *Eratogenic zones.* Regions of the body which, habitually or occasionally, prove sexually excitable.

Erotic symbolism. The process of deviation by which some object or idea normally on the verge or outside of the sexual process becomes its chief focus.

Exhibitionism. The impulse to expose a part of the body, especially the genital region, with some conscious or unconscious sexual motive.

Fellatio. Apposition of the mouth to the male genital organs.

Fetish. Some object to which a special sexually exciting influence is attached.

Frottage. Sexual pleasure derived from rubbing against some part of the body of another person.

Gamete. The reproductive cell.

Gonad. The relatively undifferentiated reproductive cell.

Heterosexual. The normal sexual attachment to a person of opposite sex.

Homogenic. A substitute for the term *Homosexual* proposed by Edward Carpenter.

Homosexual. The general term for sexual attraction to a person of the same sex.

Hormones. The internal secretions of the ductless glands which act as "chemical messengers."
Hyphedonia. A little-used term for relative sexual frigidity.
Karezza. See *Coitus reservatus.*
Kleptolagnia. The association of sexual excitement with the act of theft.
Libido. The term selected by Freud to indicate the energy of the sexual impulse manifesting itself in various forms, and subsequently used by some authors to cover vital energy in general without special reference to the sexual impulse.
Masochism. Sexual pleasure experienced in being hurt, humiliated, or dominated.
Metatropism. A term proposed by Hirschfeld for a reversed sexual attitude, a man assuming that of a woman, or a woman that of a man.
Mixoscopia. Sexual pleasure experienced in prying at sights of a sexual nature, sometimes termed *voyeurism.*
Mixoscopic zoophilia. Sexual pleasure in the spectacle of animals copulating.
Narcissism. Auto-erotic self-admiration, regarded either as a phase of sexual development or (in an extreme form) as a sexual deviation.
Necrophilia. The sexual attraction of corpses ; vampirism.
Œdipus complex. Early attachment to the mother accompanied by jealous hostility to the father, which Freud originally regarded as a general psychic phenomenon with far-reaching significance.
Osphresiolagnia. Or *Ozolagnia.* Sexual pleasure aroused by body odours.
Pædicatio. Sodomy, sexual connection by the anus, whether active or passive.
Paidophilia or *Paiderastia.* Sexual attraction to the young, not necessarily associated with any physical relationship.
Pyrolagnia. Or *Erotic pyromania.* Sexual pleasure aroused by conflagrations.
Sadism. Sexual pleasure experienced in hurting, humiliating, or subjugating the object of sexual attraction.
Scatologic. Referring to the excretions.
Scoptolagnia. An alternative and perhaps preferable term for *Mixoscopia.*
Stuff-fetishisms. Sexual fetishes constituted by various fabrics, such as silk, velvet, etc.
Transvestism. Or *Cross-dressing.* Hirschfeld's term for *Eonism,* which really involves more than cross-dressing.
Tribadism. The ancient term for female sexual inversion which was believed to involve an attempt at physical intercourse.
Tumescence. The preliminary stage of orgasm involving engorgement of vessels, and leading on to detumescence.
Undinism. Sexual pleasure associated with water and specially apt to be connected with the act of urination.
Uranism. The term for homosexuality devised by Ulrichs.
Urolagnia. Sexual pleasure associated with urination.
Venus obversa. The normal face-to-face posture in sexual intercourse.
Zooerastia. The desire for real or simulated intercourse with animals.
Zygote. The fertilised egg.

INDEX